Fiascos in Public Policy and Foreign Policy

The collection brings together scholars from Public Policy and Foreign Policy to address the theme of policy fiascos. So far research on failure and fiascos in both Public Policy and Foreign Policy has existed independent of each other with very little communication between the two sub-disciplines. The contributions aim to bridge this divide and bring the two sides into a dialogue on some of the central issues in the study of fiascos, including how to define, identify and measure policy failure (and success); the social and political contestation about what counts as policy fiascos; the causes of policy fiascos and their consequences; the attribution of blame; as well as processes of learning from fiascos. A common theme of the collection is to explore different epistemological and methodological approaches to studying policy fiascos.

This book will appeal to scholars and practitioners interested in policy failures and fiascos both within and among states and other international actors.

This book was previously published as a special issue of the *Journal of European Public Policy*.

Kai Oppermann is Reader in Politics at the University of Sussex, UK. His research interests relate to the domestic sources of foreign policy and European integration as well as British and German foreign and European policy.

Alexander Spencer is Associate Professor of Global Governance at the Ludwig-Maximilians-University Munich, Germany. His research focuses on constructivist approaches to global governance and European foreign and security policy.

Journal of European Public Policy Series

Series Editors:

Jeremy Richardson is Emeritus Fellow at Nuffield College, Oxford University, UK, and an Adjunct Professor in the National Centre for Research on Europe, University of Canterbury, New Zealand.

Berthold Rittberger is professor and chair of International Relations at the Geschwister-Scholl-Institute of Political Science at the University of Munich.

This series seeks to bring together some of the finest edited works on European Public Policy. Reprinting from Special Issues of the *Journal of European Public Policy*, the focus is on using a wide range of social sciences approaches, both qualitative and quantitative, to gain a comprehensive and definitive understanding of Public Policy in Europe.

Fiascos in Public Policy and Foreign Policy

Edited by
Kai Oppermann and Alexander Spencer

Routledge
Taylor & Francis Group

LONDON AND NEW YORK

First published 2017 by Routledge

2 Park Square, Milton Park, Abingdon, Oxfordshire OX14 4RN
52 Vanderbilt Avenue, New York, NY 10017

Routledge is an imprint of the Taylor & Francis Group, an informa business

First issued in paperback 2018

British Library Cataloguing in Publication Data
A catalogue record for this book is available from the British Library

ISBN 13: 978-1-138-20764-6 (hbk)
ISBN 13: 978-0-367-07478-4 (pbk)

Typeset in Adobe Garamond
by RefineCatch Limited, Bungay, Suffolk

Publisher's Note
The publisher accepts responsibility for any inconsistencies that may have arisen during the conversion of this book from journal articles to book chapters, namely the possible inclusion of journal terminology.

Disclaimer
Every effort has been made to contact copyright holders for their permission to reprint material in this book. The publishers would be grateful to hear from any copyright holder who is not here acknowledged and will undertake to rectify any errors or omissions in future editions of this book.

Contents

Citation Information

The chapters in this book were originally published in the *Journal of European Public Policy*, volume 23, issue 5 (February 2016). When citing this material, please use the original page numbering for each article, as follows:

Chapter 1
Studying fiascos: bringing public and foreign policy together
Kai Oppermann and Alexander Spencer
Journal of European Public Policy, volume 23, issue 5 (February 2016), pp. 643–652

Chapter 2
Revisiting the study of policy failures
Mark Bovens and Paul 't Hart
Journal of European Public Policy, volume 23, issue 5 (February 2016), pp. 653–666

Chapter 3
A public policy approach to understanding the nature and causes of foreign policy failure
Allan McConnell
Journal of European Public Policy, volume 23, issue 5 (February 2016), pp. 667–684

Chapter 4
Telling stories of failure: narrative constructions of foreign policy fiascos
Kai Oppermann and Alexander Spencer
Journal of European Public Policy, volume 23, issue 5 (February 2016), pp. 685–701

Chapter 5
'Fiasco prime ministers': leaders' beliefs and personality traits as possible causes for policy fiascos
Klaus Brummer
Journal of European Public Policy, volume 23, issue 5 (February 2016), pp. 702–717

CITATION INFORMATION

For any permission-related enquiries please visit:
http://www.tandfonline.com/page/help/permissions

Notes on Contributors

Ryan Beasley is Senior Teaching Fellow at the School of International Relations, University of St Andrews, UK.

Mark Bovens is Professor of Public Administration at the Utrecht University School of Governance, the Netherlands.

Klaus Brummer is Associate Professor of Political Science at the University of Erlangen-Nuremberg, Germany, and currently interim full Professor of Foreign Policy and International Politics at the Catholic University of Eichstätt-Ingolstadt, Germany.

Jamie Gaskarth is Senior Lecturer in International Relations and Politics at the University of Birmingham, UK.

Andreas Kruck is Assistant Professor of Global Governance at the Institute for Political Science, Ludwig-Maximilians-University Munich, Germany.

Allan McConnell is Professor in the Department of Government and International Relations, University of Sydney, Australia.

Christoph O. Meyer is Professor in the Department of European and International Studies, King's College London, UK.

Kai Oppermann is Reader in Politics at the University of Sussex, UK.

Alexander Spencer is Associate Professor at the Ludwig-Maximilians-University Munich, Germany.

Paul 't Hart is Professor of Public Administration at the Utrecht University School of Governance, the Netherlands.

Studying fiascos: bringing public and foreign policy together

Kai Oppermann and Alexander Spencer

Mistakes happen. In politics no less than everywhere else. Their causes and consequences are at the heart of what scholars in public policy and foreign policy have always been interested in. Policy decisions in either field tend to attract much greater scholarly attention if they are seen to have gone wrong than if they are considered a success. It is small wonder, then, that many of the best-studied public and foreign policy episodes are precisely those which have been linked to 'disastrous' failures or consequences. Prominent examples in public policy include 'planning disasters' such as Sydney's Opera House, San Francisco's rapid transit system or the Concorde supersonic passenger jet (Hall 1980); large-scale policy 'blunders' such as the Thatcher government's poll tax initiative and the attempt to introduce identity cards in Britain (Butler *et al.* 1994; King and Crewe 2013) or the European Union's (EU's) Common Fisheries Policy (Ritchie and Zito 1998); as well as various 'crises' such as the Swedish monetary crisis of 1992 (Baggott 1998) or the British bovine spongiform encephalopathy (BSE) crisis in the 1990s (Stern and Sundelius 1998). Well-researched cases in foreign policy, in turn, include the British policy of appeasement towards Nazi Germany in 1938 (Stedman 2011), the attempted occupation of the Suez Canal zone by Britain, France and Israel in 1956 (Gorst and Johnman 1997), the inability of the United Nations (UN) peacekeeping mission to stop the Srebrenica massacre in 1995 (Brändström and Kuipers 2003); as well as a number of cases in United States (US) foreign policy, like the failure to prevent the Japanese attack on Pearl Harbor in 1941 (Wohlstetter 1962), the Bay of Pigs invasion of Cuba in 1961 (Blight and Kornbluh 1998), the Vietnam War (Kaiser 2002; Tuchman 1984), the 1980 Iran hostage rescue mission (Smith 1985) or the 2003 Iraq War (Yetiv 2011).

In both fields, the predominant concern of research has been with understanding and explaining why policy fiascos have occurred. In public policy, scholars have, for example, focused on competing values and motives of decision-makers, unrealistic policy objectives and expectations, increasing social and technological complexity, uncertainty, implementation failures or various deficiencies in decision-making, such as undue haste, incrementalism, competing bureaucratic interests and inadequate checks and balances (Bovens *et al.* 1998; Dunleavy 1995). In foreign policy, different theories have similarly identified numerous sources of fiascos, most notably cognitive biases and misperceptions (Janis 1989; Jervis 1976) or the emotions of individual decision-makers (McDermott 2004); socio-psychological dynamics in small decision-making groups (Janis 1982; 't Hart *et al.* 1997); or bureaucratic politics and an overreliance on organizational routines (Allison and Zelikow 1999). Since decision-makers are expected to learn primarily from their own or others' past mistakes (Howlett 2012), many accounts of public and foreign policy fiascos also seek lessons to avoid such mistakes in the future.

As the reader will notice, there is, however, very little agreement in the literature on the precise conceptualization of a 'fiasco', with many authors referring to alternative concepts such as 'failure', 'mistake', 'crisis', 'disaster' or 'blunder' as synonyms. Others, in contrast, differentiate these concepts – for example, by pointing to differences in the role of agency or in the levels of severity and politicization. As there is also no agreement in this regard among the contributors to this collection, we have purposely avoided asking our authors to start out from a single definition of the constitutive elements of 'fiascos' or to use a common terminology. What unites the authors in this collection, however, is their interest in situations in which things have gone wrong, where policy has fallen short of some objective or subjective benchmark of success.

Against the background of the long research traditions in public policy and foreign policy, the aim of this collection is twofold. First, it serves to reflect on and further develop the state of the art in studying policy fiascos at a time when research in this field is at a critical juncture. Twenty years after the publication of the seminal study on 'Understanding Policy Fiascos' by Mark Bovens and Paul 't Hart (1996) the collection takes stock of the progress that has been made since and identifies the boundaries of our current knowledge about policy fiascos. It offers the first review of original research on policy failures since the volumes edited by Pat Gray and Paul 't Hart (1998) and Mark Bovens, Paul 't Hart and B. Guy Peters (2001), and comes at a time when the field experiences a noticeable and very welcome increase in research activities. The renewed interest in understanding policy fiascos is evidenced both by an increasing number of panels, workshops and major research conferences on the topic, as well as by some recent publications (e.g., Howlett 2012; Howlett *et al.* 2015; King and Crewe 2013; McConnell 2015; Walker and Malici 2011). In our view, this 'rediscovery' of policy fiascos as an object of study after years of relative neglect marks a watershed moment at which it is crucial to ensure that future research productively builds on and adds to existing knowledge in order to maximize its potential. The contributions to this collection will serve as an important milestone in the development of such a cumulative research agenda in that they bring together the most recent findings of leading experts in the field, identify the most significant gaps in the current state of the art and point to fruitful avenues for further research. Specifically, this includes questions of how to define, identify and measure policy failure (and success); the social and political contestation about what counts as policy fiascos; the causes of policy fiascos and their consequences; the attribution of blame; as well as processes of learning from fiascos. In terms of epistemology and methodology, the collection espouses a pluralist perspective and includes contributions both from positivist and post-positivist research traditions.

Second, the collection explores the potential of bridging the divide between research on public policy and foreign policy fiascos by bringing two literatures together which have so far talked very little to each other. Existing research on fiascos in the public policy field has mostly been ignored in foreign policy analysis and vice versa. This holds true no less for two of the most recent book-length studies on foreign policy mistakes in the US (Walker and Malici 2011) and on public policy blunders in Britain (King and Crewe 2013). Given the largely similar questions and research objectives of the two literatures – understanding policy fiascos and their causes and consequences – the lack of exchange between them is indeed surprising. In our view, the disciplinary divisions in analysing policy fiascos between the fields of public policy and foreign policy are unfortunate and hinder efforts at a comprehensive understanding of the phenomenon and dynamics of policy failure.

With these two purposes in mind, the collection employs a broad understanding of foreign policy that goes beyond traditional notions of diplomacy and security to include issues of international public policy. Understood in this way, we hold that the study of foreign policy fiascos has a lot to gain from recent conceptual and methodological advances in research on public policy fiascos. Similarly, the literature on public policy fiascos stands to benefit from opening up its research agenda to foreign policy fiascos which would broaden the scope of its empirical arguments and provide new opportunities for further developing and refining its conceptual frameworks. Furthermore, public policy will benefit from insights gained in foreign policy on the rising interconnectedness of national and international causes and consequences of (foreign) policy failure. Along these lines, the collection will encourage a genuine dialogue between the public policy and foreign policy literatures in two complementary ways. On the one hand, the editors have challenged contributors from the public policy field to reflect on how their research relates to foreign policy fiascos. On the other hand, foreign policy scholars were asked in their case studies on foreign policy fiascos to critically engage with the public policy literature.

OVERVIEW

The collection starts with a framing piece by Mark Bovens and Paul 't Hart, who review the study of policy failure 20 years after their seminal contributions to the field. The authors start out from a social constructivist view on policy fiascos and make the case that 'failure' is not an inherent attribute of policy but rather a judgment about policy which is debated controversially in political discourse.

Fiascos do not just 'happen', but are constructed in labelling processes that are not necessarily 'evidence-based'. Specifically, the contribution distinguishes two logics of evaluation which do not always go hand–in-hand: a political logic which focusses on the reputation conferred on policies in public discourse; and a programmatic logic which assesses observable costs and benefits. Policies which are evaluated positively on the programmatic dimension may still damage the reputation of political actors ('tragedy'), just as policies which fail to deliver beneficial outcomes can bring dividends on the political dimension ('farce'). Policy 'fiascos', in turn, are policies which are judged to have failed in terms of both the political and the programmatic logic. Moving forward, Bovens and 't Hart argue for developing mid-range theories to explain policy fiascos.

Allan McConnell offers a second conceptual contribution to this collection which considers two fundamental questions in studying 'failures' in public policy: what constitutes a failure and what causes such failures? What is more, the contribution reflects on how the insights on these two questions in public policy can be made fruitful for the analysis of fiascos in foreign policy. First, McConnell outlines a number of challenges in defining policy failures, including divergent assessment criteria ranging from the failure to achieve declared goals to the failure to garner sufficient support for a policy. In order to bring greater clarity to what constitutes policy failures, the contribution suggests to distinguish between process failures, programme/decision failures and political failures. On the second question, McConnell points to a number of methodological difficulties in pinpointing the causes of policy failures and argues for re-focusing our analytical perspective on how political actors frame the causes of such failures. Specifically, the contribution outlines three key elements which many such 'failure' narratives highlight: individual decision-makers; institutions and the policy process; as well as deeper societal values.

The next contribution by Kai Oppermann and Alexander Spencer picks up the concept of 'failure narratives' introduced in the previous contribution and reemphasizes that fiascos are not factual occurrences, but that they are constructed in political discourse. Employing the method of narrative analysis adopted from literary studies, the authors show how fiascos are told in a narrative form that is structured around three elements: the setting of a story which delimits appropriate behaviour in a given situation; the negative characterization of individual or collective actors involved in the story; and the emplotment of an event as a 'fiasco' through the attribution of cause and responsibility. In order to illustrate such a post-positivist approach to studying policy fiascos, the authors apply the suggested method in a case study on German media reporting about Germany's abstention in the UN Security Council on Resolution 1973 authorizing the military intervention in Libya in March 2011. The analysis highlights the discursive struggle of interpretation between dominant 'fiasco' narratives and marginalized counter-narratives which try to refute such claims.

The following piece by Klaus Brummer subscribes to a more objectivist understanding of foreign policy fiascos. It makes the case that explanations of policy failure should move beyond the structural perspectives commonly found in public policy and place more emphasis on the role of individual decision-makers. Specifically, Brummer argues that the personalities of individual decision-makers are an important but often neglected source of foreign policy fiascos. He substantiates his argument by employing two cognitive approaches in foreign policy analysis, leadership traits analysis and operational codes, to identify the personality traits and political beliefs of British prime ministers. Having analysed more than 900 political statements of different prime ministers, Brummer shows that individual office-holders who were responsible for major foreign policy fiascos displayed extreme scores on certain traits and beliefs. In particular, he suggests that 'fiasco prime ministers' appear to possess higher levels of self-confidence (personality trait) and an inclination for pursuing conflictual strategies (political belief).

The contribution by Jamie Gaskarth discusses the 'fiasco' of the failure of the British government in August 2013 to secure approval of the House of Commons for military action in Syria. Going back to McConnell's categorization of different types of failures, the discursive construction of this case into a fiasco mainly pointed to process failures related to how the government managed the issue in parliament. What is paradoxical, Gaskarth argues, is that the government defeat in the House of Commons was widely seen as an 'instant fiasco' despite the positive, if unintended, diplomatic consequences on the ground in Syria. This appears to confirm the usefulness of Bovens and 't Hart's distinction between a political and a programmatic dimension of policy evaluation which may lead to incongruent results. Moreover, Gaskarth argues that the vote against military action in Syria reflects longer-term trends in British foreign policy which have made it harder for British governments to mobilize domestic support for the use of military force more generally. The framing of the Syria vote as a fiasco and the highly personalized attribution of blame, however, have deflected the attention of policy-makers and commentators away from this broader context.

Christoph Meyer's contribution then moves on to consider the over- and under-reaction to transboundary threats as two inter-related types of foreign policy fiascos. Going beyond traditional issues of national security, the contribution aims at improving cross-fertilization between the foreign policy and international public policy literatures on threat response and risk management. While existing scholarship has mainly been concerned with cases of under-reaction to threats, Meyer argues that policy over-reactions can be just as costly and harmful. In fact, the pre-occupation with avoiding failures of under-reaction might lead to policy prescriptions which precisely result in failures of over-reaction. Against this background, the contribution suggests a typology of failures that can lead to either under- or over-reaction, focusing on threat diagnosis and the proportionality and timeliness of the response. Drawing on pilot case studies on a diverse set of transboundary threats, Meyer identifies three common causal factors that can contribute to fiascos of both under- and over-reaction: learning the wrong lessons from previous incidents; decision-making in institutional silos; and pre-existing preferences of decision-makers to act or not to act.

The following contribution by Andreas Kruck, like the previous one, goes beyond the traditional scope of foreign policy and extends the study of policy fiascos to transnational non-state actors. It focuses on credit rating agencies (CRAs), and asks why these agencies have not faced more negative consequences to their status as private authorities despite their widely recognized rating failures in previous financial and economic crises. Employing a historical institutionalist approach, the author argues that the surprising resilience of CRAs and the difficulties in effectively responding to their failures are owing to flawed public policy decisions in the past which have generated unintended institutional dynamics. Paradoxically, therefore, Kruck suggests that recent failures of CRAs have not weakened their status and influence, but rather contributed to their further entrenchment and institutionalization as transnational private authorities.

In the last contribution to this collection, Ryan Beasley explores how features of Ulrich Beck's world risk society increase the likelihood of public and foreign policy fiascos. Building on previous scholarship according to which policy fiascos can often be traced back to deficient policy-making processes, he argues that the macro-level conditions of globalization affect micro-level decision-making in a way that makes such processes more failure-prone. In particular, the contribution suggests that political decision-making in the risk era is marked by significant uncertainty and an awareness of the self-generated, unpredictable and uncontrollable dynamics of modern industrial society which can potentially have catastrophic consequences. Such decision contexts, in turn, heighten cognitive dissonance in policy-makers and activate psychological dynamics of dissonance avoidance and reduction which are often the source of decision-making mistakes. The contribution illustrates these arguments by discussing the 'war on terror' as a policy response to the 9/11 attacks and the 2003 Iraq war.

LESSONS LEARNED AND FURTHER RESEARCH

The main lesson that comes out of this collection is that public policy and foreign policy fiascos should not be studied as distinct categories. Rather, future research should bring to bear insights from both fields on the joint enterprise of developing middle-range theories (Bovens and 't Hart 2016) to understand and explain the causes and consequences of different types of policy fiascos. This would acknowledge the many similarities between fiascos in public and foreign policy; for example, with regard to the political contestation of policy fiascos or the role of deficiencies in decision-making processes. Understanding public and foreign policy fiascos as examples of the same category of events would also facilitate the broader application of important concepts in studying policy fiascos; for example, the distinction between process failures, programme failures and political failures (McConnell 2016).

If anything, this collection suggests that well-known 'macro' trends such as globalization and internationalization, the growing interdependencies between different levels of policy-making or the rise of transnational politics reinforce the sense that fiascos in public and foreign policy are shaped by similar dynamics. For scholarship in the public policy tradition, the implication is to put more attention on international and transnational sources of policy fiascos. For example, this may shed new light on the roles of uncertainty, complexity and risk as important contexts of such fiascos (Beasley 2016; Meyer 2016). Broadening public policy research out to the international arena might also add to recent efforts at explaining the persistence of policy fiascos (Howlett *et al.* 2015) – for example, by emphasizing international and transnational sources of path dependency or obstacles to policy learning (Kruck 2016). Research on foreign policy fiascos, in turn, would benefit from being less preoccupied with explaining programme failures on the international level and from paying more systematic attention to political failures in the domestic arena. In particular, it is worth exploring whether there is more scope for disconnect between the programmatic and political dimensions of policy evaluation in foreign policy than in public policy. This could come, for example, from the lesser control decision-makers are often said to have over policy outcomes in foreign affairs than in domestic public policy, or from a tendency towards 'symbolic' foreign policies which are primarily designed to play to the domestic gallery.

Closely related, another common theme that runs through the contributions to this collection is the role of agency and structure in the study of policy fiascos. On one hand, there is implicit agreement that policy fiascos involve agency. Foreign and public policies which 'have gone wrong' will more likely come to be seen as fiascos if they could have been avoided and if blame can be attributed to responsible actors. However, scholarship into public policy fiascos has often failed to explore causal factors on the level of individual decision-makers. To redress this imbalance, public policy research can benefit from the rich toolbox in foreign policy for understanding the influence of the personalities and cognitions of key individuals in positions of policy-making authority (Beasley 2016; Brummer 2016). At the same time, focusing explanations of policy fiascos squarely on failures of decision-makers risks masking broader structural contexts which may systematically provoke such failures (Gaskarth 2016). Research into foreign policy fiascos, in particular, would do well in taking more note of such structures on the domestic level which have been widely studied in public policy; for example, types of political systems or governance capacity.

Finally, this collection suggests that the divide between 'objectivist' and 'interpretivist' approaches to studying policy fiascos can easily be overstated. Of course, this is not to deny the important differences that exist between contributions from positivist and post-positivist research traditions. However, these differences appear to be less about ontology, but to reflect primarily differences in methodology and research questions. Specifically, 'objectivist' approaches tend to agree that the benchmarks and criteria they suggest to evaluate policies require some interpretation. Implicitly or explicitly, they often invoke intersubjective standards in defining policy fiascos – for example, when they select cases for study which are 'widely seen' to meet the defining criteria for fiascos (Brummer 2016; Kruck 2016). It is only that such contributions do not problematize the constitution of fiascos, because they are primarily interested in the causes and consequences of policy fiascos they 'take for granted'. Similarly, even contributions that clearly employ post-positivist methods do not tend to go as far as to argue that policy fiascos are completely 'in the eye of the beholder' (Oppermann and Spencer 2016). Rather, they acknowledge that policies will more likely be constructed into fiascos if they can plausibly be linked in social and political discourse to widely shared indicators for policy failure. There thus appears to be quite some common ground between the 'objectivist' and 'interpretivist' camps. Certainly, the differences between the two should not be seen as standing in the way of establishing a dialogue between scholarship on fiascos in public policy and foreign policy. Given the richness of research in the two field and the comparative strengths and weaknesses of each of them, such a dialogue looks immensely promising.

REFERENCES

Allison, G. and Zelikow, P. (1999) *Essence of Decision: Explaining the Cuban Missile Crisis*, Boston, MA: Little, Brown and Company.

Baggott, R. (1998) 'The BSE crisis: public health and the risk society', in P. Gray and P. 't Hart (eds), *Public Policy Disasters in Western Europe*, London: Routledge, pp. 63–80.

Beasley, R. (2016) 'Dissonance and decision-making mistakes in the age of risk', *Journal of European Public Policy*, doi:10.1080/13501763.2015.1127276.

Blight, J.G. and Kornbluh, P. (1998) *Politics of Illusion: The Bay of Pigs Invasion Reexamined*, Boulder, CO: Lynne Rienner.

Bovens, M. and 't Hart, P. (1996) *Understanding Policy Fiascoes*, New Brunswick, NJ: Transaction.

Bovens, M. and 't Hart, P. (2016) 'Revisiting the study of policy failures', *Journal of European Public Policy*, doi:10.1080/13501763.2015.1127273.

Bovens, M., 't Hart, P. and Peters, B.G. (1998) 'Explaining policy disasters in Europe: comparisons and reflections', in P. Gray and P. 't Hart (eds), *Public Policy Disasters in Western Europe*, London: Routledge, pp. 195–214.

Bovens, M., 't Hart, P. and Peters, B.G. (eds) (2001) *Success and Failure in Public Governance*, Cheltenham: Edward Elgar.

Brändström, A. and Kuipers, S. (2003) 'From "normal incidents" to political crises: understanding the selective politicization of policy failures', *Government and Opposition* 38(3): 279–305.

Brummer, K. (2016) '"Fiasco prime ministers": leaders' beliefs and personality traits as possible causes for policy fiascos', *Journal of European Public Policy*, doi:10.1080/13501763.2015.1127277.

Butler, D., Adonis, A. and Travers, T. (1994) *Failure in British Government. The Politics of the Poll Tax*, Oxford: Oxford University Press.

Dunleavy, P. (1995) 'Policy disasters: explaining the UK's record', *Public Policy and Administration* 10(2): 52–70.

Gaskarth, J. (2016) 'The fiasco of the two Syria votes: decline and denial in British foreign policy', *Journal of European Public Policy*, doi:10.1080/13501763.2015. 1127279.

Gorst, A. and Johnman, L. (1997) *The Suez Crisis*, Abingdon: Routledge.

Gray, P. and 't Hart, P. (eds) (1998) *Public Policy Disasters in Western Europe*, London: Routledge.

Hall, P. (1980) *Great Planning Disasters*, London: Weidenfeld and Nicolson.

Howlett, M. (2012) 'The lessons of failure: learning and blame avoidance in public policy-making', *International Political Science Review* 33(5): 539–55.

Howlett, M., Ramesh, M. and Wu, X. (2015) 'Understanding the persistence of policy failures: the role of politics, governance and uncertainty', *Public Policy and Administration* 30(3–4): 209–20.

Janis, I.L. (1982) *Groupthink. Psychological Studies of Policy Decisions and Fiascos*, Boston, MA: Houghton Mifflin.

Janis, I.L. (1989) *Crucial Decisions. Leadership in Policymaking and Crisis Management*, New York: The Free Press.

Jervis, R. (1976) *Perception and Misperception in International Politics*, Princeton, NJ: Princeton University Press.

Kaiser, D. (2002) *American Tragedy: Kennedy, Johnson, and the Origins of the Vietnam War*, Cambridge, MA: Harvard University Press.

King, A. and Crewe, I. (2013) *The Blunders of Our Governments*, London: Oneworld.

Kruck, A. (2016) 'Resilient blunderers: credit rating fiascos and rating agencies' institutionalized status as private authorities', *Journal of European Public Policy*, doi:10. 1080/13501763.2015.1127274.

McConnell, A. (2015) 'What is policy failure? A primer to help navigate the maze', *Public Policy and Administration* 30(3–4): 221–42.

McConnell, A. (2016) 'A public policy approach to understanding the nature and causes of foreign policy failure', *Journal of European Public Policy*, doi:10.1080/ 13501763.2015.1127278

McDermott, R. (2004) 'The feeling of rationality: the meaning of neuroscientific advances for Political Science', *Perspectives on Politics* 2(4): 691–706.

Meyer, C. (2016) 'Over- and under-reaction to transboundary threats: two sides of a misprinted coin?', *Journal of European Public Policy*, doi:10.1080/13501763. 2015.1127275.

Oppermann, K. and Spencer, A. (2016) 'Telling stories of failure: narrative constructions of foreign policy fiascos', *Journal of European Public Policy*, doi:10.1080/ 13501763.2015.1127272.

Ritchie, E. and Zito, A. (1998) 'The common fisheries policy: a European disaster?', in P. Gray and P. 't Hart (eds), *Public Policy Disasters in Western Europe*, London: Routledge, pp. 157–76.

Smith, S. (1985) 'Policy preferences and bureaucratic position: the case of the American hostage rescue mission', *International Affairs* 61(1): 9–25.

Stedman, A.D. (2011) *Alternatives to Appeasement: Neville Chamberlain and Hitler's Germany*, London: I.B.Tauris.

Stern, E. and Sundelius, B. (1998) 'In defence of the Swedish Crown: from triumph to tragedy and back?', in P. Gray and P. 't Hart (eds), *Public Policy Disasters in Western Europe*, London: Routledge, pp. 137–54.

't Hart, P., Stern, E. and Sundelius, B. (eds) (1997) *Beyond Groupthink. Political Group Dynamics and Foreign Policy-Making*, Ann Arbor, MI: University of Michigan Press.

Tuchman, B.W. (1984) *The March of Folly. From Troy to Vietnam*, New York: Alfred A. Knopf.

Walker, S.G. and Malici, A. (2011) *US Presidents and Foreign Policy Mistakes*, Stanford, CA: Stanford University Press.

Wohlstetter, R. (1962) *Pearl Harbor: Warning and Decision*, Stanford, CA: Stanford University Press.

Yetiv, S.A. (2011) *Explaining Foreign Policy: US Decision-Making in the Gulf Wars*, 2nd edn, Baltimore, MD: Johns Hopkins University Press.

Revisiting the study of policy failures

Mark Bovens and Paul 't Hart

ABSTRACT   The analysis of policy failures is, by definition, not a neutral endeavour, since policy fiascos are not neutral events. Moreover, they are often, usually implicitly, but sometimes explicitly, permeated with prosecutorial narratives, blame games and a search for culprits. Fiascos do not just 'happen'. They are constructed, declared, and argued over in labelling processes that are not necessarily 'evidence–based'. This presents a challenge for any academic endeavour to identify, analyse and explain policy fiascos. Against this backdrop, we assess the study of policy failure as it stands today, and offer some reflections for its further development.

POLICY FAILURES: CONTESTED CONSTRUCTS

In 2012, the Australian historian Christopher Clark published *The Sleepwalkers*, a 700-page-thick account of how the European great powers stumbled into the First World War. The book gave a very detailed description of the years, months, days and even hours that preceded the outbreak of war in August 1914. Soon after its publication, the book became the subject of controversy. Clarke's conclusion was that 'the outbreak of war was a tragedy, not a crime' (Clarke 2012: 561). The crisis that resulted in one of the world's most atrocious wars was 'the fruit of a shared political culture', according to Clarke, and could not be blamed solely on Germany and Austria, the axis powers. The other European superpowers, but also the Serbian nationalistic government, bore part of the blame, too. In Germany, with its contemporary history of soul-searching and introspection and its 'battle of the historians', Clarke was portrayed as an apologist. In Serbia, on the other hand, he was accused of anti-Serbian bias.

The reception of *The Sleepwalkers* shows how, even one century after the fact, international crises and diplomatic failures can be the topic of vehement academic debate and political controversy. The analysis of policy failures is, by definition, not a neutral endeavour, since policy fiascos are not neutral events. Moreover, they are often, usually implicitly, but sometimes explicitly, permeated with prosecutorial narratives, blame games and a search for culprits (see Oppermann and Spencer 2016). Starting 20 years ago, we published several books and papers on policy failures, successes and the politics of policy evaluation, including cross-national and cross-sectoral case comparisons (Bovens and 't Hart 1995, 1996; Bovens *et al.* 1999, 2001, 2006; Gray and 't Hart

1998). We argued in these studies that 'success' and 'failure' are not inherent attributes of policy, but rather labels applied by stakeholders and observers. Fiascos do not just 'happen'. The same goes for 'successes' (McConnell 2011). They are constructed, declared and argued over. Clearly, these labelling processes are not necessarily 'evidence-based'. Formal evaluations or benchmarking exercises are not always conducted, and when they do their results may not necessarily be widely known or accepted.

Particularly in cases of complex and contested programmes, stakeholders' views may have been shaped long before. Moreover, evidence will be met by counter-evidence. In other words, the verdict about a public policy, programme or project is shaped in ongoing 'framing contests' between its advocates and shapers on the one hand, and its critics and victims on the other (Boin *et al.* 2009). In this contribution, we re-examine this argument, review the study of policy failure as it stands today, and offer some reflections for the analysis of foreign policy failures.

IDENTIFYING FAILURE: TWO LOGICS OF EVALUATION

Governments plan, decide, do, deliver, adjust, reverse and terminate many things, all the time. Three decades of rhetoric about shrinking the scope of the state notwithstanding, their interventions cover almost every conceivable aspect of our lives and our societies. Even deregulation, privatization and more community-based public service provision require proactive and alert government, we have since discovered (Moran 2001). Only a part of this myriad of ambitions and activities unfolds as hoped, expected and planned for by policymakers. Another part throws up surprises, complications, delays, disappointments and unintended consequences. Though to our knowledge no one has ever attempted to make a comprehensive estimate of the proportion, four decades of implementation research have taught us that the share of the latter group is non-trivial at best: it has yielded a litany of 'great expectations dashed' and 'ruined hopes' (Pressman and Wildavsky 1984; see also Schuck 2014).

So, if we regard instances of delivery-and-results-as-planned as 'successes', what are we to make of the other category? Are they all, by definition, 'failures'That seems overly harsh, and hardly helpful. But how much deviation from original plans – in terms of coverage, timing, production costs, impacts, stakeholder attitudes and behaviours – can a policy stand before its reputation begins to suffer? There is no Archimedean point, no self-evident yardstick. The exercise of discretionary judgment is inevitable, and that is precisely what goes on both in the political and the academic arenas in which policy reputations are being shaped.

But this exercising of judgment in how people perceive the performance of public policies is an imperfect business. Nor does it take place in a vacuum. There are many sources of inadvertent or explicit bias in assessing policies and their outcomes (Bovens and 't Hart 1996). Values, positions, interests, time and culture come into play as much as the observable attributes (the 'facts') of a policy. Evaluation is, after all, both a normative exercise, in that it presumes standards against which performance will be assessed, and a political exercise, in that attaching certain labels to a programme or project can have significant consequences for those involved in and affected by it.

Of course, there are instances where few observers will hesitate to attach the label 'policy failure' to government operations that evidently went wrong. Think of spectacular, unambiguous and highly consequential mishaps such as the United States-led invasion of Iraq, the regulation and oversight of the banking and financial services industry, the acute collapse of public infrastructures and other man-made disasters, conspicuous public procurement and IT-innovation failures, or cases of entrenched institutional corruption. However, some analysts seem to think that this suffices, and don't bother to define what they mean when they talk about 'blunders' or 'fiascos' (e.g., Crewe and King 2013).

But more often it is fundamentally ambivalent. Think of the Australian government's suite of 'Keynesian' macroeconomic policy measures (worth A\$42 billion) taken at the onset of the global financial crisis and designed to prevent it causing an economic slump in Australia by putting money in the hands of local businesses and consumers as soon as possible. It was a marked success overall: Australia was the only Western country to avoid recession at that time. But at the same time, one of the measures – generous subsidies for home insulation – generated not just a massive uptake but also appeared to have contributed to the electrocution of four young apprentices working for several of the many electricians that scrambled to perform the work, as well as to a marked upsurge in house fires owing to improper installation of insulation materials. How to assess this latter programme? The four fatalities that had occurred across the 200,000 installations that had been performed during this period actually constituted an improvement upon the industry's average safety record. But all four incidents occurred within a few weeks, and thus became a story rather than a statistic. Massive and critical attention was trained on the programme by media and the parliamentary opposition. The government tried to counter with 'facts'. A framing contest ensued, and the image of a 'mess' was the one that stuck. It cost the responsible minister his job, the programme was shut down and the public service division that administered it was moved into a different department. Some policy analysts argued that the programme's woes were a product of avoidable failures in policy design (Lewis 2011), but others claimed that had the government conducted its impression management a little more astutely, the chips could well have fallen the other way and the story could have crumbled. What was now a major 'fiasco' could well have ended up as an incident (Tiffen 2010).

This example is the rule rather than the exception. There are many shades of grey in how we perceive public policies, programmes and projects. The study of policy success and failure is therefore one of the dynamics of *reputation* as much as it is one of *performance*. Bovens and 't Hart (1996) acknowledged this by making a distinction between the 'programmatic' and the 'political' dimensions of policy evaluation. *Programmatic* evaluation pertains to the world of facts and social balance sheets: observable costs and benefits, original intentions and eventual outcomes. Its currency is 'performance as measured'. Mark Moore's (2013) public value scorecard is just the latest in a whole series of attempts to provide policy analysts with standardized tools for programmatic assessment. Clearly, though sometimes presented as 'objective' and 'evidence-based', there is ample debate over the extent to which such technical assessment is free of political judgement/evaluation. For instance, the European Commission has introduced impact assessments for all major policy initiatives, designed to ensure that all economic, social and ecological consequences of alternative policy options are described, estimated and evaluated. However, such impact assessments have been characterized as justifications for certain pre-determined policy narratives, rather than representing an objective instrument for evidence-based policy (Radaelli *et al.* 2013).

Political evaluation, on the other hand, squarely pertains to the world of impressions: lived experiences, stories, frames, counter-frames, heroes and villains. These are constructed in the way policies are being perceived and debated among their stakeholders, in the media and in the forums where policy-makers are held to account, such as citizen and institutional watchdogs, legislatures, courts. The currency of political evaluation is 'reputation as conferred' (by those accountability forums). Performance statistics and professional judgments are only a few among many reputation-shaping forces in the politics of evaluation. In the political arena, critical, well-publicized incidents, however unrepresentative for the policy at large they might be, can make for more compelling narratives than any programmatic evaluation exercise, however richly documented and methodologically robust.[1]

That these two logics of evaluation are not necessarily highly correlated was demonstrated empirically in our six-country, four-sector comparative empirical investigation of success and failure in public governance (Bovens *et al.* 2001; see also Gaskarth 2016; Kruck 2016). Some significant programmatic successes – such as health care reforms seeking to regulate doctor's pay or government efforts to provide soft landings to sectors and regions afflicted by terminal industrial decline – were not recognized as such in the political arena. Tax collection is also a classic case. In quite a few countries, governments manage, year in, year out, to peacefully extract very significant parts of wages, profits and asset values from citizens and corporate bodies, with tax compliance rates well above 90 per cent. But tax laws and tax authorities are rarely getting any credit and remain nearly always politically controversial, loathed by the corporate sector and met with at best quiet desperation by the public. They can never be popular, regardless of their performance on the relevant performance indicators; at best, they are taken for granted and accepted as a necessary evil. Much of government policy is not about conferring benefits and delivering services, but about restricting freedoms, administering pain and eliciting compliance. To make those types of policies politically popular is a big ask.

Likewise, marked performance failures were not followed by a collapse of a programme's reputation or of its chief architects and implementers. Most of the six countries in our study experienced major banking and/or currency crises as unintended consequences of deregulation policies pursued during the 1980s and early 1990s. In some instances, major monetary and social costs were incurred by sloppy or toothless regulatory oversight of the now much more autonomous financial institutions. But in the closed, technocratic, old-boys-network world of finance, political pressures for transparency and accountability about what had happened remained limited. Twenty years on, the scenario appeared to have changed only somewhat. Programmatically, very similar causes lay at the root of the spectacular regulatory failure that allowed financial institutions to embark on the excessively complex products and risky investment strategies that triggered the 2008–9 global financial meltdown. But this time, politically, virtually all incumbent governments responsible for the lax regulatory regime were punished by the voters, particularly in hard-hit countries ('t Hart and Tindall 2009).

When programmatic and political evaluation logics are out of kilter, strange incongruities may occur. Take for example the handling of HIV-infected blood samples during the early days of the AIDS epidemic. Countries all struggled to get to grips with this new and ill-understood challenge. Technically, most adopted more or less similar measures at roughly the same time. In France, however, the limited number of HIV infections that occurred resulted in one of the most vehement post-World War 2 political scandals, with several ministers having to step down and former prime minister Fabius ending up in a criminal court. At the same time in Spain where, seen from a programmatic perspective, medical authorities were far less effective, resulting in many avoidable HIV contaminations, little or no political 'fallout' occurred (Bovens et al. 2001).

Table 1   Two logics of evaluation

Reputation: Political assessment / Performance: Programmatic assessment	++	--
++	Success	Tragedy
--	Farce	Fiasco

Table 1 visualizes the four ideal typical outcomes that result from acknowledging these two logics of evaluation. The table in effect creates a two-dimensional assessment space. Two symmetrical outcomes ('success' and 'failure') are contrasted with two incongruent, asymmetrical outcomes. One is the 'tragedy' box, consisting of policies that deliver admirable outcomes but yield little or no public or political credit. Wildavsky's (1977) political paradox of health policy – 'doing better, feeling worse' – captures this. Intelligence and counterterrorism programmes, whose accomplishments can often not be publicized, may suffer from a similar lack of community and political appreciation, particularly when salient enemies and threats seem to be lacking.

Conversely, there is also the 'farce' of a policy failing to deliver on its promises but suffering no real dent in its reputation or that of its makers. During the 1970s and '80s, industry policies seeking to resuscitate dying but publicly treasured, regionally pivotal and politically sacralized sectors like shipbuilding, car manufacturing and steel production triggered truly massive but strategically futile public expenditure. But in the short run, jobs were 'saved' and pain postponed, and so these policies for a long time enjoyed solid support across the political spectrum. It was a classic case of 'too much invested to quit', with all the cognitive dissonance reduction it entailed. Likewise, foreign policy fixtures like 'deterrence' (and its close connection to 'domino theory' thinking, however ill-grounded in misperceptions of adversaries' will power, resources and rationality), and 'economic sanctions' appear to enjoy continued popularity among policy-makers in any states, despite their chequered performance records and the complicated conditions under which they are said to be working at all (Blanchard and Ripsman 2013; Payne 2015).

Table 1 highlights what related fields of research – on agency reputation (Maor 2014), public accountability (Bovens *et al.* 2014) and the social dynamics of credit and blame (Tilly 2008) – have also found: there is no 'just world' of policy assessment in which reputation naturally reflects performance. The nexus between the two is constructed, negotiated and therefore contingent, and often variable over time. The dynamic (dis)equilibriums between performance and reputation that may result are always the result of two different and only weakly related evaluation processes: the deterioration or improvement of its programmatic accomplishments as measured in technical assessment exercises; and the political waxing and waning of the coalitions of actors lending it support or criticizing it.

Over time, a policy may thus evolve an assessment trajectory across the two-dimensional space of Table 1. One example would be NASA's space shuttle programme (1981–2011), which was the initially popular and seemingly well-performing follow up to its iconic Apollo programme. But five years after its inception, budgetary difficulties and growing vulnerabilities in the management of the programme undermined its performance. This became dramatically visible, and politically challenging, with the January 1986 Challenger explosion, which caused a major slump in both the programme's and the agency's reputation and autonomy. Reputation recovered somewhat and ostensibly performance improved as 'lessons were learned'. But the reputations of programme and organization were shattered again in 2003, when the Columbia shuttle was lost upon its re-entry to earth and the subsequent investigation revealed that the agency had learned less well than it thought it had (Starbuck and Farjoun 2005).

16

McConnell (2011) has since made three additions to the Bovens and 't Hart's framework. One, he has turned the original focus on fiascos upside down by concentrating on the other end of the spectrum, policy success. Second, he devised a continuum of assessment outcomes that comprises two intermediate positions between the two opposites of complete (in his terminology: 'durable') success and failure: conflicted and precarious success. *Conflicted* success comprises instances where, notwithstanding some demonstrable achievements, there is significant political contestation about the merits of a policy. *Precarious* success denotes instances where 'policies operate at the edge of failure', as there are major shifts or deviations from original goals and 'high-profile and bitter conflicts' among stakeholders and in the political arena (McConnell 2011: 61). Third, he supplemented the programmatic–political dichotomy with a third dimension: process assessment (see also McConnell 2016). McConnell (2011: 64):

> Process basically "gets the job done" for government in the sense that it puts in place the quality that government wants, bringing constitutional legitimacy to the outcome, with a strong coalition of interests behind it.

In our view, this way of defining process comes perilously close to what has been defined as political assessment. Each of the three criteria mentioned by McConnell essentially refers to reputational concerns, namely (ways of) getting and maintaining support and legitimacy for a policy. The technocratic side of 'process' – methodological rigour and procedural correctness in policy design, professional management of implementation and oversight – the quality of 'puzzling' to counterbalance the 'powering', to use Heclo's (1974) classic phrase – is noticeably absent.

This is not the place to debate the merits of various incarnations of the success/failure assessment framework as such (see Bovens 2010; Marsh and McConnell 2010). Suffice to say that the entire line of research discussed here makes it clear that researchers of alleged failures, fiascos, blunders and messes of governments' labour have an obligation to be methodical, transparent and clever in how they position themselves *vis-à-vis* these quintessentially political acts of applying synthetic labels to often complex, ambiguous, changeable realities of performance and reputation.

Howlett (2012) has made several important recent additions to the analytical repertoire of students of policy failure that can help in this endeavour. He observes, first of all, that one should distinguish between policy failures born out of ill will and malevolence, such as studied in the literature on state crimes (De Haven-Smith 2006), and those that arise inadvertently. Secondly, focusing on the latter class of events, Howlett (2012: 545) rightly argues that:

> [I]n many contemporary studies ... different aspects and types of failure are often poorly specified and incorrectly juxtaposed, and this conceptual confusion has stood in the way of cumulative theory-building into the causes and consequences of policy success and failure.

Table 2 Howlett's typology of policy failure

| | | Magnitude (extent and duration) | |
		High	Low
Salience (intensity and visibility)	High	Type I: major failure e.g., climate change (international treaty) policy failure	Type II: focused failure e.g., sports crowd control (riots) policy failure
	Low	Type III: diffuse failure e.g., anti-poverty policy failure	Type IV: minor failure e.g., policy service contract bid failure

To remedy this, he presents a typology (see Table 2) that employs two dimensions: highly public and widely agreed-upon versus more opaque and more ambivalent failures; and system-wide and long-lasting versus limited scope and ephemeral failures. Howlett is right. If the analytical ambition is to not only systematically identify but also explain policy failures, lumping together systemic and protracted failures (such as the creeping regulatory failure in financial sector supervision in the decade leading up to the 2008–9 global financial crisis) with a local, one-off events like, for example, the crowd disaster at the 2010 Love Parade electronic dance festival in the German city of Duisburg (a case of crowd turbulence which caused the death of 21 people by suffocation), is not a particularly helpful case selection strategy. Aiming for a grand theory covering all forms of policy failure identified in the typology is fruitless. It makes more sense to develop several mid-range theories covering particular clusters of policy failures, and Howlett's typology is one plausible way to get this process underway.

EXPLAINING POLICY FAILURE: IN SEARCH OF MID-RANGE THEORIES

With these distinctions in mind, let us explore this ambition of explaining policy failures a bit further. There are at least two forms that ambition can take. The first is to *explain specific instances of policy failure*. The literature is replete with such attempts. Some of the most impressive efforts in this vein have not only been made by academic researchers such as Vaughan(1996), but by 'post-mortem-style' public inquiries. Notable examples include the 9/11 Commission study of the roots of the US intelligence failure that failed to forestall the Al Qaeda surprise attacks on the Twin Towers and the Pentagon; and the Dutch Institute for War Studies report on the failure of the United Nations (UN) peacekeeping operation to prevent the 1995 massacre of Bosnian men by Bosnian Serb forces at Srebrenica (Netherlands Institute for War Studies [NIOD] 2002). Contemporary high-salience, high-magnitude cases, such as the failure of the US-led invasion of Iraq, now routinely elicit a multi-disciplinary array of academics seeking to explain their occurrence.

Much of this oft-admirable work is either at best implicitly using existing theory (e.g., Byman 2008 on Iraq). Much of it privileges a single explanation at a single level of analysis – for example, cognitive failure because of excessive reliance on misleading historical analogies (Khong 1992), 'risk-taking' and 'hubris' on the part of ambitious but unreflective government leaders (Boetcher 2005; Owen 2012), 'groupthink' in the inner circle élite groups in which foreign policy decisions get made (Badie 2010), or 'bureaucratic politics' marring interorganizational information exchange and co-ordination (Gabriel 1986). Piling up single case studies using single theories of failure remains useful to an extent. But it should be clear that it does not advance the field as much as do multi-perspectivist and integrative approaches (e.g., Houghton 2001; Kam 1988; Mintz and DeRouen 2010; Mitchell and Masoud 2009; Parker and Stern 2005; Walker and Malici 2011; Yetiv 2011) to analysing single instances of policy failure. Equally useful are medium-n comparative case designs, particularly ones that compare the dynamics of policy failures with those of non-failures (Patashnik 2008; Shafer and Crichlow 2010).

The second form of explanatory analysis, as we have seen, is to *develop theories explaining a range of policy failures of a certain type*. Peter Hall's (1981) classic study of planning disasters in the United Kingdom led the way. Moran's (2001) study of policy disasters of the regulatory state, Bovens *et al.*'s (2001) structured-focused comparison of successes and failures of governments dealing with four different types of governance challenges, and Flyvbjerg *et al.*'s (2003) study of failures of 'megaprojects' are all examples of controlled comparisons that enable the development of mid-range theories. Contemporary advances in causal process-tracing and fuzzy-set methodology allow for more explanatory rigour and stronger theory development than can be found in any of these examples (Blatter and Haverland 2012; Ragin 2008). The present collection's emphasis on explaining failures in foreign policy stands in a long, US-based tradition that was given momentum by Irving Janis's *Victims of Groupthink* (Janis 1972) and has reached an impressive new peak with Schafer and Crichlow (2010). It treats foreign affairs as a distinct policy endeavour and develops purpose-built models explaining instances where foreign policy initiatives are seen to have failed.

The challenges of such attempts are manifold. They entail issues of scope (does, for example, 'foreign policy' still not cover much too broad a spectrum of interventions to be a suitable target for mid-range theorizing?), typologizing (are, for instance, 'intelligence failures' or 'megaprojects' coherent enough cat-egories to be treated as types in a comparative design?) and case selection (what can we learn from a sample of 'foreign policy fiascos' in country X that includes a military misadventure, a grand development aid scheme coming unstuck and a deterrence failure?). Fortunately there are now great examples of mid-range theory construction based on rigorous comparison of (foreign) policy-making process that we can emulate and adapt for the purposes of explaining particular types of policy failure (George and Smoke 1974; Haney 2002; Kaarbo 2012).

MOVING FORWARD: LEARNING FROM POLICY FAILURES

In closing this contribution, it might be useful to reflect on the underlying purpose of studying policy failure. Most analysts who analyse policy failures probably are driven by a desire to create knowledge that will help prevent the recurrence of failure. By documenting what went wrong and explaining why, policy analysts create a knowledge base that should enable future policy-makers to do better. One cannot help but wonder if we have gotten any closer to achieving that objective. To get complex organizations and policy networks to actually *learn* from feedback, rather than make symbolic, opportunistic or minimal impact changes in response to it, (March and Olsen 1975) about their past performance is hard enough – that much we know from the spate of studies on policy change and policy learning across a wide range of sectors and jurisdictions. To induce policy (as opposed to political) learning from highly public, politically charged forms of feedback such as that produced by evaluators and public inquiries in the context of policy fiascos is proving even more difficult (Birkland 2006; Boin *et al.* 2008; Hansén 2007; Howlett 2012; May 1992; Walsh 2006).

In short: big policy failures can be, but all too seldom are, a trigger for big policy learning that reduces the likelihood of their reoccurrence. This should not deter us from trying, but it also means that in doing so we need to move 'from scientific demonstration and verification to the giving of reasons and the assessment of practical arguments' (Fischer 1995: 215). Articulating their research-based ideas about institutional and policy design, decision-making and implementation and injecting them into the right places at the right time is a challenge that students of policy failure (and success) should take to heart just as much as getting the next study underway and the next article published. Policy analysts must be prepared to make a difference in the 'real world' if they are serious about preventing fiascos (Hallsworth 2011).

This is not just frivolous sniping from the sidelines. It is about taking our own findings seriously. They tell us that the best way to avoid fiascos is to 'open up' policy-making processes to genuine contests of ideas. This is truer the more complex and interdependent the world is getting, and the bigger the stakes of avoiding the destructive potential of flawed government. Christopher Clark, the author of *The Sleepwalkers* ends on a positive note. One of the major differences between the years before World War 1 and the decades after World War 2 is that:

> decisionmakers and the general public alike grasped in a visceral way the meaning of nuclear war … As a consequence, the greatest arms race in

human history never culminated in nuclear war between the superpowers. (Clark 2012: 562)

At the same time, minute analysis of several crises and nuclear alerts during the Cold War standoff between the US and the Soviet Union suggests that this was sometimes more owing to coincidence and level-headed individuals lower down the hierarchy exercising sound professional judgments than it was a product of failure-proof weapons systems, military doctrines or far-sighted foreign and defence policy-makers (Jervis et al. 1985; Lebow and Stein 1995; Sagan 1993).

One of the founding fathers of modern policy analysis, Yehezkel Dror, has demonstrated acute awareness of the rising stakes of governance failures in the contemporary world. In his latest book, *The Avant-Garde Politician* (Dror 2014), he makes a compelling case that bad governance can now compromise the very survival of species and planet. His solution is to advocate what, in inimitable fashion, he has earlier called a 'novo-Platonic' approach to public policy-making: a circle of strong, enlightened, dedicated, disciplined, well-educated 'high-quality' rulers (Dror 2001). Only constrained by a global constitutional court, they should offset democracy's penchant for short-termism and opportunism in dealing with our future world's increasingly complex and often dangerous policy predicaments. To some this may be a tempting idea. But if the yield of several decades of studies of policy failure is anything to go on, it is likely to generate terrible unintended consequences.

The biggest fiascos are not caused by division, ceaseless debate, all too powerful checks and balances and institutional paralysis, but by the closing up of policy-making processes: concentrating authority in too few hands; constraining the scope and duration of deliberation; and shutting down diversity and dissent (*cf.* Schuck 2014). Another founding father of the field, Charles Lindblom, was absolutely right when he observed that the very 'messiness' of democratic policy-making – active citizens, wide participation, dispersed decision making, multistakeholder involvement, contending bodies of evidence and argument, persuasion and negotiation, institutional checks and balances during policy design as well as implementation – with all the suboptimization, incrementalism and prevarication it entails, is still a much better safeguard against spectacular failures than a top–down, monolithic, tightly held, 'evidence-based', linear and lean process dominated by a single small 'team' within the policy arena (Lindblom 1965). We forget this number one lesson for preventing policy failure at our own peril.

NOTE

1 To complicate things further, in the evaluation practice technical assessments will often not be free of political judgements. For instance, the European Commission has introduced impact assessments for all major policy initiatives, designed to ensure that all economic, social and ecological consequences of alternative policy options are described, estimated and evaluated. However, such impact assessments have been characterized as justifications for certain pre-determined policy narratives, rather than representing an objective instrument for evidence-based policy (Radaelli *et al.*, 2013).

REFERENCES

Badie, D. (2010) 'Groupthink, Iraq, and the War on Terror: explaining US policy shift toward Iraq', *Foreign Policy Analysis* 6(4): 277–96.

Birkland, T. (2006) *Lessons of Disaster*, Washington, DC: Georgetown University Press.

Blanchard, J.F. and Ripsman, N.M. (2013) *Economic Statecraft and Foreign Policy*, London: Routledge.

Blatter, J. and Haverland, M. (2012) *Designing Case Studies: Explanatory Approaches in Small-N Research*, Basingstoke: Palgrave.

Boetcher, W. (2005) *Presidential Risk Behavior in Foreign Policy: Prudence or Peril?* New York: Palgrave MacMillan.

Boin, A., 't Hart, P. and McConnell, A. (eds) (2008) *Governing After Crisis: The Politics of Investigation, Accountability and Learning*, Cambridge: Cambridge University Press.

Boin, A., McConnell, A. and 't Hart, P. (2009) 'Crisis exploitation: political and policy impacts of framing contests', *Journal of European Public Policy* 16(1): 81–106.

Bovens, M. (2010) 'A comment on Marsh and McConnell: towards a framework for establishing policy success', *Public Administration* 88(2): 584–85.

Bovens, M. and 't Hart, P. (1995) 'Fiascos in the public sector: towards a conceptual frame for comparative policy analysis', in J.J. Hesse and Th.A.J. Toonen (eds), *The European Yearbook of Comparative Government and Public Administration*, Baden-Baden: Nomos, pp. 577–608.

Bovens, M. and 't Hart, P. (1996) *Understanding Policy Fiascoes*, New Brunswick, NJ: Transaction.

Bovens, M., 't Hart, P., Dekker, S. and Verheuvel, G. (1999) 'The politics of blame avoidance: defensive tactics in a Dutch crime-fighting fiasco', in H.K. Anheier (ed.), *When Things Go Wrong: Failures and Breakdowns in Organizational Settings*, London: Sage, pp. 123–47.

Bovens, M., 't Hart, P. and Peters, B.G. (eds) (2001) *Success and Failure in Public Governance: A Comparative Analysis*, Cheltenham: Edward Elgar.

Bovens, M., 't Hart, P. and Kuipers, S.L. (2006) 'The politics of policy evaluation', in M. Moran, B. Goodin and M. Rein (eds), *Oxford Handbook of Public Policy*, Oxford: Oxford University Press, pp. 317–33.

Bovens, M., Schillemans, T. and Goodin, R. (eds) (2014) *Oxford Handbook of Public Accountability*, Oxford: Oxford University Press.

Byman, D. (2008) 'An autopsy of the Iraq debacle: policy failure or bridge too far?', *Security Studies* 17(4): 599–643.

Clark, C. (2012) *The Sleepwalkers: How Europe Went to War in 1914*, London: Penguin.

Crewe, I. and King, A. (2013) *The Blunders of Our Governments*, London: Oneworld.

De Haven-Smith, L. (2006) 'When political crimes are inside jobs: detecting state crimes against democracy', *Administrative Theory & Praxis* 28(3): 330–55.

Dror, Y. (2001) *The Capacity to Govern: A Report to the Club of Rome*, London: Frank Cass.

Dror, Y. (2014) *Avant-Garde Politician: Leaders for a New Epoch*, Washington, DC: Westphalia Press.

Fischer, F. (1995) *Evaluating Public Policy*, Chicago: Nelson-Hall.

Flybjerg, B., Bruzelius, N. and Rothengatter, W. (2003) *Megaprojects and Risk: An Anatomy of Ambition*, Cambridge: Cambridge University Press.

Gabriel, R. (1986) *Military Incompetence*, New York: Hill and Wang.

Gaskarth, J. (2016) 'The fiasco of the two Syria votes: decline and denial in British foreign policy', *Journal of European Public Policy*, doi:10.1080/13501763.2015.1127279.

George, A.L. and Smoke, R. (1974) *Deterrence in American Foreign Policy*, New York: Columbia University Press.

Gray, P. and 't Hart, P. (eds) (1998) *Public Policy Disasters in Europe*, London: Routledge.

Hall, P. (1981) *Great Planning Disasters*, London: Penguin.

Hallsworth, M. (2011) *Policymaking in the Real World: Evidence and Analysis*, London: Institute for Government.

Haney, P.J. (2002) *Organizing for Foreign Policy Crises*, Ann Arbor, MI: University of Michigan Press.

Hansén, D. (2007) *Crisis and Perspectives on Policy Change: Swedish Counter-terrorism Policymaking*, Stockholm: Swedish National Defence College.

Heclo, H. (1974) *Modern Social Politics in Britain and Sweden: From Relief to Income Maintenance*, New Haven, CT: Yale University Press.

Houghton, D.P. (2001) *US Foreign Policy and the Iran Hostage Crisis*, New York: Cambridge University Press

Howlett, M. (2012) 'The lessons of failure: learning and blame avoidance in public policy', *International Political Science Review* 33(5): 539–55.

Janis, I.L. (1972) *Victims of Groupthink*, Boston: Houghton Mifflin.

Jervis, R., Lebow, R.N. and Stein, J.G. (1985) *Psychology and Deterrence*, Baltimore, MD: Johns Hopkins University Press.

Kaarbo, J. (2012) *Coalition Politics and Cabinet Decision Making: A Comparative Analysis of Foreign Policy Choices*, Ann Arbor, MI: University of Michigan Press.

Kam, E. (1988) *Surprise Attack*, Cambridge, MA: Harvard University Press.

Khong, Y.F. (1992) *Analogies at War*, Princeton, NJ: Princeton University Press.

Kruck, A. (2016) 'Resilient blunderers: credit rating fiascos and rating agencies' institutionalized status as private authorities', *Journal of European Public Policy*, doi:10.1080/13501763.2015.1127274.

Lebow, R.N. and Stein, J.G. (1995) *We All Lost the Cold War*, Princeton, NJ: Princeton University Press.

Lewis, C. (2011) 'A recent scandal: the home insulation program', in K. Dowding and C. Lewis (eds), *Ministerial Careers and Accountability in the Commonwealth Government*, Canberra: ANU E Press, pp. 153–76.

Lindblom, C.E. (1965) *The Intelligence of Democracy*, New York: Free Press.

Maor, M. (2014) 'Theorizing bureaucratic reputation', in W. Arild and M. Maor (eds), *Organizational Reputation in the Public Sector*, London: Routledge, pp. 17–36.

March, J. and Olsen, J.P. (1975) 'Organizational learning under ambiguity', *European Journal of Political Research* 3(2): 147–71.

Marsh, D. and McConnell, A. (2010) 'Towards a framework for establishing policy success: a reply to Bovens', *Public Administration* 88(2): 586–7.

May, P.J. (1992) 'Policy learning and failure', *Journal of Public Policy* 12(4): 331–54.

McConnell, A. (2011) *Understanding Policy Success*, Basingstoke: Palgrave.

McConnell, A. (2016) 'A public policy approach to understanding the nature and causes of foreign policy failure', *Journal of European Public Policy*, doi:10.1080/13501763.2015.1127278.

Mintz, A. and DeRouen, K. (2010) *Understanding Foreign Policy Decision Making*, Cambridge: Cambridge University Press.

Mitchell, D. and Massoud, T.G. (2009) 'Anatomy of failure: Bush's decision-making process and the Iraq War', *Foreign Policy Analysis* 5(2): 265–86.

Moore, M. (2013) *Recognizing Public Value*, Cambridge, MA: Harvard University Press.

Moran, M. (2001) 'Not steering but drowning: policy catastrophes and the regulatory state', *Political Quarterly* 72(3): 414–27.

Netherlands Institute for War Studies (NIOD) (2002) *Srebrenica, een 'Veilig' Gebied: Reconstructie, Achtergronden, Gevolgen en Analyses van de Val van een Safe Area*, Amsterdam: Boom.

Oppermann, K. and Spencer, A. (2016) 'Telling stories of failure: narrative constructions of foreign policy fiascos', *Journal of European Public Policy*, doi:10.1080/13501763.2015.1127272.

Owen. D. (2012) *The Hubris Syndrome*, London: Methuen.

Parker, C. and Stern, E.K. (2005) 'Bolt from the blue or avoidable failure? Revisiting September 11 and the origins of surprise', *Foreign Policy Analysis* 1(2): 301–33.

Patashnik, E. (2008) *Reforms at Risk: What Happens After Major Policy Changes Are Enacted*, Princeton, NJ: Princeton University Press.

Payne, K.B. (2015) *Deterrence in the Second Nuclear Age*, Lexington, KY: University of Kentucky Press.

Pressman, J., and Wildavsky, A. (1984) *Implementation*, Berkeley, CA: University of California Press.

Radaelli, C., Dunlop, C.A. and Fritsch, O. (2013) 'Narrating impact assessment in the European Union', *European Political Science* 12(4): 500–21.

Ragin, C.C. (2008) *Redesigning Social Inquiry: Fuzzy Sets and Beyond*, Chicago, IL: University of Chicago Press.

Sagan, S.D. (1993) *The Limits of Safety*, Princeton, NJ: Princeton University Press.

Schuck, P.H. (2014) *Why Government Fails so Often, and How it can do Better*, Princeton, NJ: Princeton University Press.

Schafer, M. and Crichlow, S. (2010) *Groupthink Versus High-Quality Decision Making in International Relations*, New York: Columbia University Press.

Starbuck, W.H. and Farjoun, M. (eds) (2005) *Organization at the Limit: Lessons from the Columbia Disaster*, New York: Wiley Blackwell.

't Hart, P. and Tindall, K. (eds) (2009) *Framing the Global Meltdown*, Canberra: ANU Press.

Tiffin, R. (2010) 'A mess? A shambles? A disaster?', *Inside Story*, 26 October 2010, http://insidestory.org.au/a-mess-a-shambles-a-disaster (accessed 1 February 2015).

Tilly, C. (2008) *Credit and Blame*, Princeton, NJ: Princeton University Press.

Vaughan, D. (1996) *The Challenger Launch Decision*, Chicago, IL: University of Chicago Press.

Walker, S.P. and Malici, A. (2011) *US Presidents and Foreign Policy Mistakes*, Stanford, CA: Stanford University Press

Walsh, J.I. (2006) 'Policy failure and policy change', *Comparative Political Studies* 39(4): 490–518.

Wildavsky, A. (1977) 'Doing better and feeling worse: the political pathology of health policy', *Daedalus* 106(1): 105–23.

Yetiv, S. (2011) *Explaining Foreign Policy: Explaining US Foreign Policy in the Gulf Wars*, Baltimore, MD: Johns Hopkins University Press.

A public policy approach to understanding the nature and causes of foreign policy failure

Allan McConnell

ABSTRACT All governments are vulnerable to policy failure but our understanding of the nature and causes of policy failure is highly underdeveloped. This contribution, written from a public policy perspective, sets out a framework for understanding these issues as applied to foreign policy. In doing so, it seeks a cross-disciplinary fertilization of thinking that uses the messy and contested reality of policy failure as fundamentally a key – rather than a barrier – to advancing our understanding of a phenomenon referred to variously as policy fiascos, policy disasters, policy blunders and policy failures.

INTRODUCTION

Regardless of the extent of evidence, modelling, projections, risk assessment, expert advice and political skills that contribute to policy design and decision-making, no government is immune to the risk of policy failure (Althaus 2008). Allegations abound of policies that have failed for one reason or another. In the field of foreign policy, for example, there are seemingly never-ending allegations of failed military action, peacekeeping initiatives, troop deployment, diplomatic agreements, economic sanctions, trade agreements, aid to other nations and more.

Failures can consume huge amounts of government agenda time, create bigger problems than they seek to solve, provoke media feeding frenzies, provide 'gifts' to political opponents, damage political careers and lead to the downfall of governments. They can also wreak damage – at times fatal – to people, property, economic prosperity and nation-building. Yet, despite many case studies of failure and a small number of grander incursions into understanding 'policy fiascos' (Bovens and 't Hart 1995), 'policy disasters' (Dunleavy 1995) and 'policy blunders' (King and Crewe 2013), we know remarkably little about what actually constitutes 'policy failure' or what causes it. This gap in our understanding is compounded by the routine politics of failure which is replete with blame games, wildly different perceptions and *post-hoc* inquiries often accused of politicization and bias (Boin *et al.* 2008; Brändström and Kuipers

2003; Hood 2002). Such tendencies are hugely significant. If governments and societies have a poor understanding of *if* and *why* policies fail, there is significant risk that they will continually make the same 'mistakes' again, pursuing policies vulnerable to failure with a high risk of political backlash.

In this context, the present article focuses essentially on two separate but related sets of issues. The first is what *is* policy failure and the second is what *causes* policy failure. It presents a framework and argument to assist academic analysts seeking to tread on the 'quicksand' of both issues. Some qualifying points can be made before proceeding.

First, the key analytical value of the article can be explained with reference to Ostrom (2007), who makes the distinction between three types of intellectual contributions: (1) frameworks which address the main elements, relationships and variables that one needs to consider in approaching a problem; (2) theories which focus on explaining and predicting outcomes; and (3) models which operationalize precise assumptions about certain parameters and variables. The article provides a *framework* to advance our understanding, in the hope that it will pave the way for theoretical development and operationalization through case studies (see Bovens and 't Hart 2016). If we can gain deeper insights into policy failure and place less store, for example, on often crude arguments which oversimplify failure (e.g., 'it was a total policy fiasco' or 'the president is totally to blame for this policy disaster'), then we are better placed to reduce the likelihood of policy failures/fiascos/disasters in the future.

Second, it should be noted that the word 'fiasco' is something of a pejorative term. As Bovens and 't Hart (1996: 9) argue in their seminal work *Understanding Policy Fiascoes*: 'To call something a fiasco is to impress on it a powerful negative label, and effectively to engage in an act of allegation.' In effect, 'fiasco' implies that political agents are the causes of farce-like outcomes. In this contribution, I use instead the term 'policy failure' because it does not come primed with assumptions that individual actions (or inactions) are in effect the causes of failure.

Third, while being informed at the margins by a strand of international relations which focuses particularly on decision-making failures and aspects of their causes (e,g., Edelstein 2008; Fleitz 2002; Janis 1972; Jervis 1976; Mearsheimer 2013), the article is written from a public policy perspective by a public policy scholar. This sub-discipline of political science focuses on 'whatever governments choose to do or not to do' (Dye 2012: 12). In adopting this approach, and against the grain of policy studies where foreign policy is generally left to scholars of international relations, comparative politics and area studies, examples are drawn exclusively from foreign policy. I define this field broadly to cover multiple ways in which governments form policies that engage with others beyond state borders. It includes, but is by no means limited to, military engagements, peacekeeping missions, troop deployments, diplomatic accords, sanctions, trade deals and overseas aid. It is hoped that a by-product of this contribution is the building of some bridges across these various sub-disciplines of political science.

DEFINING POLICY FAILURE: CHALLENGES AND A WAY FORWARD

The many methodological difficulties of defining policy failure

The word 'failure' has an air of completeness about it, as though a policy either fails or doesn't fail, and that we can have access to this fact through research. Yet, there are many reasons why we cannot and should not think of policy failure as an indivisible and wholly objective phenomenon.

The existence of multiple standards for failure

The word failure implies undesirability and the breaching of a goal, aspiration or value. Defining failure would be quite straightforward if analysts could agree on such a 'standard'. In reality, however, we immediately confront an array of failure criteria. The outline below is neither exhaustive nor are the categories mutually exclusive, but it does provide a flavour of the apparent elusiveness of policy failure.

Failure to achieve the goals of government. Evaluation against what government set out to do is a standard feature or much policy analysis – especially of the rationalist–scientific tradition (e.g., see Gupta 2011), and it is the default of most intra-governmental assessment of policies. It is also a common feature of academic analysis. Pressman (2009), for example, assesses the G.W. Bush administration's goals in Iraq in precisely this manner, arguing that it did not achieve the three key goals of defeating terrorism, promoting democracy and blocking nonconventional proliferation among adversaries.

Failure to benefit particular interests or groups. At times policies may have failed to benefit the particular target group or groups that were, in theory, the formal target of the original policy design (Schneider and Ingram 1997). One of the key criticisms of foreign aid from a libertarian perspective is that it has little impact on poverty (and indeed can make the poor poorer) unless countries have in place, good governance procedures (Booth 2012).

Failure to produce benefits greater than the costs. Cost–benefit analysis is a standard tool of economic analysis (Gupta 2011), but can also be used in political discourse and often in policy evaluations, via a weighing-up of positive and negative outcomes. *De facto*, a policy is considered to fail if the costs exceed the benefits. Edelstein (2008), in his evaluation of 30 military occupations, adopts this approach, weighing up accomplishments such as mitigating threats from an occupied territory, against costs such as lives lost, financial resources deployed and damage to political reputation.

Failure to match moral, ethical or legal standards. Regardless of what government sets out to do or what it claims to have achieved, many protagonists

27

claim policy failure to be a breach of deeper values. It may be breaches of the law (the 'legal black hole' of Guantanamo Bay has led to arguments that numerous procedures fail to comply with international law) or a policy failing to live up to some higher ethical· or moral standards. A report by the UN Human Rights Committee (2013) found Australia to have breached a series of human rights Articles in its detention of refugees.

Failure to improve on what went before.   A common feature of 'failure' discourse is that we are 'worse off' as a result of what government has done (or failed to do). The benchmark here is how policy outcomes compare to a prior state of affairs. Most judgements of British Prime Minister Neville Chamberlain's policy of appeasement and the signing of the Munich Agreement in 1938 saw this move as paving the way for war rather than avoiding it (McDonough 1998).

Failure to do better than others dealing with similar issues.   The benchmark here is government doing worse in addressing a problem than another jurisdiction (usually a nation) addressing a broadly similar problem, e.g., threat from global terrorism.

Failure to garner sufficient support from those actors and interests who matter.   Policies may be considered a failure because they were unable to command sufficient support from those who either played a strategic role in the implementation process, or whose support was vital in legitimation of the policy. Policy proposals may also fail to gain approval at the executive decision making stage, e.g., 2013 defeat in the House of Commons on a government motion for the UK to join United States- (US) led air strikes on Syria (Gaskarth 2016).

The existence of multiple standards for policy failure seems to be a major barrier to our understanding. One hundred civilian casualties in a military intervention could be considered a failure if we assess this outcome against certain standards (for example, failure to produce benefits greater than the costs and failure to match moral, ethical or legal standards). Yet, such deaths may be perceived as regrettable but nevertheless successful if they contribute to broader standards, such as achieving government goals (helping restore democracy in another nation), improving on what went before (ousting a dictator) and even producing benefits greater than the costs (the long-term benefits of peace and democracy being considered more important than the lives lost regrettably along the way). I will return to such methodologically difficult issues shortly.

Ambiguities, contradictions and the relationship of failure to success

There are additional challenges to understanding what constitutes policy failure. For example, virtually every policy in the world produces some 'achievement', from the very minor to the substantial, just as there are always some 'failures', from the minor and inconsequential to the major. Failure is not 'all or nothing'. For example, the benefits to donors of providing overseas aid are often accompanied by a degree of fraud, with estimates cited in one study as varying between 0.85 per cent and 1.27 per cent (Button *et al.* 2012). A difficult analytical task, therefore, given the perennial entwining of varying degrees of 'successes' and 'failures', is ascertaining what matters most.

Policies also, and typically, have multiple goals, often changing over time, and with tensions between them (Bardach 2011). Baldwin (2000) identifies seven US foreign policy goals in the 1991 Gulf War, from forcing Saddam Hussein out of Kuwait to discouraging other nations from seeking to emulate Iraq. It is, of course, not uncommon for governments to deliver in some respects but not others. We are then faced with the task of weighing up which failures matter most. This is particularly difficult if goals are contradictory. A government paying money behind the scenes to kidnappers can succeed in freeing hostages but fail against a promise not to do deals with terrorists.

Producing unambiguous 'evidence' of failure can also be challenging. As Head (2008) argues, there are many different evidence bases (science, politics, bureaucracy), and a policy that fails the test of gaining approval from experts in the field may be politically expedient. Evidence may also point in different directions, becoming entwined with politicization and argument, and ultimately requiring a high degree of interpretation (Majone 1989). We may not even have sufficient evidence to assess. Heine-Ellison (2001), in her study of sanctions in Iraq, the former Yugoslavia, Angola and Sierra Leone, found that lack of effective monitoring in the latter two cases seriously hampered a strong judgment on the (in)effectiveness of targeted sanctions.

In sum, despite the existence of multiple standards for failure, numerous ambiguities, contradictions and disputes over what constitutes 'evidence' of failure, I would argue that we should not bemoan such difficulties or seek instead a rational scientific measure of policy failure. Our understanding of the nature of policy failure can actually be enhanced rather than hampered once we accept and work with the various standards for policy failure and the numerous methodological difficulties. As Wildavsky (1987) famously argued, in a world of complexity, uncertainty and competing moral values, we should accept that our understanding of policy (in our case policy failure) requires creativity, judgement and innovation.

Defining policy failure: a way forward

Here I modify an earlier definition (McConnell, 2010: 357) and suggest that:

> A policy fails, even if it is successful in some minimal respects, if it does not fundamentally achieve the goals that proponents set out to achieve, and opposition is great and/or support is virtually non-existent.

This definition is able to accommodate the numerous methodological challenges identified above. It is not predicated on accepting or rejecting the normative aims of government and its policies (or the normative claims of policy failure by any actor). The definition is simply an analytical anchor for the framework being proposed here to help us approach this complex and difficult topic.

To advance the analysis I have divided the phenomenon of 'public policy' in a manner reflecting significant strands of policy literature, and helping capture 'what governments do'. We can conceive, therefore, of governments engaging in three types of 'doing', i.e., seeking to (1) steer processes to produce policies, (2) enact programmes/decisions which they seek to put into practice, and (3) impact on 'politics'. They can overlap and compete (as I will argue), but of fundamental importance is that government can 'fail' in each of these three realms (see Table 1), and we can incorporate degrees of contestation to governmental norms and goals. Doing so allows us to build competing views into our understanding, with different political actors using aspects of policy ambiguity such as mixed results, competing goals, and variable evidence in ways that reflect their own, differing perspectives.

Process failure
Governments engage in the process of producing programmes and taking authoritative decisions. This process involves multiple activities from defining problems, narrowing down options for appraisal, deciding on who/when/if to consult, and so on (Althaus *et al.* 2013; Howlett *et al.* 2009). While they 'may' fail in any of these tasks, a more useful and aggregated way of thinking about the process of policy production is to conceive of several aspects of process failure.

We can conceive of failure to preserve government goals and instruments in the policy-making process, to the extent that government is either defeated in its quest to obtain authoritative approval (e.g., legislative approval to cut military funding) or the policy-making process has diluted its aspirations and the programme/decision bears little relation to its original intentions, e.g., one member fails to gain United Nations (UN) support for economic sanctions against another member state. There may also be failure to attract a viable level of legitimacy for the way government produced the policy, e.g., lacks a strong evidence base; is declared unconstitutional; in breach of norms/agreements (such as the Geneva Convention). Failure may also be an inability to build a sustainable coalition of interests during the policy-making process, e.g., inability to get warring interests to sign a peace agreement. There may also be failure to attract broader support for the way in which the policy was produced (or attempted to be produced) to the extent that opposition to the policy-making process is virtually universal and/or support is virtually non-existent, e.g., a government not only failing to gain legislative approval to send troops overseas, but in the process of doing so it is on the receiving end of a political backlash.

Programme/decision failure
Government produces *inter alia* programmes (often conventionally referred to as 'policies') and decisions. There are several ways in which they may fail. One

Table 1   Forms of policy failure

	Success criteria	Failure characteristics
Policy-making process failure	Preserving goals and policy instruments	Government unable to produce its desired policy goals and instruments
	Securing legitimacy	Policy process illegitimate
	Building sustainable coalition	No building of a sustainable coalition
	Attracting support for process	Opposition to process is virtually universal and/or support is virtually non-existent
Programme failure	Implementation in line with objectives	Despite minor progress towards implementation as intended, programme is beset by chronic implementation failures
	Achieving desired outcomes	Some small outcomes achieved as intended, but overwhelmed by failure to produce results
	Benefitting target group(s)	Small benefits are accompanied and overshadowed by damage to the very group that was meant to benefit
	Satisfying criteria highly valued in policy domain	A few minor successes, but plagued by inability to meet criteria highly valued in that policy domain
	Attracting support for programme	Opposition to programme aims, values, and means of achieving them, outweighs small levels of support
Political failure	Enhancing electoral prospects/ reputation	Despite small signs of benefit, policy proves an overall electoral and reputational liability
	Easing the business of governing	Clear signs that the agenda and business of government struggles to suppress a politically difficult issue
	Promotion of government's desired trajectory	Entire trajectory of government in danger of being compromised
	Providing political benefits for government	Opposition to political benefits for government outweighs small levels of support

Note: Original table, substantially adapted from McConnell (2010)

aspect is failure to be put into practice, to the point that despite some progress towards implementation as intended, the programme is beset by chronic implementation failures. Sharman (2011), in his study of the multiple errors produced by states in copying tax blacklists from other countries, reveals multiple failures – even to the extent that Venezuela copied a list from Mexico and blacklisted itself. Another aspect is failure to achieve the desired outcomes. Some small outcomes may be achieved as intended, but these are overwhelmed by failure to produce results, e.g., the United Kingdom's (UK's) unsuccessful application to join the three European Communities in 1961, despite the small benefit of paving the way for a further successful application lodged in 1967. There may also be failure to benefit the intended target group(s) to the point that small benefits are accompanied and overshadowed by damage to the very group(s) that was/were meant to benefit, e.g., Dutch peacekeepers and the deaths of 300 Bosnian Muslims in Srebrenica. Failure may also be an inability to meet a criterion that is highly valued in the policy sector in question, to the extent that despite a few minor successes it is plagued by an inability to meet this criterion, e.g., new intelligence agency failing to protect national security because of a series of missed warning signs. There may also be failure to attract broader support for the programme/decision, to the degree that opposition to programme aims, values, and means of achieving them outweighs small levels of support, e.g., economic sanctions not working and government under attack for pursuing this policy in the first place.

Political failure
Policies have political repercussions. Different conceptual frameworks imply different forms of impact, e.g., policy cycle implications that policy outcomes prompt policy-makers to reflect and learn (Althaus *et al* 2013), path dependency and the inference that policies generally help reproduce dominant ideological pathways (Pierson 2000). The common theme is that policy is not produced or enacted in a vacuum (Cairney 2012b). What governments 'do' has political repercussions. Again, we can capture failures in several ways.

The first and perhaps most obvious is failure to enhance electoral prospects/reputation, to the point that, despite small signs of benefit, the policy proves an overall electoral and reputational liability, e.g., extended and messy war damages government's standing in opinion polls. Perhaps less obvious but no less important is failure to ease the business of governing, to the extent that that the agenda and business of government struggles to suppress a politically difficult issue, e.g., free trade agreement leaves out a major farming producer and this industry runs a relentless and effective lobbying campaign that government cannot escape or quell. There may also be failure to promote the government's desired trajectory, to the degree that the entire trajectory of government is in danger of being compromised, e.g., 'hawkish' administration sanctions the invasion of another nation in the name of promoting democratic freedoms, only for the move to be widely criticized even by its own supporters as dictatorial and undemocratic. Finally, there can be failure for government in the sense that any political benefits it may have accrued are outweighed by substantial opposition which is critical of government and accuses it of not acting in the public interest, e.g., European Union (EU) member state promising a referendum on continuing with EU membership, widely criticized as little more than non-serious pre-election positioning to take the heat out of a contentious issue.

There are many implications for the existence of diverse forms of policy failure. I will return to this issue in the conclusion and link it to the causes of failure.

THE CAUSES OF POLICY FAILURE: CHALLENGES AND A WAY FORWARD

The methodological difficulties of ascertaining the causes of policy failure

Notwithstanding the aforementioned difficulties in determining *if* a policy has failed, approaching the issue of what *causes* policy failure brings its own special challenges. The few academic works that have tackled the issue of policy failure lean towards different causes: e.g., Dunleavy (1995) focuses essentially on political systemic issues that create vulnerability to failure; Wallis (2011) focuses on a lack of internal logic in predicting outcomes based on goals; King and Crewe (2013) look broadly but emphasize particularly the role of individual decision makers through their use of the term 'blunders' (see also Brummer 2016), and Bovens and 't Hart (1996) explicitly reject a rationalist–scientific view of causality and focus instead on differing constructions of causality.

The richest seam of research on the causes of failure tends to come from the organizational studies and decision-making literature, which also crosses over at times into disaster literature. Some of the most prominent contributions address issues such as: the capacity of organizational systems and process to cultivate the conditions of failure (Anheier 1999; Turner 1978); attempts to eliminate failures that create even greater risk of failure (Wildavsky 1988); varieties of human error and the role of organizational context (Reason 1990); cross-system similarities in understanding failure (Fortune and Peters 1995; Toft and Reynolds 1995); and failures across complex systems (Dekker 2011). If there is a common message here for understanding policy failures and fiascos, it is that we need to think of the institutional frameworks and processes within which policy-makers take decisions, rather than assuming that 'bad' decisions' exist independently of the contexts in which they are created.

Such a diversity of potential causes of failure goes against the grain of media perceptions and popular commentary, which often point to a single cause of failure and a single individual who should take the blame. All policies are formed and decided upon by individuals, but they are produced and enacted in broader institutional contexts, which in themselves operate in broader societal contexts of governing ideas, powerful groups, changing technologies, global interdependencies and so on. To say that one factor *alone* is the cause of a failure would be to neglect the range of individual, institutional and societal factors that interacted to produce that failure – as well as their complex interdependencies (Jörg 2011). Byman (2008: 601), in his study of the US intervention in Iraq, argues that failure has a 'thousand fathers' and cites a plethora of interconnected causes from 'bad choices', such as the deployment of insufficient troop numbers, to structural factors such as the divided nature of Iraqi society, torn apart by years on conflict

A related difficulty is how we understand which causes of any particular policy failure are more important than others. It might make instinctive sense, for example, to organize our analysis into primary, secondary and peripheral causal factors. However, it is difficult to do so rigorously because it assumes (a) there is a scientific means of ascertain causal priority factors and (b) that these causal factors operate in some kind of hierarchical way, rather than in a complex, mutually reinforcing way that is not easily amendable to investigation (Cairney 2012a), and indeed may be the product of decisions that are 'reasonable' on their own but their interaction within complex systems may produce a drift towards failed outcomes (Dekker 2011). Allison and Zelikow (1999), in their seminal study of the Cuban missile crisis, which approached this critical time period from the different vantage points of rational, organizational and governmental politics, recognized that a multitude of 'what ifs?' made it difficult to reconcile competing explanations and causes in a quasi-hierarchical way.

A further challenge in understanding the causes of policy failure is that failures are viewed in hindsight, with the knowledge that 'failure' has occurred. This typically leads to the construction of a narrative which begins with warning signs that were ignored, and culminates in failures that could have been prevented (Boin and Fishbacher-Smith 2011). This is exemplified in intelligence failures that emerge in the wake of terrorist attacks, where the 'bad ending' to the story leads to a search for unnecessary risks taken and warning signs ignored. While analyses of policy failures after the fact tend to put give the impression of a definitive 'whole story', one of the lessons from the methodological issues identified earlier is that a single authoritative narrative of failure is not the only one possible (Boin and Fischbacher-Smith 2011). Hindsight analysis does not often do not take into account the prior historical context (at the policy-making stage) where policy-makers anticipated a successful policy and perhaps even perceived the risk for failure to be either negligible or a risk worth taking (Althaus 2008). McDermott (2001), in her study of risk-taking and presidential foreign policy decisions, explores this issue in detail on the assumption that decision-makers will be more inclined to take risks when they are facing prospective losses. Complicating matters further, as indicated by Kitts (2006) in his work on presidential commission covering Pearl Harbour, the Iran–Contra affair, 9/11, et al. as well as Ellis (1994) on 'lightening rods' insulating the US president from blame for failures, hindsight evaluations of failures are often highly politicized (from terms of reference to committee composition) (Boin et al. 2008).

Methodologically, therefore, we seem to face real difficulties in ascertaining the causes of policy failure, because we need to juggle the hindsight biases of warning signs ignored and 'accidents waiting to happen' to the more context-sensitive stories of negligible or low risk factors being considered unproblematic in the quest for greater successes. Such methodological challenges mirror classic methodological differences within political sciences – whether the phenomenon being studied is a matter of 'fact', interpretation or both (see e.g., Marsh and Stoker 2010). Of course, we do not stop studying political phenomena because of its complexity and methodological challenges, and neither should we stop studying policy failure.

The causes of policy failure: a way forward

I would argue that we should avoid a fruitless search for a definitive, scientifically rational cause of any particular policy failure, or getting caught in the trap of saying definitively that failure has a single cause, isolated from its context. The way to advance our understanding is to consider a range of ways in which political actors frame the causes of policy failure. Doing so provides us with a heuristic framework as summarized in Table 2. The various categorizations are not mutually exclusive but, as per Ostrom (2007), the framework at least allows us to order a range of elements to help prompt deeper and subsequent theorizing and operationalizing.

Policy failure narratives (see Oppermann and Spencer 2016) tend to focus on failure being caused by one or more of three main elements: i.e., individual decision-makers; institutions/policy processes; and deeper societal values and power structures/interests. This tripartite approach allows us to think about the possibility of multiple frames and realms of multiple potential causes. For example, we could place the many analyses of the causes of the Bay of Pigs failure centred on actors (groupthink, individual miscalculations), institutions/processes (over-ambition of CIA and poor intelligence capabilities) and society more broadly (Cold War tensions, Cuba's economic realignment with the Soviet Union). Additionally, while this framework does not seek to provide definitive answers to the matter of degrees of causality, its tripartite structure does at least allow analysts to think in a more structured way about primary, secondary and peripheral causes of failure.

Some narratives are generally sympathetic and supportive in the face of policy failure, while others are much more critical. We can see these, as in Table 2, through three sub-narratives which are typically embedded (explicitly and/or implicitly) in post-failure framing contests. These relate to the causes of the failure, whether it could have been foreseen/prevented, and what can be done to learn from the failure.

Sympathetic accounts of policy failure are rather forgiving of the 'causes' of failure. The arguments proceed along similar lines. Individuals who took 'bad' decisions' were faced with unrealistic pressures or were the victims of bad luck. Institutions/processes did let us down in a small way but nevertheless they are fundamentally robust and have a difficult job to do in balancing priorities in a sometimes uncertain world. Society did drift marginally from core values/interests or fail to put them effectively into practice, but these are

Table 2 Differing frames on the causes and implications of policy failure

	Individual actor centred frame		Institution/policy process centred frame		Societal centred frame	
	Unsupportive	Supportive	Unsupportive	Supportive	Unsupportive	Supportive
What caused the failure?	Reckless self-interest, deliberate cultivation of failure, negligence, incompetence, appalling judgement	Lapse in otherwise good judgement, genuine mistake, bad luck	Institutional self-interest, institutional arrogance, major blind spots, weak capacity for good decision-making	Small weakness in otherwise solid institutions and processes	Core values/elite interests produced policy-making biases and inevitable failures	'Good society' has perhaps drifted slightly from core values and issues
Should decision-makers have foreseen and prevented the failure?	Yes, absolutely, but they pathologically ignored or were incapable of seeing the risks	Ideally yes, but they were faced with difficult circumstances; they may also have been unlucky	Yes, absolutely, but a dysfunctional institution/process, either ignored or wasn't capable of seeing the risks	Ideally yes, but small weaknesses in processes and procedures limited the capacity to foresee and prevent	Yes, in theory, but systematic biases produced a blindness to possibility of failure or even a preparedness to foresee but tolerate	Ideally yes, but in practice we can't foresee and prevent every failure
How can we learn from the failure?	Remove 'bad' individuals from office and replace them with others who are more competent	Do what we can to better train our policy-makers but we shouldn't be too harsh on them	Drastic dismantling or overhaul of institution/process	Minor refinement of institutional policy, procedures and/or processes	Causes of failure are deeply embedded in dysfunctional core values and systems of power. Learning can only happen when there is a paradigm shift	Reflection and perhaps refinement of core values/priorities and how we put them into practice, rather than fundamentally challenging them

marginal shortfalls in a complex society where our values and principles are solid and steadfast. In such accounts, the causes of failure are in essence 'good intentions' or 'good societies' that have gone marginally askew at the periphery. The corollary of such sympathetic tendencies is that we shouldn't have inflated expectations that we can foresee and prevent all failures, but once they happen we can at least reflect, learn and refine.

By contrast, alternative accounts of failure lean towards the deeply critical. Individuals took bad decisions and did so because they are fundamentally reckless, self-interested, ego-driven, incompetent and so on. For example, Glad (1989), in her psychological appraisal of mistakes made by US President Jimmy Carter in managing the Iranian hostage crisis, attributed them to Carter's ego-centric narcissistic tendencies leading to a refusal to consider alternative courses of action. Similarly, institutions and processes at the heart of failure are fundamentally pathological, consumed by empire building, arrogance, biases and more, which reduce the capacity for good decision-making. For instance, Gompert *et al.* (2014) argue that a major explanation for the flawed US 2003 intervention in Iraq was 'dysfunctional' decision-making processes surrounding intelligence, giving privilege to outdated and untrustworthy 'evidence' that Iraq held weapons of mass destruction. By the time we reach deeper core societal values and power structures in this narrative, the flaws are deep, and a severely dysfunctional society is prone to producing destructive policy failures. A detailed study by Gezari (2013: 198) of the failures of US Human Terrain System (designed to increase cultural understanding between US forces and local communities in Iraq and Afghanistan) argued that the policy is an 'expression of the national zeitgeist: American exceptionalism tempered by the political correctness of a post-colonial, globalized age'.

In such narratives, the root causes of failure are essentially dysfunctional people, 'bad' institutions and distorted or inappropriate core values/distribution of power. The corollary of unsympathetic narratives is that we should in theory be able to foresee/prevent and learn from failure, but we can only so if we get rid of bad decision-makers, overhaul our institutions/processes and produce a paradigm shift in our ways of thinking and/power structures.

There is no need in this tripartite framework to present propositions or hypotheses on the causes of policy failure. These are a matter (in the fashion of Ostrom [2007]) for theory and operationalizing. Nevertheless, it is possible to offer some potential analytical avenues that flow from a conception of process, programme and political failure. They start from the assumption that policy-makers typically need to juggle competing priorities. The framework can be used, for example, to help us think about the three forms of failure – process, programme and political – as well as connections and trade-offs between them. A government dispensing with detailed scrutiny and instead rushing through a legislative motion and marshalling all party energies to send troops into battle overseas (process success) is risking both programme failure (that the initiative will not produce the intended outcomes) and political failure (backlash). Furthermore, the prioritizing of political success (pre-election posturing, token initiatives that manage issues down policy agendas, unwavering promotion of governing ideology) can risk producing failed programme outcomes. Larson (1997: ix), in her work on spirals of mistrust during the Cold War period, argued that 'For many years I have been trying to determine why foreign policy officials make decisions that result in needless sacrifice of lives and money,' and found a key explanation in US foreign policy (unlike that of the Soviet Union) being driven by the President's need to build and reinforce trust with domestic political opponents and citizens.

The causes of policy failure are many in number, often vague, complex in their relationship and often highly contested. The framework presented here and as summarized in Table 2 does not provide definitive answers, but instead seeks to provide a framework to help us approach such issues.

CONCLUDING REFLECTIONS: LINKING THE NATURE OF FAILURE AND ITS CAUSES

The articulation of policies and their outcomes as 'failures' is part of the political fabric of societies. The different standards against which to assess policy outcomes are typically diverse, complex and 'grey' that, depending on the particular standard chosen, 'failures' can be portrayed as 'successes' – and *vice versa*. Framing a policy as 'failed' is both a judgement and a move to delegitimize the value and veracity of what government is doing. From wars and diplomacy to trade agreements, failure frames are attempts to destroy existing policy interventions (and often the values underpinning them and the reputations of those promoting them) and create political space for new policies to emerge. Defining failure and articulating its causes are inextricably linked. Those arguing, or at least agreeing, that policy has 'failed' may articulate different causes of failure, depending on whether they seek to conserve the *status quo ante* or use the failure as a springboard for reform. The more that causes of failure are framed as institutional/process or societal, the greater the case being made that reform is necessary.

Furthermore, not all policy failures are equal. They can have greater/lesser consequences and can be more/less tolerable. Some failures (casualties in times of war, corruption in overseas aid) are seen at times to be an unavoidable consequence of pursuing policy goals. Many policies carry inherent risks (Althaus 2008; Vis 2010), and such risks may be classified by policy-makers as 'acceptable risks' which need to be taken in order to satisfy broader 'success' goals. Stronger still, failure in some regard may be tolerated in an attempt to achieve broader success (or even actively pursued). Gilbert and Sharman (2014), in their study of Britain and Australia's limited compliance with the Organization for Economic Co-operation and Development (OECD) Anti-Bribery Convention, argue that governments turning a 'blind eye' to bribery used by corporate citizens is a product of seeking to protect jobs and promote export success. Policy advocates will often frame such failures as unfortunate but 'normal' by-products of pursuing broader goals, rather than being caused by fundamental flaws in the policy itself.

Our attitude to failure also tells us something about our attitude to the society in which we live. Following Bovens and 't Hart (1996), substantially different assumptions may emerge from the same set of failure phenomena. Optimistic accounts tend to see the ideological and institutional foundations of society as fundamentally solid (e.g., a belief in the benefit of free markets, or plural political systems), and when policies fail they are unfortunate and considered the product of 'weak' leaders, misguided diplomacy and so on, but they should not shatter our understanding of the deeper ways in which we are governed. By contrast, *pessimistic accounts* perceive policy failure to be the near-inevitable product of societal contradictions, whether it is clashes between civilizations/religions or even the expansionist and predatory tendencies of capitalist accumulation. Policy-makers in this account tend to be distant players/pawns and even institutional structures are a product of broader societal contradictions. In this view, ongoing failures are inevitable unless there are drastic change (or a revolution in) the fundamental organizing principles of society.

In conclusion: the nature and causes of policy failure may be a methodological minefield, but the analytical framework presented above does allow us to approach this topic in a novel way. The public policy approach adopted here – far from attempting to eschew the politics of policy failure in favour of a rational scientific approach – argues that recognizing political disputes and grey areas is the key to advancing our understanding. The extent to which policy outcomes are considered failures and explanations for the causes of any failures, are interconnected matters of politics. They are fought over by different interests as they seek to confirm or deny whether our governments are indeed acting in the public interest and protecting the rights of citizens – at home and overseas.

ACKNOWLEDGEMENTS

I would like to thank the anonymous reviewers, as well as Ben Goldsmith, Diarmuid Maguire and Jason Sharman for their very helpful comments and suggestions.

REFERENCES

Allison, G. and Zelikow, P. (1999) *Essence of Decision: Explaining the Cuban Missile Crisis*, New York: Longman.

Althaus, C. (2008) *Calculating Political Risk*, Sydney: University Of New South Wales Press.

Althaus, C., Bridgeman, P. and Davis, G. (2013) *The Australian Policy Handbook*, Sydney: Allen & Unwin.

Anheier, H.K. (ed.) (1999) *When Things go Wrong: Organizational Failures and Breakdowns*, Thousand Oaks, CA: Sage.

Baldwin, D.A. (2000) 'Success and failure in foreign policy', *Annual Review of Political Science* 3: 167–82

Bardach, E. (2011) *A Practical Guide for Policy Analysis*, Washington, DC: CQ Press.

Boin, A. and Fishbacher-Smith, D. (2011). 'The importance of failure theories in assessing crisis management: the Columbia space shuttle disaster revisited', *Policy and Society* 30(2): 77–87.

Boin, A., McConnell, A. and 't Hart, P. (eds) (2008) *Governing after Crisis: The Politics of Investigation, Accountability and Learning*, Cambridge: Cambridge University Press.

Booth, P. (2012) 'Does foreign aid make the poor poorer?', *Economic Affairs* 32(1): 1.

Bovens, M. and 't Hart, P. (1996) *Understanding Policy Fiascos*, New Brunswick, NJ: Transaction.

Bovens, M. and 't Hart, P. (2016) 'Revisiting the study of policy failures',.

Brändström, A. and Kuipers, S. (2003) 'From "normal incidents" to political crises: understanding the selective politicization of policy failures', *Government and Opposition* 38(3): 279–305.

Brummer, K. (2016) '"Fiasco prime ministers": leaders' beliefs and personality traits as possible causes for policy fiascos',.

Button, M., Lewis, C., Shepherd, D. and Brooks, G. (2012) *Measuring Fraud in Overseas Aid: Options and Methods*, Portsmouth: Centre for Counter Fraud Studies.

Byman, D. (2008) 'An autopsy of the Iraq debacle: policy failure or bridge too far?', *Security Studies* 17(4): 599–643.

Cairney, P. (2012a) 'Complexity theory in political science and public policy', *Political Studies* 10(3): 346–58.

Cairney, P. (2012b) *Understanding Public Policy: Theories and Issues*, Basingstoke: Palgrave.

Dekker, S. (2011) *Drift Into Failure: From Hunting Broken Components to Understanding Complex Systems*, Farnham: Ashgate.

Dunleavy, P. (1995) 'Policy disasters: explaining the UK's record', *Public Policy and Administration* 10(2): 52–70.

Dye, T.R. (2012) *Understanding Public Policy*, Englewood Cliffs, NJ: Pearson Prentice Hall.

Edelstein, D.M. (2008) *Occupational Hazards: Success and Failure in Military Occupation*, Ithaca, NY: Cornell University Press.

Ellis, R. (1994) *Presidential Lightning Rods: The Politics of Blame Avoidance*, Lawrence, KS: Kansas University Press.

Fleitz, F.H. (2002) *Peacekeeping Fiascos of the 1990s*, Westport, CT: Praeger.

Fortune, J. and Peters, G. (1995) *Learning from Failure: The Systems Approach*, Chichester: Wiley.

Gaskarth, J. (2016) 'The fiasco of the two Syria votes: decline and denial in British foreign policy',.

Gezari, V.M. (2013) *The Tender Soldier: A True Story of War and Sacrifice*, New York: Simon & Schuster.

Gilbert, J.L. and Sharman, J.C. (2014) 'Turning a blind eye to bribery: explaining failures to comply with the international anti-corruption regime', *Political Studies*, doi:10.1111/1467-9248.12153.

Glad, B. (1989) 'Personality, political and group process variables in foreign-policy decision making: Jimmy Carter's handling of the Iranian hostage crisis', *International Political Science Review* 10(1): 35–61.

Gompert, D.C., Binnendijk, H. and Lin, B. (2014) *Blinders, Blunders and Wars: What America and China Can Learn*, Santa Monica, CA: Rand.

Gupta, D.K. (2001) *Analyzing Public Policy: Concepts, Tools, and Techniques*, Washington, DC: CQ Press.

Head, B.W. (2008) 'Three lenses of evidence-based policy', *Australian Journal of Public Administration* 67(1): 1–11.

Heine-Ellison, S. (2001) 'The impact and effectiveness of multilateral economic sanctions: a comparative study', *The International Journal of Human Rights* 5(1): 81–112.

Hood, C. (2002) 'The risk game and the blame game', *Government and Opposition* 37(10): 15–37.

Howlett, M., Ramesh, M. and Perl, A. (2009) *Studying Public Policy: Policy Cycles and Policy Subsystems*, Ontario: Oxford University Press.

Janis, I.L. (1972) *Victims of Groupthink: A Psychological Study of Foreign-Policy Decisions and Fiascos*, Boston, MA: Houghton Mifflin.

Jervis, R. (1976) *Perception and Misperception in International Politics*, Princeton, NJ: Princeton University Press.

Jörg, T. (2011) *New Thinking in Complexity for the Social Sciences and Humanities: A Generative, Transdisciplinary Approach*, New York: Springer.

King, A. and Crewe I. (2013) *The Blunders of Our Governments*, London: Oneworld.

Kitts, K. (2006) *Presidential Commissions and National Security: The Politics of Damage Control*, Boulder, CO: Lynne Rienner.

Larson, D.W. (1997) *Anatomy of Mistrust: US–Soviet Relations During the Cold War*, Ithaca, NY: Cornell University Press.

Majone, G. (1989) *Evidence, Argument, and Persuasion in the Policy Process*, New Haven, CT: Yale University Press.

Marsh, D. and G. Stoker (eds) (2010) *Theories and Methods in Political Science*, Basingstoke: Palgrave.

McConnell, A. (2010) 'Policy success, policy failure and grey areas in-between', *Journal of Public Policy* 30(3): 345–62.

McDermott, R. (2001) *Risk-Taking in International Politics: Prospect Theory in American Foreign Policy*, Ann Arbor, MI: University of Michigan Press.

McDonough, F. (1998) *Neville Chamberlain, Appeasement and the British Road to War*, Manchester: Manchester University Press.

Mearsheimer, J.J. (2013) *Why Leaders Lie: The Truth About Lying in International Politics*, New York: Oxford University Press.

Oppermann, K. and Spencer, A. (2016) 'Telling stories of failure: narrative constructions of foreign policy fiascos',.

Ostrom, E. (2007) 'Institutional rational choice: an assessment of the institutional analysis and development framework', in P.A. Sabatier (ed.), *Theories of the Policy Process*, Boulder, CO: Westview Press , pp. 21–64.

Pierson, P. (2000) 'Increasing returns, path dependence, and the study of politics', *American Political Science Review* 94(2): 251–67.

Pressman, J. (2009) 'Power without influence: the Bush administration's foreign policy failure in the Middle East', *International Security* 33(4): 149–79.

Reason, J. (1990) *Human Error*, New York: Cambridge University Press.

Schneider, A.L. and Ingram, H. (1997) *Policy Design for Democracy*, Lawrence, KS: University Press of Kansas.

Sharman, J.C. (2011) *The Money Laundry: Regulating Global Finance in the Criminal Economy*, Ithaca, NY: Cornell University Press.

Toft, B. and Reynolds, S. (2005) *Learning from Disasters: A Management Approach*, Leicester: Perpetuity.

Turner, B.A. (1978) *Man-made Disasters*, London: Wykeham.

UN Human Rights Committee (2013) *Communication No: 2094/2011*, Geneva: United Nations.

Vis, B. (2010) *Politics of Risk-taking: Welfare State Reform in Advanced Democracies*, Amsterdam: Amsterdam University Press.

Wallis, S.E. (2011) *Avoiding Policy Failure: A Workable Approach*, Litchfield Park: Emergent.

Wildavsky, A. (1987) *Speaking Truth to Power: The Art and Craft of Policy Analysis*, New Brunswick, NJ: Transaction.

Wildavsky, A. (1988) *Searching for Safety*, New Brunswick, NJ: Transaction.

Telling stories of failure: narrative constructions of foreign policy fiascos

Kai Oppermann and Alexander Spencer

ABSTRACT   The contribution introduces narrative analysis as a discourse analytical method for investigating the social construction of foreign policy fiascos. Based on insights from literary studies and narratology it shows that stories of failure include a number of key elements, including a particular setting which defines appropriate behaviour; the negative characterization of agents; as well as an emplotment of the 'fiasco' through the attribution of cause and responsibility. The contribution illustrates this method through a narrative analysis of German media reporting on Germany's abstention in the United Nations Security Council vote on Resolution 1973 in March 2011 regarding the military intervention in Libya.

INTRODUCTION

Most studies on foreign policy fiascos have predominantly been concerned with explaining why foreign policy fiascos have occurred and how to avoid them (see Janis 1989; Walker and Malici 2011). These studies have in common that they take the assessment of a foreign policy episode as a 'fiasco' for granted. They do not problematize such assessments but take them as starting points for their explanations of foreign policy failures and for the conclusions to be drawn from these explanations. Explicitly or implicitly, therefore, the analysis of foreign policy fiascos tends to follow the foundationalist and positivist tradition that has long been dominant in policy evaluation studies (Marsh and McConnell 2010: 567). According to this perspective, policy failures are objective facts that can be independently identified and verified. Policies count as failures if they fall short of certain objective criteria or benchmarks for success (Howlett 2012: 541–2; McConnell 2010: 349–51).

Critics, however, point out, that measuring policies against the benchmark of officially stated objectives becomes difficult when such objectives are vague and multi-faceted and may have been formulated more for their strategic or symbolic functions than as a realistic guide to policy-making (Ingram and Mann 1980: 20). An objectivist approach to studying policy failures is not well-positioned to acknowledge that policy outcomes will often be ambiguous and thus do not speak for themselves. 'Failure' is not an inherent attribute of policy, but rather a judgment about policy. While it is important to point out that 'goal

43

attainment' may clearly be an important dimension of policy evaluation and that judgments on policy are also driven by observable criteria, such as indicators of the costs and benefits of a policy, it is ultimately the interpretation of policy outcomes and the meaning imbued to them in political discourse which makes policies be seen as successful or unsuccessful. This critique is the main point of departure for a constructivist and interpretivist strand in policy evaluation studies, which conceives of policy fiascos as an 'essentially contested' (Gallie 1956) concept (Bovens and 't Hart 2016). Since there are no fixed or commonly accepted criteria for the success or failure of a policy, such judgments are always likely to be open to dispute (Bovens and 't Hart 1996: 4–11).

Foreign policies that are seen as successful by some may thus well be dismissed as fiascos by others. Such opposite judgments can come, for example, from differences in the timeframes or geographical and social boundaries of assessing the impacts of a policy, as well as from cultural biases, diverging evaluations of available alternatives or by uneven levels of expectation or aspiration (*ibid.*: 21–32; Marsh and McConnell 2010: 575–7). Most notably, however, the designation of (foreign) policy as success or failure is inescapably intertwined with politics (Bovens *et al.* 2001: 10; Brändström and Kuipers 2003: 279–82). Policy evaluations will thus be influenced by the values, identity and interests of the evaluator and may reflect underlying power relations in the political arena or in society at large (Marsh and McConnell 2010: 566-–8). In particular, labelling a policy or decision a 'fiasco' is an intensely political act (Gray 1998: 16). It makes for a powerful semantic tool in political discourse to discredit opponents and seek political advantage (Howlett 2012: 547; McConnell 2016).

The contribution follows this constructivist critique of objectivist approaches to policy evaluation and conceptualizes foreign policy fiascos not as facts to be discovered and explained, but rather as social constructs which are constituted in political discourse (Bovens and 't Hart 2016). While the discursive construction of fiascos will be subject to contestation, the characterization of a foreign policy decision as a fiasco depends on the extent of intersubjective agreement in this regard, in particular among powerful political and social actors. Political discourse, in this sense, can be seen as a struggle between competing claims which either attribute the 'fiasco' label to foreign policy decisions or reject such a label. Borrowing from a well-known definition of policy fiascos in public policy (Bovens and 't Hart 1996: 15), this contribution thus understands *foreign policy fiascos* as significant foreign policies or foreign policy decisions which are widely seen by socially and politically relevant actors to involve blameworthy failures and mistakes of the responsible decision-makers. Against this background, we suggest that foreign policy fiascos are constructed through narratives.

Specifically, the main purpose of the contribution is to emphasize the discursive nature of policy fiascos and to show that such constructions are structured in the form of narratives. This is to provide the first building blocks of a more general theory of fiasco constructions in foreign policy. At this stage of theory development, however, the objective is not to explain *why* some foreign policy decisions may be more susceptible to fiasco narratives than others. Still, the analysis offers some initial pointers to this question, in that it expects fiasco narratives to be more compelling if they can draw on arguments and character-izations that are widely seen in a certain context as plausible criteria and ingre-dients of foreign policy failures. The ambition of the contribution, therefore, is to build on the interpretivist work of Bovens and 't Hart (1996) and address the gaps left by positivist attempts to judge foreign policy fiascos from objective cri-teria, in particular in the many situations where policy outcomes are unclear or contested. We hold that a better understanding of the political and discursive logic of fiasco constructions is not only academically important but also prom-ises to be of practical relevance for foreign policy decision-makers and commen-tators, as it highlights their agency in the constitution of policy fiascos.

In order to substantiate our argument, the remainder of the contribution is divided into two parts. First, the following section introduces the method of narrative analysis and shows how it can contribute to the study of foreign policy fiascos. Second, the contribution presents an illustrative case study on the narrative construction as a foreign policy fiasco of Germany's abstention on United Nations (UN) Security Council Resolution 1973 on 17 March 2011, which authorized member states to 'take all necessary measures' to protect civilians from the Gaddafi regime in Libya. This abstention ranks among the highest-profile and most controversial foreign policy decisions in post-unification Germany, and there is widespread agreement among academic and non-academic observers in Germany and beyond that the abstention was a serious mistake which came at a significant diplomatic cost. This negative assess-ment of Germany's non-support for intervention is somewhat puzzling, however, considering the country's longstanding culture of military restraint, as well as the precedent of Germany's opposition to the 2003 Iraq War, which is widely regarded in Germany as a major foreign policy success. In other words, there was nothing inevitable about what has become the common wisdom to see the Merkel government's approach to Libya as a failure. The question in need of clarification, therefore, is *how* this policy was still constructed into a fiasco.

NARRATIVE ANALYSIS

Narratives are a 'mode of verbal representation' (White 1987: 26) which offer humans a way of comprehending their environment. While narrative analysis is one among many different discourse analytical methods including critical dis-course analysis (Fairclough 2010) or metaphor analysis (Oppermann and Spencer 2013), we hold that a narrative is a means of structuring discourse. While discourse includes a vast number of different representations and it is unclear where to draw a line delimiting discourse, narratives include a number of key elements which offer anchor points for the empirical analysis of phenomena such as policy fiascos.

We are by no means the first to look at the discourse and language of fiasco constructions. As Edelman (1988: 31) argues, 'a policy failure, like all news developments, is a creation of the language used to depict it; its identification is a political act, not a recognition of a fact'. So far, this analytical perspective has predominantly focused on the notion of framing (Goffman 1974). The main argument behind frame analyses of fiascos 'is that the reaction to an event is determined not – or hardly at all – by the event itself but by the way in which such events are interpreted and given meaning' (De Vries 2004: 596–7). Frame analysis is the attempt to unmask the underlying framework which is used in reporting to make sense of a certain empirical event such as a crisis or policy fiasco.

While there are clear overlaps between frame and narrative analysis which are sometimes used in a similar fashion (Boin *et al.* 2009: 82–3; Brändström and Kuipers 2003; De Vries 2004), we hold that the concept of 'narrative' in particular has a number of advantages. It offers an opportunity for cross disciplinary learning by incorporating insights from literary studies, a discipline which predominantly concentrates on textual modes of literature and writing, and narratology, the theory of narrative, into political science. While the analysis of the arts in the form of poetry, literature or film has made inroads into the political sciences, discourse analytical methods have generally been adopted from sociology and linguistics rather than literary studies. However, research on narratives in literary studies offers both theoretical and analytical arguments for why narratives can be helpful for the analysis of political events.[1] From a theoretical perspective it provides arguments for why narratives are important for the analysis of human behaviour in the first place. Essentially, there are two interrelated lines of argumentation one may pursue: a cognitive perspective and a cultural perspective (Patterson and Monroe 1998: 315). The first emphasizes that narratives are an important part of human mental activity, in the sense that the human brain 'captures many complex relationships in the form of narrative structures' (Fludernik 2009: 1). The second perspective considers narratives as culturally embedded phenomena which are part of every society. Myths and stories of the past including stories about political representatives and nations on the international stage are an essential part of all forms of community-building where the constitution of a common identity is sought.

In that view, actors in foreign policy are (co-)authors and 'subjects' of identity-constructing self-narratives, as well as objects of public narratives which constitute a particular understanding of states and their representatives. Foreign policy actors, specifically, seek to develop and communicate strategic narratives about the past, present and future of international politics and about their country's identity as an international actor in order to shape their discursive environment and the behaviour of other actors both domestically and internationally (Miskimmon *et al.* 2013: 1–11). The analysis of how narratives of failure are told and how they establish a dominant position in a struggle for interpretation of complex events in international politics while other alternative stories are sidelined ultimately helps to understand the distribution of discursive power (Patterson and Monroe 1998: 315–16).

From an analytical perspective, another advantage of narrative analysis is that the definition of 'narrative' in literary studies and narratology provides clear categories which can be used to guide empirical research including a *setting* or context of a story, agents that are *characterized* in different ways as well as the causal and temporal *emplotment* of events (Toolan 2001). All of these elements are elaborated on in the narrative discourse in order to give them a more specific character and a certain evaluative implication. The dimensions of *setting, characterization* and *emplotment* can be empirically analysed and are representative of an overall narrative.

With regard to the *setting* the idea is that, similar to a stage play or film, the background or location in front of which the story unfolds is of importance for the narrative as a whole because it gives audiences clues about the kind of story in which they are about to indulge. For example, a setting such as the diplomatic realm has important implications for what is considered to be suitable behaviour on the international stage. The representation of the setting indicates the set of norms and values the reader considers to be appropriate for the situation. The constitution of the setting of diplomacy as one of hard power politics among untrusting actors or as a realm of co-operative friendship amongst long standing allies thus has implications for what is and what is not considered a failure in such a setting.

More specifically, narratives on foreign policy fiascos will likely be more powerful if they involve settings allowing for the possibility of alternatives, choice and different behaviour. Narratives in which agents are left with no alternative but to act the ways they did are generally not told as a fiasco (Ingram and Mann 1980: 14; Tuchman 1984: 5). The very notion of 'failure' is often seen to imply the existence of 'better' alternatives which decision-makers have failed to identify or implement. Compared to events which are construed as being beyond the control of decision-makers, the construction of the narrative setting of foreign policy failures as avoidable makes it more difficult for decision-makers to escape blame by invoking mitigating circumstances such as misfortune or structural constraints (see Hood 2002). For example, in the case of US policy towards Iraq, some argue that the Gulf War in the early 1990s was a 'war of necessity' making it less susceptible to fiasco narratives, while the second Iraq war in 2003 was a 'war of choice', implying the possibility of alternative behaviour and therefore inviting constructions as an avoidable fiasco (Haass 2009).

The second essential part of narratives is the *characterization* of the agents involved in a story. While there are a number of ways in which the characterization of actors can be influenced, the most straightforward is giving them a name or label rather than referring to them simply by the role they play in the story. The giving of a name or label informs the relationship between the audience and the agent in the story. For example, referring to Margaret Thatcher as the 'Iron Lady' or George W. Bush as a 'cowboy' constitutes them in a particular fashion, making failures more or less easy to stick. Moreover, an agent is characterized by being placed in relation to others. For example, this can involve hierarchical relationships such as in the family (mother/child), in society (government/public), or in international politics (leader of the free world); it may also point to more equal relations such as business partners, allies or friends (Fludernik 2009: 44– 6). A third possibility of characterizing agents is through what they say and how they act (Herman and Vervaeck 2007: 227). Ultimately, the words and deeds of characters in a story, such as foreign policy-makers, greatly influences our perception of what these characters are like.

Narratives of foreign policy fiascos thus crucially depend on the identification and characterization of agents both on the individual and collective level who have been influential in formulating the policy in question (Gray 1998: 8). On the individual level such narratives are often facilitated by the personification of foreign policy issues (Bovens *et al.* 1998: 204; see Gaskarth 2016). Given their leading· position in the decision-making process, the actors who will likely be most prominent in stories of foreign policy failure include the members of the foreign policy executive consisting of the head of government and the departmental ministers responsible for foreign policy, most notably the foreign minister (Hill [2003: 56–62]; on the role of prime ministers in foreign policy fiascos, see Brummer [2016]). Specifically, the narrative construction of foreign policy fiascos can be driven by characterizations of decision-makers which cast doubt on their competence, credibility and sincerity. Examples include allegations of inexperience, weakness, dishonesty or arrogance, as well as the imputation of personal or domestic political motives for foreign policy decisions. Such characterizations will likely resonate best if they can pick up on low levels of public trust in the government and pertain to agents who command only little political capital (Boin *et al.* 2009: 96–100; Dunleavy 1995: 61–4). Finally, the characterization of agents may include references to self-declared ambitions. While stated objectives are a problematic benchmark for policy evaluation, the reminder that these objectives have not been met is still a powerful narrative tool to characterize agents as hubristic, out-of-touch or incompetent. For example, the construction of the European Community's (EC) foreign policy response to the Yugoslav crisis in 1991–2 as a 'fiasco' was very much aided by the overly optimistic and self-confident portrayal which the EC set for itself at the onset of the crisis (Selm-Thoburn and Verbeek 1998).

On the collective level, the characterization can focus in particular on deficient process characteristics of policy-making found in institutions such as government departments. Prime examples include undue haste, excessive informality, biased information processing, ineffective checks and balances and lack of broader consultation (see Dunleavy 1995: 59–68; Janis 1989: 3– 24). A case in point is the 'fiasco' of the unsuccessful and very costly effort by the Swedish government at avoiding the devaluation of the Swedish Krona amidst intense currency speculation in November 1992, which has been traced, among other things, to overly rapid, secretive and centralized decision-making procedures (Stern and Sundelius 1998).

The third constitutive element of narratives is the event and its *emplotment*: in a narrative something has to happen (see Fludernik 2009: 5). What is more, the event understood as an action has to lead to more action. The events in a narrative do not stand on their own, they have to be placed in relation to each other. Here, the causal dimension, commonly termed 'causal emplotment', is of major importance as it elaborates the causal relationship between the elements of a narrative. Emplotment allows the audience to weigh and explain events rather than to just list them, i.e., to turn a set of propositions into an intelligible sequence of connected events about which one can form an opinion.

In the case of a fiasco narrative, the emplotment starts out with the labelling of an event or action as a fiasco, mistake, disaster or similar concept, which highlights the significance of the policy in question and the severity of the damage done (Howlett 2012: 543–4). A fiasco has to be worth telling, i.e., it has to be about a rupture in the everyday and normal. Thus, a foreign policy is being linked to gross violations of core interests or norms which go 'beyond the normal "zones of tolerance"' (Bovens and 't Hart 1996: 12). The event or policy which is constituted as a fiasco and its consequences are described as highly negative. The fiasco is emplotted into a chain of events which have led to results considered undesirable. In particular, 'fiasco' narratives may put foreign policy decisions in the context of doing harm to a country's national interests, of not being effective in addressing the foreign policy problem at hand or of being inappropriate in view of international or domestic norms and expectations.

What is more, the emplotment of powerful narratives of foreign policy fiascos involves the explanation of why a failure has occurred (causal emplotment) and importantly who is blameworthy (normative implications). Firstly, narratives of foreign policy fiascos depend on establishing a causal link between the actions or non-actions of one or more agents and the policies or consequences which are described as undesirable (Gray 1996: 77–8). Secondly, the narrative needs the allocation of responsibility and blame as a crucial ingredient to any social construction of policy fiascos (Gray 1998: 8–9).

Importantly, the causal explanation of fiascos and the attribution of blame are interconnected (Bovens and 't Hart 1996: 129). Fiasco narratives are most compelling if they make plausible claims to the effect that the negative implications of a foreign policy were foreseeable and controllable at the time when the policy was formulated (*ibid.*: 73–90; Howlett 2012: 543). Also, the attribution of blame is facilitated if the selected policy was widely criticized already in its own time and went against the advice of relevant observers or participants of decision making (Tuchman 1984: 5). For example, the 1995 Srebrenica massacre is often partly ascribed to failings in Dutch foreign policy, not least because the decision to contribute troops to the UN peacekeeping mission in Bosnia passed over the warnings of military experts and failed to sufficiently explore alternative responses to the ethnic conflict in former Yugoslavia (Bränd-ström and Kuipers 2003: 286–89).

The emplotment of fiasco narratives must thus allow for responsibility to be attributed squarely to individual and collective decision-makers. Linking up to the narrative elements of setting and characterization, the causal emplotment of foreign policy fiascos may not least point to personality traits of the decision-makers or avoidable deficiencies in the process of foreign policy-making which can be held responsible for negative policy outcomes.

In the following case study we will apply such a method of narrative analysis to the German media narrative on the German abstention on UN Security Council Resolution 1973, including the counter-narratives proposed by the German government and Foreign Minister Guido Westerwelle in particular. The narrative elements of setting, characterization and emplotment are used to structure the analysis of the textual material. In the analysis the text material is dissected into individual words or phrases which fit into the three narrative categories. Following several rounds of dissection, one is able to gain an insight into the dominance of certain representations within each category. Having filled the categories, we identify the main elements found in the texts and engage in retelling the story by using the quotes as a collage. While there are overlaps in the categories and the placing of some of the phrases into one category or the other is open to challenge, the analysis nevertheless provides a verifiable representation of existing narrative elements through the extensive use of footnotes which make each of our narrative claims traceable.

GERMANY'S ABSTENTION ON UN SECURITY COUNCIL RESOLUTION 1973 ON LIBYA

Germany's abstention on United Nations Security Council Resolution (UNSCR) 1973 was considered by many in Germany as a 'complete debacle' (Fischer 2011: 26) and a 'diplomatic disaster' (Müller 2011: 2). The focus of the critique against the Merkel government was that its Libya policy marked the first occasion in which the Federal Republic stood against all three of its main Western allies, the US, France and the UK, simultaneously on a major foreign policy issue. This, in turn, was expected to damage Germany's reputation as a trustworthy member of the Western alliance and to risk isolating the country from its partners. To avert such negative consequences, the widespread suggestion was that the Merkel government should have voted in favour of UNSCR 1973, which would still have left it with sufficient diplomatic room either to refuse becoming involved in the military implementation of the resolution at all or to make only a symbolic contribution to it (Stelzenmüller 2011: 2).

From a positivist perspective, however, the widely held view of Germany's policy on Libya as a major fiasco must remain somewhat surprising, since the 'objective' grounds for such a judgment appear far less clear-cut than the dominant discourse would suggest. First, the decision to abstain on UNSCR 1973 reflected rather than contradicted the stated objective of the Merkel government and in particular its junior coalition partner, the Free Democrats, to privilege civilian instruments of foreign policy and to advocate the use of military force only as a means of last resort. Second, realist accounts of the decision have suggested that the abstention made sense in terms of Germany's geo-economic interests and grand strategy (Miskimmon 2012: 401–3). Third, it is easy to overstate the diplomatic costs of the abstention, given that Germany was actually far less isolated within the North Atlantic Treaty Organization (NATO) and the European Union (EU) than critics of the abstention acknowledge and that the Merkel government was quick to make good for any potential damage to its international reputation by reinforcing its engagement in Afghanistan (Hansel and Oppermann 2014: 7–15).

Against the background of this discrepancy between 'objectivist' and 'interpretative' perspectives on the Merkel government's decision to abstain in the vote on UNSCR 1973, the following analysis will examine the media narrative in Germany through which this foreign policy decision was constructed into a fiasco, as well as the government's counter-narrative which, however, remained marginal to the media discourse. We focus on media narratives because the reporting of the media is both a good indicator for the prevalent narratives in public discourse at large, as well as a crucial arena for the social construction of foreign policy fiascos. We selected the following six large newspapers which represent the mainstream political spectrum in Germany: *Süddeutsche Zeitung*, *Frankfurter Allgemeine Zeitung*, *Tagesspiegel*, *Welt*, *Tageszeitung*, and *Zeit*. Specifically, we employed the Nexis database to identify the 50 most relevant articles in those newspapers that are included in this database. For the search we used the keywords 'Germany', 'Libya' and 'Security Council'. In the case of the two newspapers that are not in Lexis Nexis – the *Süddeutsche Zeitung* and the *Frankfurter Allgemeine Zeitung* – we used their archives to examine the 25 most relevant articles in each of the two papers. For all six newspapers, our analysis covers the entire timeframe of the intervention from 17 March to 31 October 2011.[2]

Setting

In the fiasco narrative, the setting of the UN Security Council is constituted as 'the stage of world politics', the 'highest UN body' or the 'most powerful body of the international community of states' where the 'powerful' take responsibility to deal with 'nothing less than the maintenance of world peace'. This setting provides the 'chance to shape one's profile' and gain 'prestige'. Correspondingly, this implies high expectations towards Germany to live up to its responsibilities as a member of the UN Security Council and to act in a way that is seen as appropriate.

What is more, the setting of the UN Security Council allows for highly visible agency of its members. Specifically, the vote on UNSCR 1973 confronted Germany with an explicit choice between different behaviours. The main alternative to the selected policy of abstention, which was widely discussed in the fiasco narrative, was that Germany should have voted in favour of the Resolution without committing military troops to its implementation. In particular, the media narrative brings in the views of prominent members of Angela Merkel's Christian Democratic Union (CDU) and of foreign policy practitioners to challenge the government's claim that no such alternative existed and that political support for the Resolution would have made a military contribution to the NATO mission unavoidable. According to the president of the German Bundestag, Norbert Lammert (CDU), for example, there is no direct link 'between supporting the Resolution and deciding about the participation of German troops'. This point was also made, among others, by Wolfgang Ischinger, the chairman of the Munich Security Conference and a former junior minister in the German Foreign Office:

> Since the government has in any case declared that it backs many parts of the UN-Resolution, it would have been more elegant, if Germany had voted in favor. [...] The German ambassador could have pointed out that the agreement holds in principle, but that there is no consideration of contributing troops to a military operation.

In contrast, the German government and in particular Guido Westerwelle tell a very different counter-narrative, constituting the *setting* as unclear and dangerous with a possibility of unforeseen consequences. Specifically, he warned of the 'risks of a lengthy mission' and of a military escalation towards the deployment of ground troops which would make the Bundeswehr 'a party in a civil war'. 'I want to protect Germany from such a slippery slope.' Moreover, Westerwelle denies that there would have been the alternative of voting in favour of Resolution 1973 without participating in its military implementation. If Germany had supported the resolution, according to Westerwelle, it could then not have avoided sending troops to Libya. Overall, however, this attempt of the German government to constitute a particular narrative setting around the abstention on UNSCR 1973 is not taken up much by the media and remains marginal. The dominant narrative is situated in a setting that highlights the high stakes involved in the German decision on UNSCR 1973 and suggests that the foreign policy fiasco would have been avoidable.

Characterization

With regard to agent characterization, one encounters three important actors in the fiasco narrative: Foreign Minister Guido Westerwelle, Chancellor Angela Merkel and the collective agent Germany or the German government. Here, Guido Westerwelle is characterized as a 'clueless', 'tired out' and 'weakened foreign minister' who had the opportunity to 'stage himself as an active formative driver of world politics' but who 'was not willing to take political responsibility'. He is constituted as 'narrow-minded', 'naïve', a 'dilettante', a 'strategic trainee' and a 'catastrophe'. After the fiasco he is considered a 'minister on parole' who is 'alone with his defiance' and whose 'self-opinionatedness' is 'highly embarrassing'. Angela Merkel, in turn, is characterized by some as unreliable, indecisive ('Mrs. Flip-Flop'), cowardly and embarrassing as she 'follows only the augurs of the polling institutes'.

> Angela Merkel's course testifies to cowardice. If the [German] Federal Government considers the intervention to be wrong, it should say so and bring forward its objections. ... What is embarrassing, however, is the hemming and hawing which is driven by the desire to leave loopholes open in case something goes wrong. There are decisions which have to be made. Those who evade such decisions by trying to have it both ways, give up the claim to be taken serious any longer'.

On the collective level the German government is characterized as 'evasive, absent and unpredictable' and as suffering from 'cacophonous leadership'. Its policy is described as an 'emotional act' and a 'panicky about-turn' which speak to Germany's 'unbridled propensity to give itself up to irrational currents'. The government is also accused of 'an element of cowardice', of 'disappearing into the bushes' and of 'hiding behind' the German culture of military restraint. The German behaviour in the crisis is represented as 'cynical' and the question is raised whether Germany 'knuckles under to a murderous dictator'. Government decision-making, in turn, is marked by 'the heated Berlin atmosphere ... in which Germany's navel-gazing has reached its apotheosis'. It is described as 'opportunism' dominated by 'domestic political considerations'.

Most commonly, the characterization of Germany focuses on its alleged unreliability as 'alliance partner'. It is suspected of forging a 'new alliance' with China and Russia at the expense of its traditional partners in the West: 'Instead of being at the side of NATO, Germany in its policy on Libya embarrassingly sees itself in the company of China and Russia.' This is considered indicative of Germany's 'affectations of a great power' and as evidence that, according to former German Chancellor Helmut Kohl, 'Germany lacks a compass.'

There are again elements of a marginalized counter-characterization. Here, Westerwelle emphasizes that he has not taken the decision on Resolution 1973 lightly, but that it was the result of an 'intense, in-depth and also difficult process of deliberation'. Germany has a 'responsible position' and 'has to act cleverly and also act thoughtfully'. Furthermore, he emphasizes that other states were also sceptical about Resolution 1973, including NATO and EU partners, as well as other large democracies. He thereby places the character of Germany in relationship with other respectable actors which one is able to identify with: 'Please do not forget that also Brazil and India abstained.' In comparison to the fiasco narrative, however, these characterizations remain marginal. By far the prevalent narrative in the media discourse is a story which emphasizes the shortcomings of actors on both the individual and the collective level and in which the negative portrayal of these actors is dominant.

Emplotment

Throughout the narrative the abstention in the UN Security Council is considered a violation of normal legitimate behaviour and labelled as a 'grave', 'scandalous', 'fundamental', 'fatal' or 'big mistake of historical dimension' and 'of the highest order'. Not only is the event constituted to be 'strategically' and 'tactically wrong' and a 'moral and political failure', but it is said to be a far larger 'foreign policy debacle' or 'diplomatic disaster'. The abstention 'will go down in history as a low point in German statesmanship'.

> To oppose the closest partners, to ignore the change of mind of the most important ally, to find oneself in a spontaneous value community with Russia and China and receive congratulations for that from Hugo Chávez – no Federal Government has ever produced such a diplomatic write-off.

The abstention is made into a fiasco with reference to its 'immeasurable political costs' as well as 'shame' and 'embarrassment'. This involves at best 'ridicule', 'mockery' and 'disgrace' and at worst 'alienation', 'resentment', 'outrage' or 'incomprehension and anger' among Germany's allies the relations with which are now 'severely disturbed'. Through its decision, Germany is said to have 'rebuffed', 'appalled' and 'enraged' its 'old alliance partners' and 'closest friends' in the world and has led to a 'grudge', 'quarrel' and 'affront against the Atlantic alliance'. The fiasco narrative tells a story in which Germany has 'abandoned' and 'does not stand by' its friends and has 'isolated' itself in the 'Western world'. Germany has become an 'outsider' who 'stands on the side-lines'. It has 'renounced' its alliance partners, 'subverted' a common position of the West and has 'embarrassingly' joined ranks with 'Putin, China's autocrats, Le Pen and Gaddafi'.

Thereby it has greatly 'damaged its reputation', 'image' and 'standing', which will 'have consequences for how serious Germany is taken as a partner'. The 'refusal of alliance solidarity' has led to a political 'loss of trust' in Germany as its behaviour has created the impression that it is 'not reliable', 'unpredictable' and fails to live up to its 'responsibility'. As a result, Germany has done harm to its position on the world stage and is in danger of becoming part of the 'second tier': 'In the concert of the powerful the country at the most plays the triangle.' The negative consequences are seen not only to affect Germany's reputation and friendships but also its position of power in the world, since its behaviour has 'not helped' or even 'significantly reduced' Germany's chances for a permanent seat in the UN Security Council.

In the media narrative the cause of the fiasco was either attributed to 'fatal misjudgments', which wrongly expected a Russian or Chinese veto or an outright rejection of intervention by Arab countries, the ignoring of a 'late change of policy of the Americans, Russians and Chinese on the Libyan question' or 'domestic political reasons' linked to a possible negative effect of military intervention for the governing coalition in upcoming regional elections. Some of the responsibility is attributed to 'orders from Berlin', to the government as a whole who have made the decision 'against the advice of their closest advisors', as well as to Angela Merkel personally who 'realized that she had committed a huge mistake'.

Most of the time, however, the blame for the fiasco is primarily placed on Foreign Minister Guido Westerwelle as 'Chancellor Angela Merkel has somehow managed not to be associated with it.' 'The policy on Libya by the Federal Government has triggered harsh criticism and calls for the resignation of Foreign Minister Westerwelle.' The fiasco is said to be 'due to the clumsy procedures of the strategic trainee Guido Westerwelle ... who misjudged the situation on every level'. 'He forced his civil servants to abstain in the vote on the resolution on Libya in the Security Council against their advice'. Westerwelle is seen guilty of having surrounded himself with the 'wrong friends' in the domestic and international arena and is scolded for giving 'embarrassing explanations' for his policy. 'It would have been the job of a chief diplomat to spot the danger of isolation, warn the Chancellor and devise a counter strategy'. He is made 'directly responsible' and 'has to take the blame for the trouble' as '[n]o Foreign Minister has ever let it come this far.'

With regard to counter-*emplotment*, Westerwelle unsurprisingly denies that the decision was a fiasco. Rather, he argues that it was in the best German interest not to support Resolution 1973 and that 'our policy of sanctions was right'. The decision to abstain in the UN Security Council is constituted as a 'responsible' and 'difficult foreign policy decision following deliberation'. He argues that Germany's abstention was driven by his belief that other Arab and African states in the region have a responsibility to react and that political means had not yet been exhausted. Specifically, according to Westerwelle, sanctions were a better alternative to a military intervention. He also cited the danger of 'civilian casualties' and the 'risk of escalation' owing to Western military intervention as a reason for the German abstention. Furthermore, he denies the negative consequences of the abstention. Specifically, he rejects claims about the alleged damage this decision has caused: 'I explicitly do not see this damage which you describe'. He emphasizes that it is 'completely wrong' to see Germany as being isolated on Libya and that other NATO and EU states understand why Germany abstained: 'We are not isolated'. With regard to the question of responsibility and blame Westerwelle acknowledges that it was his 'most difficult foreign policy decision', but he also states that Angela Merkel played an active role in the abstention: 'We took the decision together'. Despite these attempts at telling a different story, the dominant emplotment of the media narrative was that the German abstention on Resolution 1973 was a fiasco that will have negative diplomatic consequences for which Guido Westerwelle in particular was made responsible.

CONCLUSION

The contribution has introduced the method of narrative analysis to the study of foreign policy fiascos. It argues that foreign policy fiascos are socially constructed in political discourse and that fiasco constructions take the form of narratives which are made up of setting, characterization and emplotment. In each of these dimensions, fiasco narratives consist of a number of essential discursive elements. In particular, the setting represents the context of foreign policy decisions which has implications for what is considered appropriate behaviour. Also, it brings into play alternatives to the selected policy suggesting that a fiasco was avoidable. The characterization of agents in the narrative is marked by negative and derogatory descriptions of influential individual or collective decision-makers and the decision-making process. The emplotment of fiasco narratives, finally, involves the labelling of foreign policies as extraordinary failures with highly negative consequences, as well as the closely interrelated elements of establishing a causal link between agent behaviour and undesirable outcomes and of attributing blame and responsibility. The case study on the media construction of Germany's abstention on UNSCR 1973 on Libya as a foreign policy fiasco and the attempted counter-narration serves to illustrate key discursive patterns of fiasco narratives and how the method of narrative analysis can be applied to the study of foreign policy.

In order to further develop narrative analyses of foreign policy fiascos and to examine their empirical and methodological usefulness, the contribution identifies three avenues for future research. In our view, these are essential next steps towards a broader theory of the narrative construction of fiascos in foreign policy. First, the empirical scope of analysis needs to be expanded from a single case study to a broader comparative case study design. Ideally, this should focus on 'least likely cases' of fiasco constructions that constitute the toughest tests for narrative analysis, in particular foreign policies which 'objectivist' evaluations would not identify as obvious fiascos. Similarly, future analyses should involve cases that are empirically 'most dissimilar' in that they investigate the narrative construction of foreign policy fiascos in different countries, at different points in time and in different issue areas. This can also fruitfully be extended to European-level cases, for example the EU's attempts at brokering a cease-fire in the civil wars in former Yugoslavia in the 1990s or at resolving the Cyprus conflict, as well as currently its role in the Ukraine conflict or its external borders policy. Most notably, such a comparative endeavour would make it possible to establish the extent to which the discursive elements of fiasco narratives identified in this contribution are common to narrative constructions of foreign policy fiascos.

Second, more emphasis than was possible within the scope of this contribution should be put on studying the relationship between 'fiasco' narratives and counter-narratives. As indicated above, counter-narratives contest the construction of foreign policy as a 'fiasco' and represent the legitimation discourse of foreign policy decision-makers. Future research should pay particular attention to the conditions under which they succeed or fail in avoiding the construction of foreign policy decisions as 'fiascos' in political discourse.

Third, it would be fruitful to investigate cases of attempted but ultimately 'unsuccessful' narrative constructions of foreign policy fiascos. In particular, the inclusion of 'near misses' and 'non-fiascos' would promise insights into the discursive and contextual conditions under which fiasco narratives will likely be most compelling. Given the far-reaching practical and political consequences of constituting foreign policy decisions as 'fiascos', more extensive efforts at understanding the narrative construction of such fiascos are called for.

SUPPLEMENTAL DATA AND RESEARCH MATERIALS

Supplemental data for this article can be accessed on the Taylor & Francis website, doi: 10.1080/13501763.2015.1127272.

NOTES

1 There are a number of very different approaches to narrative analysis within political science. While some highlight the role of the narrator or the aspect of changing narratives over time (Miskimmon *et al.* 2013; Patterson and Monroe 1998), our approach emphasizes the narrative elements of setting, characterization and emplotment as analytical categories for the empirical analysis, as these give an insight into a dominant narrative on particular empirical events during a certain time period.
2 All references to the quoted material can be found in the online appendix.

REFERENCES

Boin, A., 't Hart, P. and McConnell, A. (2009) 'Crisis exploitation: political and policy impacts of framing contests', *Journal of European Public Policy* 16(1): 81–106.
Bovens, M. and 't Hart, P. (1996) *Understanding Policy Fiascoes*, New Brunswick, NJ: Transaction Publishers.
Bovens, M. and 't Hart, P. (2016) 'Revisiting the study of policy failures', *Journal of European Public Policy*, doi:10.1080/13501763.2015.1127273.
Bovens, M., 't Hart, P. and Peters, B.G. (1998) 'Explaining policy disasters in Europe. Comparisons and reflections', in P. Gray and P. 't Hart (eds), *Public Policy Disasters in Western Europe*, London: Routledge, pp. 195–214.
Bovens, M., 't Hart, P. and Peters, B.G. (2001) 'The state of public governance', in M. Bovens, P. 't Hart and B.G. Peters (eds), *Success and Failure in Public Governance*, Cheltenham: Edward Elgar, pp. 3–11.
Brändström, A. and Kuipers, S. (2003) 'From "normal incidents" to political crises: understanding the selective politicization of policy failures', *Government and Opposition* 38(3): 279–305.

Brummer, K. (2016) '"Fiasco prime ministers": leaders' beliefs and personality traits as possible causes for policy fiascos', *Journal of European Public Policy*, doi:10.1080/13501763.2015.1127277.

De Vries, M.S. (2004) 'Framing crisis. Response patterns to explosions in fireworks factories', *Administration and Society* 36(5): 594–614.

Dunleavy, P. (1995) 'Policy disasters: explaining the UK's record', *Public Policy and Administration* 10(2): 52–70.

Edelman, M. (1988) *Constructing the Political Spectacle*, Chicago, IL: Chicago University Press.

Fairclough, N. (2010) *Critical Discourse Analysis: The Critical Study of Language*, 2nd ed., London: Routledge.

Fischer, J. (2011) 'Ein einziges Debakel', *Spiegel-Gespräch mit Joschka Fischer, Der Spiegel*, 35/2011, 29 August, 26.

Fludernik, M. (2009) *An Introduction to Narratology*, London: Routledge.

Gallie, W.B. (1956) 'Essentially contested concepts', *Proceedings of the Aristotelian Society* 56: 167–98.

Gaskarth, J. (2016) 'The fiasco of the two Syria votes: decline and denial in British foreign policy', *Journal of European Public Policy*, doi:10.1080/13501763.2015.1127279

Goffman, E. (1974) *Frame Analysis*, New York: Harper & Row.

Gray, P. (1996) 'Disastrous explanations – or explanations of disaster? A reply to Patrick Dunleavy', *Public Policy and Administration* 11(1): 74–82.

Gray, P. (1998) 'Policy disasters in Europe. An introduction', in P. Gray and P. 't Hart (eds), *Public Policy Disasters in Western Europe*, London: Routledge, pp. 3–20.

Haass, R.N. (2009) *War of Necessity. War of Choice*, New York: Simon & Schuster.

Hansel, M. and Oppermann, K. (2014) 'Counterfactual reasoning in foreign policy analysis: the case of German nonparticipation in the Libya intervention of 2011', *Foreign Policy Analysis*, doi: 10.1111/fpa.12054.

Herman, L. and Vervaeck, B. (2007) 'Ideology', in D. Herman (ed.), *The Cambridge Companion to Narrative*, Cambridge: Cambridge University Press, pp. 217–30.

Hill, C. (2003) *The Changing Politics of Foreign Policy*, Basingstoke: Palgrave.

Hood, C. (2002) 'The risk game and the blame game', *Government and Opposition* 37(1): 15–37.

Howlett, M. (2012) 'The lessons of failure: learning and blame avoidance in public policy-making', *International Political Science Review* 33(5): 539–55.

Ingram, H.M. and Mann, D.E. (1980) 'Policy failure: an issue deserving analysis', in H.M. Ingram and D.E. Mann (eds), *Why Policies Succeed or Fail*, London: Sage, pp. 11–32.

Janis, I.L. (1989) *Crucial Decisions. Leadership in Policymaking and Crisis Management*, New York: Free Press.

Marsh, D. and McConnell, A. (2010) 'Towards a framework for establishing policy success', *Public Administration* 88(2): 564–83.

McConnell, A. (2010) 'Policy success, policy failure and grey areas in-between', *Journal of Public Policy* 30(3): 345–62.

McConnell, A. (2016) 'A public policy approach to understanding the nature and causes of foreign policy failure', *Journal of European Public Policy*, doi:10.1080/13501763.2015.1127278.

Miskimmon, A. (2012) 'German foreign policy and the Libya crisis', *German Politics* 21(4): 392–410.

Miskimmon, A., O'Loughlin, B. and Roselle, L. (2013) *Strategic Narratives. Communication Power and the New World Order*, New York: Routledge.

Müller, H. (2011) 'Ein Desaster. Deutschland und der Fall Libyen', *HSFK-Standpunkte 2/2011*, Frankfurt am Main: Hessische Stiftung Friedens- und Konfliktforschung.

Oppermann, K. and Spencer, A. (2013) 'Thinking alike? Salience and metaphor analysis as cognitive approaches to foreign policy analysis', *Foreign Policy Analysis*, 9(1): 39–56.

Patterson M. and Monroe K.R. (1998) 'Narrative in political science', *Annual Review of Political Science*, 1: 315–31.

Selm-Thorburn, J. van and Verbeek, B. (1998) 'The chance of a lifetime? The European Community's foreign and refugee policies towards the conflict in Yugoslavia, 1991–95', in P. Gray and P. 't Hart (eds), *Public Policy Disasters in Western Europe*, London: Routledge, pp. 175–92.

Stelzenmüller, C. (2011) 'Libyen, Eine Deutschstunde', *Süddeutsche Zeitung*, 15 April, 2.

Stern, E. and Sundelius, B. (1998) 'In defence of the Swedish Crown. From triumph to tragedy and back?', in P. Gray and P. 't Hart (eds), *Public Policy Disasters in Western Europe*, London: Routledge, pp. 135–51.

Toolan, M. (2001) *Narrative. A Critical Linguistic Introduction*, London: Routledge.

Tuchman, B.W. (1984) *The March of Folly. From Troy to Vietnam*, New York: Alfred A. Knopf.

Walker, S.G. and Malici, A. (2011) *US Presidents and Foreign Policy Mistakes*, Stanford, CA: Stanford University Press.

White, H. (1987) *The Content of the Form: Narrative Discourse and Historical Representation*, Baltimore, MD: Johns Hopkins University Press.

'Fiasco prime ministers': leaders' beliefs and personality traits as possible causes for policy fiascos

Klaus Brummer

ABSTRACT Against the predominantly structural explanations of policy fiascos in the public policy literature, this contribution questions whether idiosyncrasies of individual decision-makers should be considered as alternative sources of foreign policy fiascos. The contribution uses the leadership trait approach and the operational code approach from the field of foreign policy analysis (FPA) to discern the personality traits and political beliefs respectively of British prime ministers who ended up with major foreign policy fiascos. The computer-aided content analysis of more than 900 speech acts shows that British 'fiasco prime ministers' do indeed exhibit certain 'extreme' personality traits (e.g., a considerably higher level of self-confidence) and political beliefs (e.g., a greater inclination to pursue conflictual strategies) that distinguish them from British 'non-fiasco prime ministers' and other world leaders. This suggests that the public policy literature might benefit from allowing for a greater role of individual decision-makers in their analyses of policy fiascos.

INTRODUCTION

This contribution discusses the role of individual decision-makers in the context of policy fiascos. More specifically, it enquires whether decision-makers who were responsible for foreign policy fiascos exhibit personality traits or political beliefs that are different from those of leaders who did not end up with policy fiascos, and that thus might have contributed to the fiasco. In so doing, with literature from the field of foreign policy analysis (FPA), it contributes to this collection's goal of bringing into dialogue the public policy literature which tends to overlook individuals as possible sources or causes of fiascos.

Conceptually, this contribution draws on two prominent FPA concepts: the leadership trait approach, which focuses on stable personality traits; and the operational code approach, which highlights decision-makers' more flexible political beliefs.[1] Empirically, the article focuses on British foreign policy fiascos, such as the failure of the appeasement policy under Neville Chamberlain, the rejection of the membership applications to the European Economic

Community (EEC) under both Harold Macmillan and Harold Wilson, and the Iraq intervention under Tony Blair. To establish the leadership traits and political beliefs respectively of the 13 British decision-makers under scrutiny (six in a 'fiasco group' and seven in a 'non-fiasco group') this article uses the automated 'Profiler Plus' content analysis system whose coding schemes were applied against some 900 speech acts comprising almost 370,000 words.

One reason for selecting leaders from the United Kingdom (UK) is that, according to the typology by Arend Lijphart (2012), the British political system belongs to the most majoritarian systems of government in Europe. Among the key characteristics of such systems is the predominant position of the prime minister in governmental decision-making. Thus, if the idiosyncrasies of individual leaders do actually lead to fiascos, this should be observable in a political system like the British, owing to the strong influence of prime ministers on (foreign) policy-making. A second reason for choosing the UK is that this country seems especially prone to commit policy fiascos. In this sense, Dunleavy (1995: 52) refers to the UK 'as a state unusually prone to make large-scale, avoidable policy mistakes' (see also Moran 2001). While foreign policy fiascos are not often related to specific idiosyncrasies of decision-makers, this contribution shows that certain individual characteristics (above all, over-confidence and conflict-proneness) might indeed increase the likelihood of leaders ending up with fiascos.

The remainder of the contribution is structured as follows. The next section reviews the public policy literature regarding the role of leaders in the context of policy fiascos. Thereafter, the leadership trait approach and the operational code approach are introduced. The subsequent section discusses the method and data employed in this contribution, followed by a presentation and discussion of the leadership traits and operational codes of the British 'fiasco' and 'non-fiasco' prime ministers respectively. The concluding section briefly summarizes the argument and points to avenues for future research.

LEADERS AND POLICY FIASCOS: A REVIEW OF THE PUBLIC POLICY LITERATURE

According to the public policy literature, policy failure can be assessed along different dimensions (see Bovens and 't Hart 2016). In a highly influential contribution Bovens *et al.* (2001) distinguish between a programmatic and a political dimension, to which Marsh and McConnell (2010: 570–5; also McConnell 2010) later added a third dimension, namely process. For the purpose of this contribution, what is striking about those works on different dimensions of policy failure and the latter's operationalization is that *individual* decision-makers are hardly mentioned in the public policy literature as possible sources for policy failure (for an exception, see McConnell 2016), let alone the specific idiosyncrasies of policy-makers.

In the process dimension, groups of decision-makers (e.g., 'governments') play a role in contributing to policy failures; for instance, by setting out unattainable policy agendas or objectives, engaging in deficient decision-making processes, or failing to address implementation problems (Howlett 2012: 547). Why governments as a group or predominant actors within government (e.g., the prime minister) would succumb to those errors, and whether certain characteristics of the individual actors increase the likelihood of that happening, is not being addressed. In the programmatic dimension, specific actors come into play only in the sense of whether a policy benefited certain interests that can be associated with a specific group of actors (Marsh and McConnell 2010: 571). And in the political dimension, the impression arises that individual decision-makers 'solely' have to bear the consequences of failure, for instance by seeing their credibility diminished or the popularity of their government decrease (Howlett 2012: 549; Marsh and McConnell 2010: 571), rather than being possible causes of failure in the first place.

In short, in the public policy literature, the failure of a policy is usually ascribed to factors other than individual decision-makers, such as legitimacy, resources, implementation, goal attainment, coalition building or public support. For the most part, references to actors remain unspecific, referring either to generic groups of actors (e.g., 'leaders', 'policy-makers', 'political executives') or, at a still higher level of abstraction, institutions as a whole (e.g., 'government', 'organizations', 'agencies').

Somewhat of an exception to the general neglect of individuals in the public policy literature on policy failure is an article by Patrick Dunleavy (1995), which focuses on the origins of policy failures in the UK. Among the five factors identified in the text, the most important one for the purpose of this article is 'hyperactivism' on the ministerial level. Dunleavy (1995: 61) sees this phenomenon occurring not only on the part of junior ministers or state secretaries, which leads them to propose 'new initiatives almost for their own sake', but also on the part of '[s]uccessor ministers [who] tend to be keen to demonstrate political virility by achieving even faster action, and hence they eliminate previously included safeguards'. However, Dunleavy does not go into the personality traits that make junior or senior ministers more or less predisposed to becoming hyperactive. Such a discussion seems necessary, though, unless the assumption is that all ministers are uniformly hyperactive. Instead, in line with the reasoning to be found in other strands of the public policy literature, Dunleavy (1995: 62) sees the key enabling factor for hyperactivism not in the personality of individual decision-makers but in structural factors, notably the 'divorce between initiation and implementation, combined with the premium on speedy and large-scale change'.

Another partial exception is the literature on learning and blame avoidance (e.g., Hood 2002; Weaver 1986) which also places greater emphasis on individual actors. Blame avoidance refers to the 'desire of decision-makers and implementers to emulate positive exemplars of successful policies and avoid negative exemplars of failed ones' (Howlett 2012: 542). Thus, it is decision-makers who 'do' the learning, with the goal being to avoid repeating the past mistakes committed by their predecessors or in other institutions or even in other countries.

However, this literature also does not really engage with the idiosyncratic features of decision-makers, in the sense of asking, for instance, which 'type' of decision-maker is more or less likely to examine practices of others in order to identify successful or failed policies. Yet, simply assuming that all decision-makers engage in – or refrain from – such activity seems unrealistic.

In short, the overall picture that emerges from this brief review of the public policy literature on policy failure is that little emphasis is being placed on individual decision-makers as possible sources or causes of policy failure. This is why the discussion now shifts to two approaches from the field of FPA that could contribute to discerning certain personality traits or political beliefs of decision-makers which could increase the likelihood of the latter being embroiled in fiascos. More specifically, the idea is that 'extreme' manifestations of individual idiosyncrasies – relating to personality traits and/or political beliefs – increase the likelihood of decision-makers to engage in low-quality decision-making processes that in turn increase the likelihood of ending up with policy fiascos as outcomes (see also Schafer and Crichlow 2010).

THE ANALYTICAL APPROACHES

The leadership trait approach

The goal of the leadership trait approach is to associate decision-makers with certain leadership styles that in turn impact the substance and style of their foreign policy. The main proponent of the approach, Margaret Hermann (2005: 181), defines leadership style as 'the ways in which leaders relate to those around them – whether constituents, advisers, or other leaders – and how they structure interactions and the norms, rules, and principles they use to guide such interactions'.

Three dimensions are taken into account in order to identify the leadership styles of decision-makers: the degree to which decision-makers are responsive to constraints (challenge vs respect); and open to new information (open vs closed); as well as their motives for seeking office (problem focus vs relationship focus). Those three dimensions are operationalized through seven leadership traits (Table 1; for details, see Hermann [2005]). Taken together, the combination of insights into those seven traits, and thus into the three dimensions to which the individual traits are linked, leads to a total of eight distinct leadership styles of decision-makers. For instance, whereas leaders who challenge constraints, are closed to information and are problem-focused are called 'expansionistic', leaders who challenge constraints, are open to information and are relationship-focused are termed 'directive' (Hermann 2005: 185). However, previous research has shown that analytical purchase can also be gained from focusing on leadership traits individually by linking certain manifestations of traits to certain types of behaviour or policy decisions, as, for example, Yang (2010) did by connecting leaders' conceptual complexity with the initiation of policy change.

Table 1 Leadership traits

Dimensions	Traits
Responsiveness to constraints	Belief in one's ability to control events
	Need for power and influence
Openness to information	Conceptual complexity (i.e., the ability to differentiate things and people in one's environment)
	Self-confidence
Motivation for seeking office	Task focus/orientation
	General distrust or suspiciousness of others
	In-group bias

Source: Based on Hermann (2005).

This contribution also focuses on individual leadership traits. However, rather than arguing that only one specific manifestation of a certain trait (i.e., very high or very low) might increase the propensity of leaders ending up with policy fiascos, the argument is that 'extreme' manifestations of a trait – that is, either a very high *or* a very low score – can be linked to low-quality decision-making processes (Schafer and Crichlow 2010) and ultimately to fiascos (Kaarbo and Beasley 2008).[2] To illustrate this point, the trait 'self-confidence' refers to a leader's self-importance and perceived ability to cope with situations and people in his/her environment. The argument evolving around extremity posits that leaders with either a very high or a very low score on this trait might be predisposed to ending up with fiascos. Leaders with a high level of self-confidence are content with themselves and have confidence in their reading of a situation, which is why they tend to ignore incoming information that runs counter to their views and refrain from questioning or evaluating their positions or actions. Conversely, leaders whose self-confidence is low lack a well-developed understanding of who they are and what they stand for, which is why they continuously seek information and advice from others, which could lead to erratic or indecisive behaviour (Hermann 2005: 195). While the former might lead to a fiasco based on doing too much or too soon, the latter might lead to a fiasco based on doing too little or acting too late (Walker and Malici 2011: 10–13).

The operational code approach

The operational code approach starts from the assumption that 'beliefs matter' (Walker 2003: 275) for the analysis of foreign policy. Operational codes can be defined as 'a set of general beliefs about fundamental issues of history and central questions of politics as these bear, in turn, on the problem of action' (George 1969: 191). More specifically, the approach focuses on the *political* beliefs of decision-makers.

George (1969) grouped the political beliefs of decision-makers into two categories (Table 2). On the one hand, philosophical beliefs refer to decision-makers' assumptions concerning the fundamental nature of politics. Those beliefs are crucial for the definition of a situation. On the other hand, instrumental beliefs relate to decision-makers' beliefs about ends–means relationships regarding action in the political realm. These are decisive for the selection of the appropriate responses or instruments for the situation at hand. The underlying assumption in operational code analysis is that the beliefs of decision-makers strongly influence their policy preferences and thus impact a country's foreign policy decisions and actions (Walker and Schafer 2006: 7).

As was the case in the discussion on leadership traits, the argument is that extreme manifestations of political beliefs may increase the propensity of leaders to end up with fiascos. To give but a few illustrations, leaders who perceive the world in overly friendly terms might downplay or ignore the malignant intentions of other actors and therefore refrain from taking precautionary measures. Conversely, leaders who perceive the world in highly conflictual terms see dangers lurking 'everywhere', which is why they might be incapable, for instance, of grasping opportunities for settling conflicts peacefully (P-1). Turning to instrumental beliefs, leaders who pursue a highly co-operative strategy (I-1) and employ a corresponding set of instruments (I-5) might end up with a fiasco if the situation would have required a more assertive response.

Table 2 Philosophical and instrumental beliefs in an operational code

---

Philosophical beliefs

P-1 What is the 'essential' nature of political life? Is the political universe essentially one of harmony or conflict? What is the fundamental character of one's political opponents?

P-2 What are the prospects for the eventual realization of one's fundamental political values and aspirations? Can one be optimistic, or must one be pessimistic on this score; and in what respects the one and/or the other?

P-3 Is the political future predictable? In what sense and to what extent?

P-4 How much 'control' or 'mastery' can one have over historical development? What is one's role in 'moving' and 'shaping' history in the desired direction?

P-5 What is the role of 'chance' in human affairs and in historical development?

Instrumental beliefs

I-1 What is the best approach for selecting goals or objectives for political action?

I-2 How are the goals of action pursued most effectively?

I-3 How are the risks of political action calculated, controlled, and accepted?

I-4 What is the best 'timing' of action to advance one's interest?

I-5 What is the utility and role of different means for advancing one's interests?

Source: Based on George (1969).

Conversely, placing too strong an emphasis on conflictual strategies and instruments might have the adverse effect of actually causing conflict that could have been avoided through more co-operative behaviour.

METHOD AND DATA

The question that follows from the above discussion is whether leaders who were responsible for foreign policy fiascos do indeed exhibit more 'extreme' personality traits or political beliefs than leaders who are not linked to fiascos. With the empirical focus of this contribution resting on the United Kingdom, the following discussion revolves around two groups of British prime ministers. The classification of prime ministers is based on what the literature suggests as being major British foreign policy fiascos;[3] the leaders who were in power at the time of the fiascos are thus referred to as 'fiasco prime ministers'. Those prime ministers and 'their' fiascos are:

- Neville Chamberlain (1937–40) and the failure of his appeasement policy toward Nazi Germany, including the signing of the Munich Agreement in September 1938;
- Anthony Eden (1955–7) and the failed Suez intervention of November 1956;
- Harold Macmillan (1957–63), as well as Harold Wilson (1964–70, 1974–6), and their failed applications respectively in August 1961 and May 1967 to join the EEC;
- John Major (1990–7) during whose tenure the UK had to leave the European Exchange Rate Mechanism (ERM) on 16 September 1992 ('Black Wednesday'); and
- Tony Blair (1997–2007) and the decision to intervene alongside the United States in Iraq in March 2003.

For the purpose of comparison, a reference group was set up comprising seven modern-day British prime ministers who typically are not associated with major foreign policy fiascos ('non-fiasco prime ministers'). Those are: Winston Churchill (1940–5, 1951–5); Clement Attlee (1951–5); Edward Heath (1970–4); James Callaghan (1976–9); Margaret Thatcher (1979–90); Gordon Brown (2007–10); and David Cameron (since 2010).[4]

Before going into specifics on data selection and processing, a general comment on the 'appropriate' source material for leadership trait analysis and operational code analysis is in order. Both approaches belong to the 'at-a-distance' assessment techniques for individual characteristics of decision-makers (Schafer 2000). Probably the biggest challenge that researchers face when analysing current or past political leaders, such as heads of states or government, is that this group of persons is hardly ever available for interviews, let alone psychological testing. Notwithstanding this lack of direct access to the subject of study, at-a-distance techniques argue that it is nonetheless possible to gain systematic insights into 'who' decision-makers are. This can be done by analysing the verbal statements of decision-makers (Hermann 2005: 178–9), which usually exist in large numbers and are available in the public domain.

While the focus on verbal statements by decision-makers is shared by the two approaches employed in this contribution, they stipulate different requirements of the type of source material (i.e., spontaneous 'versus' prepared speech acts) to be used for arriving at adequate assessments of a decision-makers' personality traits or political beliefs respectively. Proponents of the leadership trait approach argue that spontaneous speech acts, such as live television interviews or impromptu exchanges during parliamentary debates, convey the most genuine representations of 'who' leaders are, and are therefore best suited for discerning their personality traits.[5]

Proponents of the operational code approach do not dispute that spontaneous statements are well-suited to discern leaders' characteristics (Schafer 2000: 515–16). Yet, of greater importance still from this perspective is that the individual speech acts are at least 1,500 words in length, so that short statements do not exert a disproportionate influence (Renshon 2009: 655). Moreover, based on the insight from earlier studies that the political beliefs of leaders can be domain-specific (Walker and Schafer 2000), the analysed statements should address one issue area only, rather than cover different subject matters as suggested by the leadership trait approach. Since it is oftentimes challenging to find long spontaneous speech acts that deal exclusively with foreign policy, most operational code studies are based on prepared speeches, such as government statements in parliament.

The implication of the preceding discussion on source material is that two separate text corpuses were compiled for this article. The identification of leadership traits of the 13 British prime ministers under scrutiny is based on spontaneous speech acts made during different periods of their tenure and in addressing different issue areas. While some transcripts of television interviews were available (e.g., for Major and Blair, with the British Broadcasting Corporation [BBC]), most of the prime ministers' spontaneous remarks gathered for this contribution were made during parliamentary debates in the House of Commons (as shown in 'Hansard') in response to *follow-up* questions from the floor by members of the political opposition. For identifying the operational code beliefs of the prime ministers, prepared speeches were gathered on broadly conceived foreign policy issues. The speeches were compiled from a number of sources, including 'Hansard,', 'British Political Speech', and 'UKpolitics.org'.[6]

For each of the 13 British prime ministers, at least 50 spontaneous statements comprising a minimum of 100 words each,[7] as well as at least five prepared speeches of a minimum of 1,500 words each were gathered. Since previous research has shown that operational codes in particular can vary over time, for instance following traumatic events (Renshon 2008: 837–9) such as major policy fiascos, for the 'fiasco prime ministers' only spontaneous statements and prepared speeches were considered that were made between the respective prime minister entering into office and the occurrence of the fiasco with which the prime minister is associated. Overall, 802 spontaneous statements totalling some 118,000 words were used to identify the leadership traits of the 13 British prime ministers covered in the analysis, and 109 speeches comprising more than 250,000 words for their operational code beliefs.

The source material was processed using the automated 'Profiler Plus' content analysis system. Profiler Plus, which contains coding schemes for both the leadership trait approach and the operational code approach, performs frequency counts for the text corpuses that are inputted in the program. Drawing on those frequency counts, the program constructs indices for the seven leadership traits and the 10 elements of the operational code approach. The coding scheme for leadership trait analysis links particular words or phrases with the traits covered by the approach. For example, words like 'approximately' or 'possibility' are indicative of a leader with a high conceptual complexity, while words such as 'absolutely' or 'irreversibly' point in the opposite direction, with the specific score for the trait being the percentage of high- and low-complexity terms used in the speech acts of the decision-maker (for details, see Hermann 2005). The coding scheme for the operational code analysis is based on the 'Verbs in Context System', which extracts from decision-makers' verbal statements values for six different attributes for each verb. They include: whether the speaker refers to himself/herself ('Self') or to another actor ('Other'); whether verbs are 'positive' (appeal, promise, or reward) or 'negative' (oppose, threaten, or punish); and also whether the verbs refer to 'conflictual' or 'co-operative' behaviour. For instance, the score for P-1 is based on the net attribution of positive/co-operative versus negative/conflictual valences to other actors (for details, see Walker *et al.* 1998, 2005).

RESULTS AND DISCUSSION

Table 3 shows the empirical results for the leadership trait analysis of the six British 'fiasco prime ministers'. For the purpose of comparison, it also shows the mean scores (including standard deviations) of a group of 284 leaders from around the world[8] and of the seven British 'non-fiasco prime ministers' introduced above. The British 'non-fiasco prime ministers' group is used to establish whether the British 'fiasco prime ministers' exhibit traits different from their predecessors or successors, and the 'world leaders' group is used to examine whether the British 'fiasco prime ministers' are more generally different from other political leaders. If the mean score of the 'fiasco prime ministers' is more than one standard deviation above the mean score of a comparison group, they are high on the trait; conversely, if the mean score is more than one standard deviation below the mean score of a comparison group, they are 'low' on the trait. Finally, if the means score of the 'fiasco prime ministers' is around the mean score of a comparison group, they are 'moderate' on the trait (Hermann 2005: 204).

Table 3 shows both similarities and differences in the leadership traits of the two groups of British prime ministers. In three traits (control over events, distrust of others, in-group bias) the scores are very similar. In the other four traits,

Table 3 Leadership trait scores of world leaders, British 'non-fiasco prime ministers' and British 'fiasco prime ministers'

Decision-makers	Trait						
	Control over events	Need for power	Conceptual complexity	Self-confidence	Task orientation	Distrust of others	In-group bias
'World leaders' (N = 284)*	Mean = 0.35 High > 0.40 Low < 0.30	Mean = 0.26 High > 0.31 Low < 0.21	Mean = 0.59 High > 0.65 Low < 0.54	Mean = 0.36 High > 0.46 Low < 0.26	Mean = 0.63 High > 0.70 Low < 0.56	Mean = 0.13 High > 0.19 Low < 0.07	Mean = 0.15 High > 0.20 Low < 0.10
British 'non-fiasco prime ministers' (N = 7)*	Mean = 0.36 High > 0.39 Low < 0.33	Mean = 0.24 High > 0.27 Low < 0.21	Mean = 0.56 High > 0.60 Low < 0.52	Mean = 0.42 High > 0.51 Low < 0.33	Mean = 0.68 High > 0.72 Low < 0.64	Mean = 0.09 High > 0.12 Low < 0.06	Mean = 0.10 High > 0.14 Low < 0.06
British 'fiasco prime ministers' (N = 6) (mean score)	0.36	0.21	0.60	0.52	0.64	0.10	0.10
→ compared to 'world leaders'	Moderate	**Lean low**	Moderate	**High**	Moderate	Moderate	**Lean low**
→ compared to British 'non-fiasco prime ministers'	Moderate	**Lean low**	**Lean high**	**High**	**Lean low**	Moderate	Moderate

however, the scores diverge. Indeed, 'fiasco prime ministers' exhibit less need for power and a lower task orientation than the 'non-fiasco prime ministers'. At the same time, 'fiasco prime ministers' are more conceptually complex and, above all, display a significantly higher level of self-confidence than 'non-fiasco prime ministers'. Thus, there are considerable differences between the two groups of British prime ministers. What is more, there are also differences between the British 'fiasco prime ministers' and the group of 'world leaders', albeit in only three traits rather than four. The British 'fiasco prime ministers' show less of an in-group bias as well as, as was the case when they were compared to British 'non-fiasco prime ministers', less need for power along with a considerably higher level of self-confidence.

Overall, the results suggest that fiasco leaders might indeed exhibit certain personality traits which set them apart from other leaders. This holds particularly true for two traits, namely the need for power and, above all, self-confidence, where the 'fiasco prime ministers' score respectively lower (need for power) and *significantly* higher (self-confidence) than the average member of either of the comparison groups. Linking the established manifestations of those traits to fiascos seems straightforward. Decision-making by leaders low in the need for power might be plagued by indecisiveness and a lack of control of the decision group (e.g., the cabinet) over whom he or she presides. Hence, such leaders might refrain from taking timely decisions, or from pushing well enough to get an effective decision. Turning to the implications of the even more significant empirical finding, leaders with a high level of self-confidence might rush to conclusions without a proper prior screening of information and options. However, it is less obvious how the two traits might interact in promoting fiascos, since the former suggests that leaders might do too little or act too late, or do not try hard enough to get a decision, while the latter points to leaders doing too much or acting too soon. Maybe fiascos are the result of a lack of individual leadership exhibited by prime ministers who fail to provide direction to their decision group (owing to a low need for power) and refrain from changing their approach (owing to high self-confidence).

Table 4 shows results of the operational code analysis for the 'fiasco prime ministers' and the 'non-fiasco prime ministers'.[9] Again, the results point to several differences between the two groups. Beginning with the philosophical beliefs, there are already certain differences pertaining to the nature of political life (P-1), which 'fiasco prime ministers' see somewhat more conflictual than 'non-fiasco prime ministers'. The differences regarding the realization of political values (P-2) and the exertion of control over historical developments (P-4) are more pronounced. 'Fiasco prime ministers' are less optimistic on both counts, which seems to be in line with their generally more pessimistic characterization of political life. The findings for the philosophical beliefs are mirrored in the instrumental beliefs, where 'fiasco prime ministers' exhibit a *signficantly less co-operative* strategic approach to political goals (I-1) and are more inclined to employ negative sanctions (I-5d, I-5e). However, the high score for 'fiasco prime ministers' on I-4a indicates that they might be capable of altering their

Table 4 Operational code scores of British 'fiasco' and 'non-fiasco' prime ministers

Element of the operational code	P-1 Nature of Political Universe	P-2 Realization of Political Values	P-3 Predictability of Political Future	P-4 Control over Historical Development	P-5 Role of Chance	I-1 Strategic Approach to Goals	I-2 Tactical Pursuit of Goals	I-3 Risk Orientation
British 'non-fiasco' prime ministers' (n = 7)*	Mean = 0.46 High > 0.61 Low < 0.31	Mean = 0.26 High > 0.37 Low < 0.15	Mean = 0.12 High > 0.15 Low < 0.09	Mean = 0.28 High > 0.32 Low < 0.24	Mean = 0.97 High > 0.98 Low < 0.96	Mean = 0.61 High > 0.68 Low < 0.54	Mean = 0.28 High > 0.36 Low < 0.20	Mean = 0.27 High > 0.34 Low < 0.20
British 'fiasco' prime ministers' (n = 6) (mean score)	0.36	0.18	0.12	0.24	0.97	0.52	0.22	0.24
→ compared to British 'non-fiasco' prime ministers'	moderate	**Lean low**	Moderate	**Lean low**	Moderate	**low**	**Lean low**	Moderate

Element of the operational Code	I-4a Timing of action: cooperation/Conflict	I-4b Timing of action: words/deeds	I-5a Utility of means: reward	I-5b Utility of means: promise	I-5c Utility of means: appeal	I-5d Utility of means: oppose	I-5e Utility of means: threaten	I-5f Utility of means: punish
British 'non-fiasco' prime ministers' (n = 7)*	Mean = 0.39 High > 0.46 Low < 0.32	Mean = 0.53 High > 0.64 Low < 0.42	Mean = 0.18 High > 0.24 Low < 0.12	Mean = 0.06 High > 0.12 Low < 0.00	Mean = 0.57 High > 0.65 Low < 0.49	Mean = 0.10 High > 0.13 Low < 0.07	Mean = 0.01 High > 0.02 Low < 0.00	Mean = 0.09 High > 0.13 Low < 0.05
British 'fiasco' prime ministers' (n = 6) (mean score)	0.48	0.54	0.16	0.04	0.55	0.12	0.02	0.11
→ compared to British 'non-fiasco' prime ministers'	High	Moderate	Moderate	Moderate	Moderate	Lean high	Lean high	Moderate

Note: * 'High' and 'low' indicate one standard deviation from the mean score.

basically more conflictual strategies in response to changes in the environment. Overall, the operational code analysis presents British 'fiasco prime ministers' as having a gloomier perception of the political universe and pursuing a *more conflictual approach* to politics than 'non-fiasco prime ministers', which might predispose them to acting too soon or doing too much.

Finally, it also seems possible to link the findings of the separate analyses of the leadership traits and operational codes of the British 'fiasco prime ministers'. Leaders with a markedly high level of self-confidence (leadership trait) are more likely to jump to conclusions and subsequently maintain their course of action even in the light of contradictory new information. If such a highly self- or, rather, over-confident leader's preferred course of action is to pursue goals through conflictual strategies based on a pessimistic, conflict-prone view of the political universe (operational code), the odds are that policy changes will not be forthcoming even though, for instance, the situation on the ground would suggest otherwise. Leaders who are inflexible to adapting their course of action and exhibit deficiencies in information gathering and processing indeed seem more likely to end up with fiascos than less 'extreme' leaders. How this rather coherent linkage between traits and beliefs can be reconciled with the reported low score of 'fiasco prime ministers' on the need for power trait and the high score on the timing of action warrants further research.

CONCLUSION

Against the paucity in the public policy literature on the role of individuals in the context of policy fiascos, this contribution explores whether links exist between the idiosyncrasies of decision-makers and (foreign) policy fiascos. The article uses the leadership trait approach and the operational code approach from the field of FPA to discern the personality traits and political beliefs respectively of a total of 13 British prime ministers who did ('fiasco prime ministers') or did not ('non-fiasco prime ministers') end up embroiled in major foreign policy fiascos. The computer-aided content analysis of more than 900 speech acts comprising some 370,000 words shows that 'fiasco prime ministers' do indeed exhibit certain 'extreme' personality traits (above all, a considerably higher level of self-confidence) and political beliefs (pointing to a more conflictual perception of political life and a correspondingly greater inclination to engage in more conflictual strategies when pursuing their goals) which set them apart from 'non-fiasco prime ministers'.

While certainly not representing conclusive evidence, the results of this contribution nonetheless indicate that certain individual characteristics might indeed increase the likelihood of leaders to engage in low-quality decision-making processes that in turn lead to major policy fiascos. In the light of these findings, future FPA research should further examine the interactive effects of the extreme manifestations of certain personality traits and political beliefs as possible causes of policy fiascos. In turn, the public policy literature might benefit from moving beyond its predominantly structural explanations of fiascos by acknowledging a greater role played by individual decision-makers. Indeed, it seems that, in all three dimensions used in the public policy literature to assess policy failure (programme, politics and process), individual leaders can have important effects, for instance, by predetermining programmes/policies based on their (in some instances 'extreme') political beliefs or by establishing or influencing decision-making processes within the decision group based on their (in some instances 'extreme') leadership traits.

NOTES

1 These approaches have rarely been used in British cases. The most notable exceptions are works by Dyson (2006, 2009; Dyson and Raleigh 2012) who, however, did not specifically address the issue of policy fiascos.

2 While Kaarbo and Beasley (2008) discuss 'extremity' regarding the impact of coalition cabinets on the substance of a country's foreign policy (with extremity referring to the more conflictual or co-operative behaviour of coalition cabinets compared to single-party cabinets), the idea also seems to provide explanatory leverage in this contribution's discussion on individual decision-makers.

3 A discussion on whether the cases discussed in this contribution actually qualify as 'policy fiasco' – be it from a rationalistic or an argumentative perspective (Bovens *et al.* 2006: 325–8) – is beyond the scope of this contribution (see the introduction to this collection for details on the respective perspectives). Rather than seeking to establish whether the cases under scrutiny 'are' fiascos, the contribution takes corresponding claims in the literature as its point of departure and examines whether the British prime ministers that are commonly associated with fiascos exhibit certain idiosyncrasies that set them apart from prime ministers who are usually not linked to foreign policy fiascos. For literature that classifies the cases under scrutiny as fiascos, see, for instance, Stedman (2011) on appeasement; Gorst and Johnman (1997) on Suez; Ashton (2005) on Macmillan's failed EEC application; Wincott *et al.* (1999) on ERM; and Coates and Krieger (2009) on Iraq.

4 Since his time in office was less than a year, Alex Douglas-Home (1963–4) was not included.

5 At least 50 spontaneous speech acts containing at least 100 words each should be analysed for each decision-maker. Furthermore, the statements should cover a decision-maker's full tenure, or at least different time periods, and address different subject matters (Hermann 2005: 180).

6 A list of the speech acts used in this article is available from the author on request.

7 The exceptions are Neville Chamberlain and Clement Attlee, for each of whom only 50 statements of at least 50 words could be identified.

8 Since the names of the individual leaders comprising the 'world leaders' group are not available, it is impossible to discern how many of them are associated with foreign policy fiascos. Besides, the 'world leaders' group includes 15, albeit non-specified

'Anglo-American leaders' (presumably mainly from the United States and the UK) and thus maybe also a few of the prime ministers analysed in this article. However, their number is too small to significantly bias the mean score of the group. The scores for the 'world leader' group are made available when downloading the Profiler Plus programme from the website of Social Science Automation (http://socialscience.net). This article used the version of the table: 'Leadership Trait Analysis Scores (Means and Standard Deviations)' as of October 2012.

9 For operational code analysis there is no 'world leaders' group available.

REFERENCES

Ashton, N.J. (2005) 'Harold Macmillan and the "golden days" of Anglo-American relations revisited, 1957–63', *Diplomatic History* 29(4): 691–723.

Bovens, M. and 't Hart, P. (2016) 'Revisiting the study of policy failures',.

Bovens, M., 't Hart, P. and Peters. B.G. (eds) (2001) *Success and Failure in Public Governance: A Comparative Analysis*, Cheltenham: Edward Elgar.

Bovens, M., 't Hart, P. and Kuipers, S. (2006) 'The politics of policy evaluation', in M. Moran, M. Rein and R.E. Goodin (eds) *The Oxford Handbook of Public Policy*, Oxford: Oxford University Press, pp. 319–35.

Coates, D. and Krieger, J. (2009) 'The mistake heard round the world: Iraq and the Blair legacy', in T. Casey (ed.) *The Blair Legacy. Politics, Policy, Governance, and Foreign Affairs*, Basingstoke: Palgrave, pp. 247–59.

Dunleavy, P. (1995) 'Policy disasters: explaining the UK's record', *Public Policy and Administration* 10(2): 52–70.

Dyson, S.B. (2006) 'Personality and foreign policy: Tony Blair's Iraq decisions', *Foreign Policy Analysis* 2(3): 289–306.

Dyson, S.B. (2009) 'Cognitive style and foreign policy: Margaret Thatcher's black-and-white thinking', *International Political Science Review* 30(1): 33–48.

Dyson, S.B. and Raleigh, A. (2012) 'Blair, Brown, Cameron and the War on Terror', in K. Oppermann (ed.) *British Foreign and Security Policy. Historical Legacies and Current Challenges*, Augsburg: Wißner, pp. 190–206.

George, A.L. (1969) 'The "operational code": a neglected approach to the study of political leaders and decision-making', *International Studies Quarterly* 13(2): 190–222.

Gorst, A. and Johnman, L. (1997) *The Suez Crisis*, Abingdon: Routledge.

Hermann, M.G. (2005) 'Assessing leadership style: trait analysis', in J.M. Post (ed.) The Psychological Assessment of Political Leaders, Ann Arbor, MI: University of Michigan Press, pp. 178–212.

Hood, C. (2002) 'The risk game and the blame game', *Government and Opposition* 37(1): 15–37.

Howlett, M. (2012) 'The lessons of failure: learning and blame avoidance in public policy-making', *International Political Science Review* 33(5): 539–55.

Kaarbo, J. and Beasley, R. (2008) 'Taking it to the extreme: the effect of coalition cabinets on foreign policy', *Foreign Policy Analysis* 4(1): 67–81.

Lijphart, A. (2012) *Patterns of Democracy: Government Forms and Performance in Thirty-Six Countries*, New Haven, CT: Yale University Press.

Marsh, D. and McConnell, A. (2010) 'Towards a framework for establishing policy success', *Public Administration* 88(2): 564–83.

McConnell, A. (2016) 'A public policy approach to understanding the nature and causes of foreign policy failure',.

McConnell, A. (2010) 'Policy success, policy failure and grey areas in-between'. *Journal of Public Policy* 30(3): 345–62.

Moran, M. (2001) 'Not steering but drowning: policy catastrophes and the regulatory state', *Political Quarterly* 72(4): 414–27.

Renshon, J. (2008) 'Stability and change in belief systems. The operational code of George W. Bush', *Journal of Conflict Resolution* 52(6): 820–49.

Renshon, J. (2009) 'When public statements reveal private beliefs: assessing operational codes at a distance', *Political Psychology* 30(4): 649–661.

Schafer, M. (2000) 'Issues in assessing psychological characteristics at a distance: an introduction to the symposium', *Political Psychology* 21(3): 511–27.

Schafer, M. and Crichlow, S. (2010) *Groupthink Versus High-Quality Decision Making in International Relations*, New York: Columbia University Press.

Stedman, A.D. (2011) *Alternatives to Appeasement: Neville Chamberlain and Hitler's Germany*, London: I.B. Tauris.

Walker, S.G. (2003) 'Operational code analysis as a scientific research program. A cautionary tale', in C. Elman and M.F. Elman (eds) *Progress in International Relations Theory. Appraising the Field*, Cambridge, MA: MIT Press, pp. 245–76.

Walker, S.G. and Malici, A. (2011) *US Presidents and Foreign Policy Mistakes*, Stanford, CA: Stanford University Press.

Walker, S.G. and Schafer, M. (2000) 'The political universe of Lyndon B. Johnson and his advisors: diagnostic and strategic propensities in their operational codes', *Political Psychology* 21(3): 529–43.

Walker, S.G. and Schafer, M. (2006) 'Belief systems as causal mechanisms in world politics: an overview of operational code analysis', in M. Schafer and S.G. Walker (eds) *Beliefs and Leadership in World Politics*, Basingstoke: Palgrave, pp. 3–22.

Walker, S.G., Schafer, M. and Young, M.D. (1998) 'Systematic procedures for operational code analysis: measuring and modeling Jimmy Carter's operational code', *International Studies Quarterly* 42(1): 175–90.

Walker, S.G., Schafer, M. and Young, M.D. (2005) 'Profiling the operational codes of political leaders', in J.M. Post (ed.) *The Psychological Assessment of Political Leaders*, Ann Arbor, MI: University of Michigan Press, pp. 215–45.

Weaver, R.K. (1986) 'The politics of blame avoidance', *Journal of Public Policy* 6(4): 371–98.

Wincott, D., Buller, J. and Hay, C. (1999) 'Strategic errors and/or structural binds? Major and European integration', in P. Dorey (ed.) *The Major Premiership. Politics and Policies under John Major, 1990–97*, Basingstoke: Macmillan, pp. 87–107.

Yang, Y.E. (2010) 'Leaders' conceptual complexity and foreign policy change: comparing the Bill Clinton and George W. Bush foreign policies toward China', *Chinese Journal of International Politics* 3(4): 415–46.

The fiasco of the 2013 Syria votes: decline and denial in British foreign policy

Jamie Gaskarth

ABSTRACT On 29 August 2013, the British parliament voted against two motions to censure the Syrian government which were expected to lead to military action. The result was a shock to external commentators and quickly interpreted as a fiasco. This article charts the construction of the severity and agency involved in this fiasco and notes the extremely personal nature of efforts to attribute blame for the outcome. It argues that this process enabled policy-makers to ignore underlying trends impacting on foreign policy, including the breakdown of bipartisanship, increasing public scepticism about government use of intelligence and the utility of force, severe reductions in Britain's capacity to act, as well as a deeper identity crisis about what kind of actor Britain should be in the world. Constructing this event as a fiasco can be seen as a form of denial of Britain's loss of agency in global affairs.

INTRODUCTION

The British government's failure to secure parliamentary approval for military action in Syria on 29 August 2013 was widely viewed at the time as a fiasco. Journalists and commentators routinely used the term to describe this event, such that the London Mayor Boris Johnson mocked the coverage as saying: 'We were finished as a world player ... It was the biggest fiasco since Suez ... the most epic parliamentary cock-up since Lord North' (Johnson 2013). Negative interpretations of the event were evident not just in Britain but also in Europe and the wider world (Open Europe 2013). Yet, one of the curious aspects of this case is that it had positive diplomatic results – in the form of the decommissioning of Syria's chemical weapons stockpiles – and some commentators now perceive that if air strikes had been undertaken they might have exacerbated the emerging Islamist threat to the region (Hain 2014). Furthermore, the result seemed to accord with the feelings of the general public – making British foreign policy appear more democratic – and was welcomed for adding to the debate on Britain's global influence (Defence Committee 2014: 34). This case is therefore interesting for two reasons. Firstly, it is seen as a fiasco despite its positive outcomes (see Bovens and 't Hart 2016). Most fiascos, such as Gallipoli, Suez, Vietnam and Iraq are defined as such owing to their negative results. Secondly, this fiasco relates to the absence of action rather than its presence.

Justifications for labelling the event a fiasco mostly refer to the process by which parliament voted against two motions that could have led to military action (on process failures, see McConnell [2016]). It is here that critics identify the 'avoidable and blameworthy failures' that Bovens and 't Hart (1998: 15) see as characteristic of fiascos. It is less what was done than how that appears to render the votes in these terms. This article questions that argument on the same basis on which Oppermann and Spencer (2016) critique the positivism of policy evaluation studies in their contribution to this collection. As they note, failure is 'not an attribute of policy, but rather a judgment about policy' (*ibid.*). Criticism of how policy-makers behaved often assumes that if they had only acted differently the 'right' result might have been achieved. What this ignores is the broader context to decision-making. The votes against military action were arguably not an aberration but the result of a number of cumulative processes which emerged in the 2000s and are having a significant impact on the UK's will and capacity to use force. Seen in that light, the framing of this event as a fiasco, and the politicized blame game that ensued, are understandable as ways of avoiding the trauma of Britain's decline.

This contribution begins with a brief summation of the relevant policy literature on fiascos as a prelude to an analysis of how the Syria votes were constructed in these terms. A series of actors are evoked in public discourse to apportion blame for the outcome in ways that emphasize agency and, so, culpability. However, it will be argued that this understates the extent to which a fiasco emerges as a result of the loss of agency (Gray 1998). It is the gap between policy-makers' assertion of control and the reality of the power of circumstances that perhaps led to the 'Syria votes fiasco'.

POLICY FIASCOS

Bovens and 't Hart (1998: 15) define a policy fiasco as a 'negative event that is perceived by a socially and politically significant group of people in the community to be at least partially caused by avoidable and blameworthy failures of public policymakers'. The importance of perception in this definition underlines the socially constructed nature of these cases. The same authors distinguish fiascos from failures more generally as the former involve subjectively significant social damage and are highly politicized, whereas the latter could simply be routine performance errors that are corrected without much fuss (*ibid.*). The negativity of fiascos is demonstrated by the emotional reaction they are said to evoke; as Bovens and 't Hart (1998: 11) put it: 'some series of actions must have occurred that somehow aroused or upset a certain number of people'. For these authors, 'what sets policy 'fiascoes' apart as a special category of events is intense public and political arousal' (1998: 148). In our case study, arousal is certainly evident, both among the political eélite and the public at large.

When it comes to defining the temporal parameters of a fiasco, this depends on whether the focus is on a particular event or the longer causal chain of actions and processes that fed into the outcome. The Syria debate of August 2013 has the character of an 'instant fiasco', described by Bovens and 't Hart (1998: 60) as 'events concentrated in place and time where the evidence of failure is immediate and unmistakeable'. Put simply, the government sought approval from parliament for its policy, failed to secure it, and attracted negative publicity as a result; all in the space of 24 hours. Yet, this fiasco is linked to earlier fiascos, such as Britain's military ventures in Iraq and Afghanistan, as well as broader processes outside the control of the actors blamed for the Syria case. This is potentially problematic since Bovens and 't Hart (1998: 12) note that 'It is only when one accepts that human intervention (could have) made a crucial difference in producing the damage that one labels the episode in such an accusatory manner.' If structural forces provide a better explanation of events, then the construction of outcomes as a fiasco owing to human agency is misleading. The question arises as to whose interest, or what purpose, is served by limiting the time frame to this event and attributing agency and blame on an individual basis? One explanation put forward in this article is that individual blame can be seen as a coping mechanism to offset the psychological impact of British decline.

The literature on policy fiascos is notable for its range of different frameworks of analysis. Bovens and 't Hart (1998) originally set out four key questions pertinent to fiascos, namely: how bad was the policy failure? Who were the agents? Why did they act? And, who is to blame? (1998). These were later condensed in an analysis of crises to three criteria: severity; agency; and responsibility (Boin et al. 2005: 103). Here, the analyst ponders: how bad was the situation? How was it brought it about? And who sanctioned the behaviour and so bears responsibility for outcomes? The difficulty in separating out these questions into distinct responses is that they are mutually constitutive. Thus, actors are often identified in order to attribute blame rather than simply to ascertain their involvement. For this reason, the analysis that follows seeks to adapt existing frameworks by examining the construction of the severity of the situation, the agency invoked, and the political consequences of these frames. It is this essay's contention that constructing this event as a fiasco helps to obfuscate the underlying trends which led to the outcome.

THE SYRIA VOTES – 29 AUGUST 2013

The growing death toll in Syria and the failure of the Security Council to respond was a cause of heated discussion in international policy circles. The President of the United Nations (UN) General Assembly, Nassir Abdulaziz Al-Nasser, described the UN Security Council (UNSC) as 'not fit for purpose' due to its failure to act (Lakhani 2012). Meanwhile, William Hague, the British foreign secretary, stated in August 2012 that 'we have failed in this Council

... in our responsibility to address the causes of the conflict' and warned of 'months of greater bloodshed, greater suffering, and greater danger to international peace and security' (Hague 2012). However, it wasn't until the summer of 2013 that the international community proposed military action.

On 21 August 2013, chemical weapons attacks using the nerve agent Sarin occurred in Ein Tarma, Zamalka and Moadamiya on the outskirts of Damascus, Syria (United Nations 2013). Estimates of casualties vary, but Médecin Sans Frontières (MSF) suggested their hospitals treated approximately 3,600 patients for neurotoxic symptoms, 355 of whom died (MSF 2013). Given the nerve agent used, and the origin and direction of travel of the rockets used to deliver it, most policy-makers concluded that the Assad government was to blame. The British Joint Intelligence Committee (JIC) wrote a letter to the British prime minister stating that 'there are no plausible alternative scenarios to regime responsibility' (JIC 2013). On Thursday 29 August, the UK parliament was recalled from its summer break to debate how the British government should respond. The opposition Labour party tabled an amendment to the government motion, which they felt defined clearer steps to any use of force. The government opposed this, as it didn't mention the attack involved chemical weapons, or that the Assad government was to blame. The opposition amendment was voted down by 332 votes to 220. The government then put its own motion to parliament, which called for a 'strong humanitarian response' from the international community which may 'require military action'. It was rejected by 285 votes to 272.

Severity

Immediate interpretations of this event saw it as constituting a major shift in British foreign policy with profoundly negative consequences. Commentators pointed out that no government had been defeated on a House of Commons motion for military action since 1782 (Kaarbo and Kenealy 2015; Strong 2015). Early analyses posited this would have serious impacts on Britain's global status. Then Defence Secretary Philip Hammond hinted it would damage the 'special relationship' with the US (*Economist 2013*). The most prominent response was that of Lord Ashdown, a former leader of the Liberal Democrats. In a series of messages on Twitter, he stated: 'In 50 years trying to serve my country I have never felt so depressed/ashamed. Britain's answer to the Syrian horrors? None of our business!' and averred that 'We are a hugely diminished country this am' (Carter 2013).

The criticism implied both a failure in the actual policy itself – since the government was unable to get its motion passed – as well as a political failure to appreciate the context and address the concerns of key actors prior to the vote. Bovens and 't Hart (1998: 35) note a distinction between political and programme failures, whereby a policy could fail in one aspect but succeed in another. When it comes to the political aspect, they assert that policy-makers must 'provide different political stakeholders with such information, and present the information in such a way as to secure their support' (Bovens and 't Hart 1998: 35). Clearly, this is something the government failed to do. Moreover, there were important international political ramifications. Having been one of the most ardent supporters of action to confront Assad throughout 2012 and 2013, the UK had to adopt a more circumspect role and was sidelined in later negotiations over Syria's decommissioning of its stockpiles of chemical weapons. This was a serious loss of face, both in terms of its relationship with the US – its long term security partner – as well as its links with France, its new collaborator on security and defence projects. However, it is less clear whether the programme as a whole was a failure, given that it provided space for diplomacy to be conducted that led to this decommissioning.

In subsequent days, there was a concerted effort among Conservative politicians to downplay any negative effects and emphasize continuity. Daniel Hannan, a critic of British policy on Syria, asserted: 'Parliament's rejection of military action in Syria has been good for David Cameron and ... it has been good for our standing in the world' (Hannan 2013). The basis of his argument was that the general public was not in favour of action; significant figures in the US policy sphere, such as Donald Rumsfeld and John Bolton, were also opposed; and that Cameron's acceptance of the result showed that he listened to the public and reaffirmed 'democratic values'. The Conservative mayor of London, Boris Johnson, took up this theme, arguing that the votes were 'good for Britain' as they would lead to a pause before action (Johnson 2013). Rather than see this as evidence of the UK's declining influence, Johnson put forward the counter notion that Obama's decision to delay and consult Congress meant that he was emulating Cameron and that 'the views of London were too important to ignore' (*ibid.*). In other words, the event was portrayed less as a fiasco than an anomaly without lasting significance.

Assessments of the seriousness of the Syria votes faded soon after the event. By 7 September, the *Spectator* columnist James Forsyth noted it was damaging for the prime minister but also for the leader of the opposition, and suggested that 'all the party leaders seem to want to forget that last week's drama ever happened' (Forsyth 2013). The fiasco's declining salience with the general public, and the absence of a vote of no confidence in Cameron, were cited as evidence that its negative effects would be short term. However, commentators have highlighted constitutional and practical implications which are yet to be resolved (Defence Committee 2014; Perkins 2014). The lack of clarity about whether prime ministerial commitments to foreign leaders are subject to parliamentary approval, and Britain's credibility as a military actor, are still to be tested.

Agency

The fiasco of the Syria vote is notable for the extreme personalization of responsibility for the outcome, as well as the bitter and uncivil tone of recriminations that followed. This invective was overwhelmingly focused around Cameron and

Miliband; but Conservative backbench rebels were also criticized. Beyond these groups, a number of other individuals are apportioned blame for the failure to secure support for action, including the Conservative chief whip, Sir George Young, the UN secretary general, Ban Ki-moon, President Barack Obama, and even the general public themselves as agents influencing decision-making via their letters to parliamentarians and responses to opinion polls.

As the leading proponent of action, David Cameron attracted criticism for the failure to secure support for his policy. Negative comments are divisible into those emphasizing procedural failures – the 'how' of Cameron's policy – and those highlighting political problems – the 'what'. In procedural terms, Cameron's recall of parliament was criticized for being hasty, as UN inspectors had not had time to investigate and report their findings and the UN process was ongoing (Ralph 2013). The leader of the opposition described Cameron as 'cavalier and reckless' in promoting action before the UN could consider the situation. However, Douglas Alexander, the shadow foreign secretary, had asked for parliament to be recalled on the Monday before so that Cameron could 'make the case' for UK involvement in military operations (Watson 2013). The timing of this debate is usually portrayed as owing to a desire on the part of the US president to act militarily over the weekend, with Cameron having made a personal commitment that the UK would contribute to this effort (Strong 2014). In this way, Cameron shared the blame for the timing of the votes with President Obama – as well as opposition figures.

Another procedural problem attributed to Cameron was his failure to secure the support of the leader of the opposition for his policy. Bipartisanship has long been a tradition in British foreign policy and governments are expected to consult with opposition figures to ensure their support (Gaskarth 2006: 329–31). Cameron was informed by Miliband on the day before the debate that Labour would not support the government's motion. Commentators have interpreted this as a lost opportunity for Cameron to negotiate a compromise, perhaps even if it meant accepting a motion written by the opposition (Dixon 2013; Strong 2015). Critics also note Cameron's failure to shore up support among his own backbenchers. Here, Hague and Hammond, along with Young, are drawn in as agents failing to advise Cameron about the likelihood of a sizeable rebellion among his own members of parliament (MPs) (Heffer 2013). Yet, this apparent lack of political nous is often conveyed as a personal failing of Cameron's and feeds into a negative impression of his leadership (Clarke 2013). A Labour source argued: 'His approach had all the subtlety of Flashman ... It was the character of David Cameron – his stubbornness, his anger and his rush towards war – which was the central cause of his defeat' (Helm 2013).

In addition to these procedural errors, Cameron is held responsible for the fiasco on the basis that the policy itself was flawed. On a practical level, parliamentarians and media commentators questioned how far air strikes could achieve the goal of deterring the use of chemical weapons or protecting civilians (Clarke 2013). Moreover, evidence from polling of public disquiet about action risked undermining the success of any military operations that followed (Jordan 2013). Recent interventions in Iraq and Afghanistan had been labelled fiascos and lack of public support was seen as a contributory factor to these earlier failures (Defence Committee 2014: 35–6; Phillips 2005; Ricks 2007).

On the broader level of how this fitted with wider British foreign policy aims, there were concerns about whether the basis for decision-making was sufficiently robust. The idea of engaging in a further intervention in the region was controversial owing to the echoes of previous fiascos mentioned above. Cameron acknowledged this in his opening statement, arguing: 'I am deeply mindful of the lessons of previous conflicts and, in particular, of the deep concerns in the country that were caused by what went wrong with the Iraq conflict in 2003' (Hansard 2013). One of the problems here for the government was the lack of learning that had taken place in response to these fiascos. Whilst the organizations involved may have conducted internal reviews and adapted their behaviour (see Bailey *et al.* 2013), publicly reviews of government performance were either highly focused on one aspect (e.g., the 2004 Butler Inquiry), not directly related to policy (e.g. the 2004 Hutton Inquiry), entirely absent (to date there has been no official inquiry into Britain's involvement in Afghanistan) or substantially delayed (the Iraq inquiry begun in July 2009 has still not reported its findings at the time of writing). Thus, any claim to have learnt lessons encountered a credibility problem, given the lack of tangible and public demonstrations of such a process.

One can see this in the continual questioning of the premise that there was a solid intelligence basis to action (Hansard 2013). In light of how discredited intelligence had been by the Iraq fiasco of 2003, it might have been wiser for Cameron to downplay this aspect and focus on this decision as a policy judgment based on evidence from non-governmental organizations (NGOs) on the ground. Instead, by releasing intelligence assessments the government mirrored previous influence attempts by their New Labour predecessors which had proven to be flawed (Clarke 2013; Glees and Davies 2004). Thus, political and programme errors were combining to build a sense of fiasco.

Furthermore, Cameron's response did not appear to be founded on a rigorous appraisal of Britain's national interests. A central question surrounding earlier fiascos was how far they really advanced the interests of the British people directly, as opposed to indirectly, via the benefits that flowed from maintaining the special relationship with the US, supporting international police actions, and fulfilling the role of a great power on the world stage. Recent British military operations were critiqued for lacking a strategic sense of how they could (and could not) further foreign policy goals (Strachan 2009). In a period of austerity, the threat of embroiling the UK in expanding and expensive commitments to wider milieu goals would struggle to achieve support. Despite Cameron's rhetorical efforts to distinguish his proposed course of action from previous fiascos, the similarities (regional location, intelligence basis, pressure from the US, lack of clarity about long term goals) continued to resonate in the debate.

A further attribution of blame to Cameron concerned his behaviour after the votes. When Miliband asked Cameron to confirm he would not use the royal prerogative to order military action prior to another vote, the prime minister went further by asserting: 'It is very clear tonight that, while the House has not passed a motion, the British Parliament, reflecting the views of the British people, does not want to see British military action. I get that, and the Government will act accordingly' (Hansard 2013). In a subsequent debate, Hague echoed this, stating: 'The House has made its decision, and we respect that decision ... we are not planning to return to the same vote or the same debate again' (Hague 2013). Cameron's closing down of the possibility of future action could be praised as reflective of wider public opinion. It also allowed Cameron to put the debate behind him quickly (Bennister and Heffernan 2015: 34). However, Labour critics pointed out that '492 out of 577 Members of this House supported, or did not rule out, the potential use of force in Syria' and questioned why 'the Prime Minister has been so categorical in ruling it out, including refusing even to contemplate bringing the matter back to the House, whatever the circumstances' (Bradshaw 2013). According to this logic, Cameron underlined the importance of the event – and cemented its status as a fiasco – by refusing to revisit it.

To deflect criticism of Cameron's handling of the votes, and the policy that underpinned them, the government engaged in a highly personal briefing campaign against Ed Miliband. Before the debate, a government source described Miliband as a 'f****** c***', as well as a 'copper-bottomed s***' in a briefing to *The Times* (Tahir 2013). Another source was quoted as asserting: 'Labour has been playing politics when they should have been thinking about the national interest. ... Their position has changed consistently over the last 24 hours, finally ending in demands they had not even hinted at before' (Tahir 2013). The government apparently believed they would have the support of the opposition until 17:15pm on the evening before the vote, when Miliband rang Cameron to say this was not the case and that his party would be tabling an amendment (Watson 2013). Although the Conservative Whips Office had sensed the government motion may not be supported and so had been calling for MPs to return to vote, the late confirmation of the opposition's position was seen as designed to wrong-foot the government (rather than reflecting internal deliberation in the Labour party leadership). Thus, the blame for the fiasco was attributed both to Miliband's supposed character as a duplicitous individual, as well as his desire to exploit this situation for political advantage.

In this light, changes to Miliband's stance during the days prior to the votes are viewed as political manoeuvring. However, another explanation was posited at the time. A plea by UN Secretary General Ban Ki-moon for more time to complete inspections of the attack site on 28 August 2013 is said to have changed the Labour leader's calculus on whether military action was justified at that moment (Dixon 2013). Furthermore, one commentator for the right-wing *Spectator* magazine defended Miliband's change of heart as a pragmatic response to the political situation in the Commons:

I don't think it speaks badly of Miliband that, after sampling opinion in his party, he believed he was unable to say that Labour was for intervention. He seems to have realised the strength of the opinion before the Tory whips alerted David Cameron to the rebellion in his own benches. (Nelson 2013)

According to this logic, Miliband was less culpable for the fiasco, since he had judged the mood of his party (in contrast to Cameron and his whips) and adjusted his policy accordingly.

Others were less charitable and saw Miliband's stance as opportunistic. This was seen as highlighted by his insistence that the votes meant the UK should not take part in military action. Having proposed a motion himself that might have led to this outcome, Miliband appeared to be departing from his earlier policy – a course that seemed to question his commitment to taking robust action against the Syrian government for their use of chemical weapons. Facing a Labour party and public hostile to military intervention abroad, Miliband is said to have had a 'lucky escape' when Cameron refused to revisit the debate, and one writer argued 'While some interventionists will despair at the apparent lack of prin-ciple involved, his political logic was impeccable' (Eaton 2013). Conservative sources accused him of being 'incoherent', 'flipping and flopping', 'buggering around' and 'playing politics', descriptions which were seen as a deliberate strat-egy to pin the blame for the fiasco on Miliband and portray him as 'weak, opportunistic and unstatesmanlike' (Dunt 2013; Helm 2013).

Beyond the charge of political opportunism, Miliband and his shadow foreign secretary, Douglas Alexander, were also viewed as contributing to the fiasco via their tabling of a separate motion despite the government having amended their own to take into account Labour's concerns. Miliband and Alex-ander asserted that the government motion was designed to enable military action and failed to delineate a full process of UN consultation prior to this (Ralph 2013). The government responded by emphasizing that a second vote would be held prior to Britain's participation in military operations. Given this concession, the Labour motion was widely panned for manufacturing a dispute when the parties seemed substantially to agree on the process that must be followed.

Just as with Cameron, Miliband's stance was criticized for going against the tradition of bipartisanship in British foreign policy. The basis for this tradition was that domestic disputes over foreign affairs might be used by foreign powers to undermine the coherence and effectiveness of Britain's external policies and so should not be aired publicly. Thus, Philip Hammond, then defence secretary, asserted: 'Anything that stops us from giving a clear united view of the British Parliament tonight will give some succour to the regime' (Chorley and Duell 2013). In tabling an alternative motion, Hammond suggested Miliband had ensured: 'we don't have a clear, united and unified opinion from the British Par-liament' (*ibid.*). The emphasis on unity here underscores the importance placed on bipartisanship. This framing provoked an angry reaction from the Labour party and was raised in the debate itself (Hansard 2013). Charges of opportunism on the part of Miliband were regularly countered by the portrayal of Cameron as a reckless leader who had failed to listen. Thus, the personal agency of these protagonists was continually evoked to explain the fiasco.

However, this emphasis on Miliband obscured the extent to which the government defeat was enabled by opposition from its own backbenchers. The initial response to the votes was acrimonious, with Michael Gove, then education secretary, apparently shouting 'You're a disgrace!' at rebels from his own party (*Economist 2013*). A total of 30 Conservative MPs and nine Liberal Democrats voted against the government – if only seven had voted in favour the motion would have carried. Despite the reaction from Gove, both the government and backbenchers sought to downplay their internal party divisions, with the latter praising Cameron's 'conviction' and the government focusing its attacks on Miliband (Martin 2013). Another individual attracting criticism was Nick Clegg, then leader of the Liberal Democrats and deputy prime minister, who was panned for his performance at the end of the debates. It was alleged that he failed to emphasize the UK would not use force without a second vote (Watt *et al.* 2013). In addition, Clegg was blamed for not attaching more conditions to his support – such as a defined UN route to action (Dixon 2013).

An element of farce pervaded the votes when it was discovered that two ministers had missed the government vote as they were having a private meeting and missed the division bell – one of whom, the international development secretary, Justine Greening, had driven back from France at the Whips Office's behest to be there. Although not vital to the final result, they contributed to a sense of a loss of control and authority on the part of the government. In all, 10 members of the government, including six ministers, did not vote – figures that could have counted (Heffer 2013).

The final prominent agents that are apparent in discussion are the public at large. Continual reference points in the parliamentary debate were constituents' letters expressing disapproval of British involvement in intervention (Hansard 2013). This direct and personal intervention by members of the public clearly resonated with those debating the motions and contributed to the sense that the government – and the political élite – were out of step with public opinion. This added to the sense of the votes as a fiasco, since they were intended to represent a firm commitment to action when in reality a lack of public support and political will would have undermined anything but a token British involvement in the use of force. This was underlined by the speed with which party leaders ruled out military action in Syria and sought to move on from the debate.

Political consequences

The primary political consequence of framing the Syria debate as a fiasco appears to have been the loss of face experienced by individuals. Since the result was attributed to failings by key personnel such as Cameron, Miliband

and, to a lesser extent, Hague, Alexander and Young, it was they who bore the brunt of criticism. Whilst Cameron did make errors in judgment over the timing of the debate, assessing the support of the opposition, and presenting the case to parliament – and his interactions with Miliband were not harmonious – it is arguable that far more was obstructing agreement between the two, and provoking dissent among backbenchers, than simply procedural issues. Although most parliamentarians seemed prepared to vote for some form of motion that could have led to military action, there were significant factors militating against anything but a token contribution to the proposed military operations. As the comments by Hannan, Johnson and Forsyth indicate above, the overall tone of coverage seemed to welcome the outcome – even whilst acknowledging political errors in how it came about.

In this light, the extreme personalization of the fiasco and the suggestion that it was simply the result of a procedural dispute between the two leaderships, could have problematic political consequences, since there were clearly wider processes at work that fed into the outcome. Firstly, as Jason Ralph (2013) has pointed out, there were real differences in the motions put to the vote when it came to exhausting the UN process prior to engaging in action without specific UN authorization. The government seemed to have learnt the importance of legal cover and regional support in the case of Libya (Daddow 2013), but was now appearing to act precipitately. Looking only at individual failings of timing or tone in the debate ignores the wider legitimacy issues surrounding military action in the international sphere – especially when UN approval is ambiguous or absent – that informed voting outcomes.

In addition, the above framing conceals the backdrop of significant changes to the domestic and international environments in which foreign policy discussion takes place, including the breakdown of bipartisanship, increasing public scepticism about government use of intelligence and the utility of force, severe reductions in Britain's capacity to act, as well as a deeper identity crisis about what kind of actor Britain should be in the world.

In relation to the decline of bipartisanship, this was arguably sparked in 2003 by the Liberal Democrat opposition to Britain's participation in the invasion of Iraq. A major party opposing the government's policy on a matter of national security was extremely rare and established a precedent for the freer expression of dissent across the political spectrum. However, other influences also fed into this; for instance, the Eurosceptic wing of the Conservative party and their longstanding practice of opposing their own government's policies on foreign affairs, going back to the acrimonious vote on the Maastricht treaty in 1993. Ashdown specifically associated the votes against action in Syria with isolationism and the desire to withdraw from the European Union (Carter 2013). Combined with a far more rebellious parliament, in which MPs now vote against their own government more regularly and in greater numbers than past decades (Cowley 2014), it is increasingly difficult for governments to assume consensus on foreign policy, deference to the leadership and bipartisanship between parties.

Following the fiasco of Iraq and the false intelligence used to justify action to the public, UK governments now also face a crisis of authority when it comes to presenting their case for war. On the one hand, the public and parliamentarians will call for strong evidence to support the use of force. On the other hand, references to intelligence and attempts to present documentary proof inevitably recall earlier influence attempts by the New Labour government to put intelligence material in the public domain to serve their policy ends. Thus, there is a paradox at work in which the more the government seeks to justify its actions, the more suspicion it arouses about the strength of its case. Frequent references to public opinion during and after the debate highlight the significance of this factor to the outcome; but, this was lost in the rush to attribute individual blame and the government did not subsequently consider the future implications for foreign policy of shifts in public attitudes towards the use of force. Although public opinion is changeable and there is disagreement over how far it has really moved against intervention, this was clearly a major enabler of dissent against the two motions (Gaskarth 2016; Jordan 2013). If either motion had carried, this would potentially have given rise to a split between the public and the parliamentary élite which might have threatened the legitimacy and efficacy of action – as in the previous cases of Iraq and Afghanistan.

Focusing on individual character and behaviour further obfuscates the significant changes in the geopolitical environment in which the UK operates. The increasing economic and political power of China, India and Brazil in recent years, as well as the greater assertiveness of Russia, has changed the climate wherein the UK promotes its normative initiatives (Thakur 2013). In the past, the UK achieved some success in advancing the international criminal justice regime and the norm of the responsibility to protect. These are now openly opposed or undermined in international forums, as the veto on referring Syria to the International Criminal Court (ICC) attests. Were it not for the anticipated Chinese and Russian vetoes over Syria, policy-makers would likely have pushed for the support of the UN Security Council prior to any parliamentary votes and so the issues of legitimacy and legality that were a concern for many parliamentarians would have been far less prominent.

The UK's economic difficulties during the recent financial crisis have also created problems of capacity and political will to pursue intervention abroad. Globally, the contraction of its economy led to questions over whether it should retain its permanent member status at the UNSC (Deo and Pradhan 2014). Domestically, the cost of previous interventions weighed against taking on new commitments in a time of economic austerity. Combined with severe cuts to the capabilities of the armed forces in the medium term – prior to an enhanced capacity in 2020 – it appeared that the opportunities for the UK to be a significant global actor were diminishing (Cornish and Dorman 2009; Edmunds 2010).

These processes highlight and exacerbate a deeper crisis of identity that pervades British foreign policy-making. In the decades since the UK ceased to be an imperial power, there have been efforts to reappraise Britain's position in world affairs but none have resulted in changes to the basic assumptions that govern its foreign policy, namely: that the UK should have a significant military capability, that it must exert global influence, and that it should align itself with the US (Daddow 2010). These aims have been undermined in recent years by the pressures of austerity, the less-receptive international environment, and the clear differences in outlook between the US and the UK on a whole series of political and military issues. The wider policy community have made frequent calls for the government to examine national identity rigorously as a prelude to national strategy-making (Defence Committee 2014: 3; Joint Committee on the National Security Strategy [JCNSS] 2012: 18–19). Yet, these have so far gone unheeded. In the meantime, splits have emerged between public and élite attitudes to foreign policy priorities (Chatham House 2012). Indeed, the frequent references to public opinion during the Syria debate are perhaps evidence that this was a major factor behind the failure to agree action.

In sum, the construction, by all parties, of the Syria votes as a fiasco attributable to individual failings serves to deny or ignore the important underlying trends that fed into the result. The government was acting within a context of reduced global influence, reduced capacity, public disquiet about the use of force, and a legitimacy and authority gap derived from previous fiascos. Rather than using this event as a cathartic opportunity to provoke an open debate about their implications for British identity and how Britain should act – a therapeutic exercise in which blame is replaced with understanding – policy-makers chose to personalize the outcome and thereby trivialize it. Such suppression is unhelpful both in political and psychological terms. Senior defence figures have noted Britain's influence is diminishing even as foreign policy-makers continue to deny that 'strategic shrinkage' is taking place (e.g., Hennessey 2014). Depicting this outcome as a fiasco caused by personal character failings meant the political élite avoided the difficult task of acknowledging Britain's relative decline and rethinking its foreign policy. Moreover, from a psychological perspective, it allowed political élites to suppress difficult questions about future British national identity (on the role of cognitive dissonance in policy fiascos, see Beasley [2016]).

CONCLUSION

This contribution has outlined the construction of the 'Syria votes fiasco' and examined its political consequences. It began by noting how the severity of this fiasco was at first emphasized and then downplayed by commentators, and charted the extreme personalization of this event around a few key figures said to be exerting agency in a negative fashion. Although these people may have committed individual political and programmatic errors of timing, presentation and policy, the broader context of Britain's relative decline means that this country will face further difficulties in using military force in the service of its foreign policy goals in future. Whilst there still appears to be a strong desire among élites for Britain to exert global influence and be a military actor, other trends, including economic austerity, lack of public support and a global environment containing significant veto actors, are making it harder for it to act internationally. The framing of this event as a fiasco had the effect of denying or suppressing this context to avoid the difficult debates and choices that might flow from confronting this new reality. As such, it may have been a useful psychological coping mechanism, but is only likely to lead to further fiascos until élite expectations, public attitudes and material circumstances are properly aligned.

REFERENCES

Bailey, J., Iron, R. and Strachan, H. (2013) *British Generals in Blair's Wars*, Farnham: Ashgate.

Beasley, R. (2016) 'Dissonance and decision-making mistakes in the age of risk', *Journal of European Public Policy*, doi:10.1080/13501763.2015.1127276.

Bennister, M. and Heffernan, R. (2015) 'The limits to prime ministerial autonomy: Cameron and the constraints of coalition', *Parliamentary Affairs* 68(1): 25–41.

Boin, A., 't Hart, P., Stern, E. and Sundelius, B. (2005) *The Politics of Crisis Management*, Cambridge: Cambridge University Press.

Bovens, M. and 't Hart, P. (1998) *Understanding Policy Fiascoes*, New Brunswick, NJ: Transaction.

Bovens, M. and 't Hart, P. (2016) 'Revisiting the study of policy failures', *Journal of European Public Policy*, doi:10.1080/13501763.2015.1127273.

Bradshaw, B (2013) 'Question in the House of Commons.' *Hansard*, Column 694, September 9, available at http://www.publications.parliament.uk/pa/cm201314/cmhansrd/cm130909/debtext/130909-0001.htm (accessed 21 October 2015).

Carter, C. (2013) 'Syria crisis: Paddy Ashdown 'ashamed' of Britain over Commons vote', *Telegraph*, 30 August, available at http://www.telegraph.co.uk/news/politics/10275565/Syria-crisis-Paddy-Ashdown-ashamed-of-Britain-over-Commons-vote.html (accessed 15 December 2015).

Chatham House (2012) 'British attitudes towards the UK's International Priorities Survey Results', *YouGov Survey, July 2012*, London: Chatham House.

Chorley, M. and Duell, M. (2013) 'The humbling of David Cameron', *Daily Mail*, 29 August, available at http://www.dailymail.co.uk/news/article-2405633/Syria-conflict-David-Cameron-humiliated-losing-Commons-vote-possible-military-action.html (accessed 15 December 2015).

Clarke, M. (2013) 'No 10's shifty and rushed battle plan', *The Sunday Times*, 1 September.

Cornish, P. and Dorman, A. (2009) 'National defence in the age of austerity', *International Affairs* 85(4): 733–53.

Cowley, P. (2014) 'Queen's speech: can David Cameron handle the most rebellious house since 1945?', *The Conversation*, 4 June, available at https://theconversation.com/queens-speech-can-david-cameron-handle-the-most-rebellious-house-since-1945-27551 (accessed 21 October 2015).

Daddow, O. (2010) 'Dodging the bullet and ducking the question' *RUSI Analysis*, 19 August, available at https://www.rusi.org/analysis/commentary/ref:C4C6D0795721 B3/#.VRkvOo7F-So (accessed 21 October 2015).

Daddow, O. (2013) 'The use of force in British foreign policy: from New Labour to the coalition' *The Political Quarterly* 84(1): 110–18.

Defence Committee. (2014) *Intervention: Why, When and How? Fourteenth Report of Session 2013–14*, HC952, 28 April, London: Stationery Office, available at http://www.publications.parliament.uk/pa/cm201314/cmselect/cmdfence/952/952. pdf (accessed 21 October 2015).

Deo, N. and Pradhan, K. (2014) 'Should India give up on the UN Security Council?', *The Diplomat*, 9 November, available at http://thediplomat.com/2014/11/should-india-give-up-on-the-un-security-council/ (accessed 21 October 2015).

Dixon, H. (2013) 'Cameron, UK hurt by Syria vote fiasco', *Reuters*, 30 August, available at http://blogs.reuters.com/hugo-dixon/2013/08/30/cameron-uk-hurt-by-syria-vote-fiasco/ (accessed 21 October 2015).

Dunt, I. (2013) 'Syria debate verdict: a terrible moment for Ed Miliband', Politics.co.uk, 29 August, available at http://www.politics.co.uk/comment-analysis/2013/08/29/ syria-debate-verdict-a-terrible-moment-for-ed-miliband (accessed 21 October 2015).

Eaton, G. (2013) 'Syria: Ed Miliband has had a lucky escape', *New Statesman*, August 30, available at http://www.newstatesman.com/politics/2013/08/syria-ed-miliband-has-had-lucky-escape (accessed 15 December 2015).

Economist (2013) 'Britain will not fight' *The Economist*, 30 August , available at http://www.economist.com/blogs/blighty/2013/08/intervention-syria (accessed 21 October 2015).

Edmunds, T. (2010) 'The defence dilemma', *International Affairs* 86(2): 377–94.

Forsyth, J. (2013) 'Syria vote? What Syria vote? David Cameron's strategy is to forget it ever happened', *Spectator*, 7 September, available at http://www.spectator.co.uk/ columnists/politics/9012871/after-his-syria-defeat-cameron-faces-a-battle-to-win-over-his-mps/ (accessed 21 October 2015).

Gaskarth, J. (2006) 'Discourses and ethics: the social construction of British foreign policy', *Foreign Policy Analysis* 2(4): 325–41.

Gaskarth, J. (2016) 'Intervention, domestic contestation and Britain's national role conceptions', in J. Kaarbo and C. Cantir (eds), *Domestic Role Contestation, Foreign Policy, and International Relations*, London: Routledge.

Gray, P. (1998) 'Policy disasters in Europe', in P. Gray and P. 't Hart (eds), *Public Policy Disasters in Western Europe*, London: Routledge, pp. 3–20.

Glees, A. and Davies, P.H.J. (2004) *Spinning the Spies: Intelligence, Open Government and the Hutton Inquiry*, London: Social Affairs Unit.

Hague, W. (2012) 'UK Intervention at the United Nations Security Council meeting on Syria', Speech to UNSC, 29 August, available at https://www.gov.uk/ government/news/uk-intervention-at-the-united-nations-security-council-meeting-on-syria (accessed 21 October 2015).

Hain, P. (2014) 'Remarks in the House of Commons.' *Hansard*, Column 1278, 26 September, available at http://www.publications.parliament.uk/pa/cm201415/ cmhansrd/cm140926/debtext/140926-0001.htm (accessed 21 October 2015).

Hannan, D. (2013) 'The United Kingdom stands taller in the world today', *Telegraph*, 31 August, available at: http://blogs.telegraph.co.uk/news/danielhannan/100233 524/the-united-kingdom-stands-taller-in-the-world-today/ (accessed 15 December 2015).

Hansard (2013) 'Syria and the use of chemical weapons.' 29 August, available at http:// www.publications.parliament.uk/pa/cm201314/cmhansrd/cm130829/debtext/ 130829-0001.htm (accessed October 2015).

Heffer, S. (2013) 'Hague should have told the PM to retreat', *Daily Mail*, 30 August, available at http://www.dailymail.co.uk/debate/article-2407373/Syria-vote-William-Hague-told-David-Cameron-retreat.html (accessed 15 December 2015).

Helm, T. (2013) 'No 10 launches bitter assault on Ed Miliband over Syria vote' *Guardian*, 31 August, available at http://www.theguardian.com/politics/2013/aug/31/syria-commons-vote-cameron-miliband (accessed 15 December 2015).

Hennessey, Lord. (2014) 'Lord Hennessey meets ... Lord Richards', *Civil Service World*, 1 October, available at: http://www.civilserviceworld.com/articles/interview/lord-hennessy-meets-lord-richards (accessed October 2015).

Johnson, B. (2013) 'The delayed attack on Syria is good for Britain – and the PM', *Telegraph*, 1 September, available at http://www.telegraph.co.uk/news/worldnews/middleeast/syria/10279546/The-delayed-attack-on-Syria-is-good-for-Britain-and-the-PM.html (accessed 15 December 2015).

Joint Intelligence Committee (JIC) (2013) 'Syria: reported chemical weapons use', 29 August, available at https://www.gov.uk/government/uploads/system/uploads/attachment_data/file/235094/Jp_115_JD_PM_Syria_Reported_Chemical_Weapon_Use_with_annex.pdf (accessed October 2015).

Joint Committee on the National Security Strategy (JCNSS) (2012) *First Review of the National Security Strategy 2010*, February 27, HC 1384, available at http://www.publications.parliament.uk/pa/jt201012/jtselect/jtnatsec/265/265.pdf (accessed October 2015).

Jordan, W. (2013) 'Public opinion drove Syria debate', YouGov, 30 August, available at https://yougov.co.uk/news/2013/08/30/public-opinion-syria-policy/ (accessed October 2015).

Kaarbo, J. and Kenealy, D. (2015) 'No, prime minister: explaining the House of Commons' vote on intervention in Syria', *European Security*, doi:10.1080/09662839.2015.1067615.

Lakhani, Nina. (2012) 'Top UN official says it is "not fit for purpose".', Independent, 5 March, available at http://www.independent.co.uk/news/world/politics/top-un-official-says-it-is-not-fit-for-purpose-7536442.html (accessed 15 December 2015).

Martin, I. (2013) 'Syria vote: David Cameron's authority is in tatters', Telegraph, 29 August, available at http://blogs.telegraph.co.uk/news/iainmartin1/100233281/syria-vote-david-camerons-authority-is-in-tatters/ (accessed 15 December 2015).

McConnell, A. (2016) 'A public policy approach to understanding the nature and causes of foreign policy failure', *Journal of European Public Policy*, doi:10.1080/13501763.2015.1127278.

Médecin Sans Frontières (MSF) (2013) 'Syria: thousands suffering neurotoxic symptoms treated in hospitals supported by MSF', 24 August, available at http://www.msf.org/article/syria-thousands-suffering-neurotoxic-symptoms-treated-hospitals-supported-msf (accessed October 2015).

Nelson, F. (2013) 'David Aaronovitch: Syria vote shows Ed Miliband is a "vulture" not a "leader"', *Spectator*, 5 September, available at http://blogs.spectator.co.uk/coffeehouse/2013/09/david-aaronovitch-syria-vote-shows-ed-miliband-is-a-vulture-not-a-leader/ (accessed 15 December 2015).

Open Europe (2013) 'Europe reacts to David Cameron's defeat on Syria', 30 August, available at http://openeuropeblog.blogspot.co.uk/2013/08/david-camerons-defeat-on-syria-europe.html (accessed October 2015).

Oppermann, K. and Spencer, A. (2016) 'Telling stories of failure: narrative constructions of foreign policy fiascos', *Journal of European Public Policy*, doi:10.1080/13501763.2015.1127272.

Perkins, A. (2014) 'The full impact of the UK's vote against intervention in Syria has yet to be felt', *Guardian*, 1 January, available at http://www.theguardian.com/commentisfree/2014/jan/01/uk-syria-vote-impact-parliament (accessed 15 December 2015).

Phillips, D.L. (2005) *Losing Iraq: Inside the Postwar Reconstruction Fiasco*, New York: Basic Books.

Ralph, J. (2013) 'The vote was not British isolationism. It was about the legitimacy of international action', *Foreign Policy Centre Briefing*, available at http://fpc.org.uk/fsblob/1566.pdf (accessed October 2015).

Ricks, T.E. (2007) *Fiasco: The American Military Adventure in Iraq*, London: Penguin.

Strachan, H. (2009) 'The strategic gap in British defence policy', *Survival* 51(4): 49–70.

Strong, J. (2014) 'Still 'pivotal'? Still the 'first ally'? The significance of Syria for Britain's global role', Paper presented at BISA, Dublin, 16–17 May.

Strong, J. (2015) 'Interpreting the Syria vote: parliament and British foreign policy', *International Affairs* 91(5): 1123–39.

Tahir, T. (2013) 'No. 10 attacks Ed Miliband after Labour leader withdraws support for military intervention in Syria', *Metro*, 29 August, available at http://metro.co.uk/2013/08/29/no-10-attacks-ed-miliband-after-labour-leader-withdraws-support-for-military-intervention-in-syria-3941637/ (accessed 15 December 2015)..

Thakur, R. (2013) 'R2P after Libya and Syria: engaging emerging powers', *Washington Quarterly* 36(2): 61–76.

United Nations (2013) 'United Nations mission to investigate allegations of the use of chemical weapons in the Syrian Arab Republic', 13 September, available at http://www.un.org/disarmament/content/slideshow/Secretary_General_Report_of_CW_Investigation.pdf (accessed October 2015).

Watson, I. (2013) 'Syria crisis: Downing Street fury over Labour stance', BBC News, 29 August, available at http://www.bbc.co.uk/news/uk-politics-23862114 (accessed October 2015).

Watt, N., Mason, R. and Hopkins, N. (2013) 'Blow to Cameron's authority as MPs rule out British assault on Syria', *Guardian*, 30 August, available at http://www.theguardian.com/politics/2013/aug/30/cameron-mps-syria (accessed 15 December 2015).

Over- and under-reaction to transboundary threats: two sides of a misprinted coin?

Christoph O. Meyer

ABSTRACT When states over- and under-react to perceived transboundary threats, their mistakes can have equally harmful consequences for the citizens they mean to protect. Yet, studies of intelligence and conventional foreign policy tend to concentrate on cases of under-reaction to threats from states, and few studies set out criteria for identifying cases of under- and over-reaction to other kinds of threats or investigate common causes. The paper develops a typology of over- and under-reaction in foreign policy revolving around threats assessment, response proportionality and timeliness. Drawing on pilot case studies, the contribution identifies combinations of factors and conditions that make both over- or under-reaction more likely. It is hypothesized that three factors play significant causal roles across the cases: (1) institutions have learned the wrong lessons from previous related incidents; (2) decision-making is organized within institutional silos focused on only one kind of threat; and (3) actors have strong pre-existing preferences for a particular outcome.

INTRODUCTION

This contribution is concerned with two particular types of foreign policy 'fiascos' which appear, at first glance, very different and may therefore require distinct explanations. The first type is a foreign policy under-reaction epitomized by states failing to deter, repel or prepare for a 'surprise attack' by another state, even though such an attack could have been foreseen and means were available to avoid much of the harm caused at comparatively little costs and risks. The second type is a foreign policy over-reaction, which until recently has been less frequently studied and could be illustrated by the case of states launching highly costly and risky pre-emptive or retaliatory attacks against a perceived threat, even though the target of the attack was no actual threat or any potential threat could have been addressed with significantly less costly or risky means. When states and international organizations over- and under-react to perceived transboundary threats and hazards that emanate from or easily spread beyond a given state's territory, their mistakes can have equally harmful consequences for the citizens they mean to protect. We do not know empirically which kind of failure is more frequent, but the tendency to focus on warning failures and under-response can lead to problematic prescriptions; ever more warning, higher receptivity, better preparedness and commitment to act early could lead to, first, costly over-reaction and ultimately paralysis, as warnings will outstrip preventive capacities. Therefore, it would be desirable to identify a combination of factors or conditions that substantially increase the probability of both under- and over-reaction and thus give greater confidence to take remedial action.

It is not new to argue that failures of perceptions may cause either under- and over-reaction in foreign policy since Robert Jervis's seminal work on psychological biases and recurrent errors of judgement in foreign affairs (Jervis 1976). However, the extensive United States- (US-) dominated strategic surprise literature still tends to concentrate on cases of under-reaction to impending attacks and treats insights about over-reaction as a by-product (Betts 1982; Kam 2010; Wohlstetter 1962). More recently, a number of authors have characterized the US-led war on terror as an over-reaction and highlighted its various discontents, in terms of solving the original problem, but also in terms of creating new problems on the way (Aradau and Van Munster 2007; Desch 2007). However, this literature does not offer us a systematic theory of how under- and over-reaction might be linked and the difficulties of successfully navigating the boundary between them.

Moreover, there is still insufficient cross-fertilization between intelligence, security studies and foreign policy analysis on the one hand, and the literature on risk management, regulatory policy and emergency response to diverse types of transboundary threats such as unsafe drugs and foods, flooding, climate change, pandemics or financial system collapse (Bazerman and Watkins 2008; Weick and Sutcliffe 2007). The lack of attention to these threats is all the more problematic given the shifting and expanding nature of transboundary threats and the concomitant rise of an all-risks approach to foreign affairs visible in states' national security strategies (Dunn Cavelty and Mauer [2009]; on policy fiascos in the risk era, see Beasley [2016]). The recognition and response to such threats pose particular challenges as compared to predominantly domestic threats (De Franco and Meyer 2011).

This contribution aims to improve cross-fertilization between scholars working on warning failures in the area of national security and those working on risk and disaster management in international public policy. In a first step it develops a single definition of failures to deal adequately with uncertain threats whilst avoiding 20/20 hindsight. It will elaborate which performative acts are most important to what might be called 'calibrated prevention' and suggest a typology of failures that could lead to either over- or under-reaction. It will then discuss how to search for common causes. The second section will put these criteria into action by selecting six pilot studies and identifying three common mechanisms at play in both over- and under-reaction cases: (1) institutions have learned the wrong lessons from previous incidents; (2) decision-making is organized within institutional silos focused on only one kind of threat; and (3) actors have strong pre-existing preferences to act or not act. These hypotheses will require more extensive empirical testing in future research.

CONCEPTUALIZING OVER- AND UNDER-REACTION TO TRANSBOUNDARY THREATS

How to define and conceptualize the phenomena of over- and under-reaction in foreign policy? The existing literature on intelligence failures (Betts 2007; Jervis 2010), foreign policy mistakes (Baldwin 2000; Walker and Malici 2011), success and failure in public policy (Bovens *et al.* 2001; McDonnell 2010) and over- and under-reaction specifically (Maor 2012, 2014) offers useful starting points. However, the literature also has limitations for our research question and disagrees on the issue of whether objectivity in case identification and policy evaluation is possible and desirable. Constructivist approaches to policy fiascos (Bovens and 't Hart 1996: 10–11) highlight the non-linear, competitive and ideational nature of the goal-setting process in policy-making, where the meaning and valuation attached to policy goals vary amongst actors as well as over time and policy failure seems to lie 'largely in the eye of the beholder' as McDonnell criticizes (2010: 6). In contrast, most scholarship in foreign policy analysis and intelligence studies starts from the premise that the identification of failure or success is both possible and necessary, despite criticism of using unsophisticated frameworks for such judgements (Baldwin 2000). Maor aims to reconcile 'the tension between the objective and subjective dimensions of "overreaction"' by defining it as 'policies that impose objective and/or perceived social costs without producing objective and/or perceived benefits' (Maor 2012: 235).

However, the subjective/objective divide stands for quite different research designs in terms of the sampling criteria for cases and the evaluation of mistakes and failures. While it can be illuminating to better understand how and when political actors, public and news media 'construct' foreign affairs fiascos as a first cut, such an analysis needs to be juxtaposed with or followed by a scientifically sound assessment of failure rather than substituting such an assessment with subjective views of practitioners or publics. Scholarship can and should provide a more rigorous, transparent, nuanced and cautious assessment of policy successes or failures and their causes than politicians, journalists or other experts with less time, appropriate training or awareness of cognitive biases. This is particularly true for the study of foreign policy mistakes where the risk of unfair accusations and attribution errors is higher than in domestic policy because of greater uncertainty affecting analytical judgements and the higher probability of unavoidable mistakes (Betts 1978). It also more difficult here to identify what was known and communicated by whom, given the arguments to maintain a degree of secrecy about man-made threats to safeguard intelligence sources, methods and relations to foreign governments. More encouragingly, scholars in this policy area will find it easier to identify a widely shared agreement about the undesirability of the harm given its severity and typically symmetric effects. Contestation in foreign policy tends to focus more on the threat assessment and the means to be used for a given goal, rather than the policy goal itself.

A useful starting point for identifying different kinds of 'failure' in foreign policy is Walker and Maliki's (2011) study of US president's foreign policy mistakes. They advance a useful typology by distinguishing between mistakes of omission ('too little too late') and commission ('too much too soon'). They furthermore highlight two cross-cutting dimensions in mistakes of threat diagnosis and policy prescription (*ibid.*: 54). Using this distinction as a starting point, a more nuanced typology appropriate to the study of over- and under-reaction is developed below and used to select pilot cases (see Table 1).

Walker and Maliki's (2011) first dimension of *threat diagnosis* is in principle applicable to all kinds of threats and hazards, but should be further differentiated into failures of probability assessment and misjudgements of the severity and nature of a given threat. The accuracy of threat diagnosis, can only be measured *post-hoc*, even though *ex ante* we can gauge expert's confidence in the quality of the available evidence coupled with past reliability of applicable theories or models to interpret evidence. Genuinely novel threats are more difficult to accurately forecast, as theories could not be previously tested and may

Table 1   Typology of over and under-reaction with cases

Type of mistake		Under reaction	Over reaction
		Timeliness	
		Too late	Too early
Threat assessment	Probability	*Under-estimated probability* 9/11 attacks Ukraine 2014	*Over-estimated probability* Iceland Ash Clouds 2010
	Severity	*Under-estimated severity* Financial crisis 2008 9/11 attacks	*Over-estimated severity* Swine flu 2009
Response proportionality	Scope	*Under-scoped response* Financial crisis 2008	*Over-scoped response* Iraq WMD 2003 Iceland ash clouds 2010
	Scale	*Under-scaled response* Ukraine 2014	*Over-scaled response* Iraq WMD 2003 Swine flu 2009

Source: The author.

not be applicable. Transboundary threats are more likely to be novel because of the complexity and pace of the interplay between new phenomena such as globalization, technological and demographic change, as well as the expanded range of actors who can influence outcomes (Dunn Cavelty and Mauer 2009; Fishbein 2011). Furthermore, domestic authorities face greater difficulties in identifying relevant information (because of complexity), accessing information (because of secrecy, linguistic barriers or remoteness), or validating it (because of deception and lack of experience). These problems affect not only man-made but also biological threats. In the case of swine flu, the World Health Organization (WHO) accurately assessed the probable spread of the virus, but did not recognize and communicate early enough that it was no more lethal than a normal flu virus, thus causing over-reaction in many countries. While uncertainty will always be a significant problem in foreign affairs, it does not imply that associated risk assessment is futile or that cost–benefit analysis can be dispensed with, only that the epistemological basis for probabilistic methods may be fragile, contested or highly variable over time (Posner 2004: 175–87). So while it may be easy to see that an over-reaction was caused by an error of threat assessment, the real difficulty lies in deciding whether this error was avoidable and at what point mistakes can be described as 'failures' in terms of nature and scale.

Secondly, Walter and Maliki (2011) are right to attend to policy itself ('prescription'), but their focus on defence and security is too narrow for our purposes and insufficiently sensitive to the 'too little/too much' dimension of under- or over-reaction. It is proposed instead to focus first on the *proportionality of the response* in terms of scale and scope. Some types of policy problems, such as protection from floods or vaccination programmes, require a minimum scale of response to be effective at all, whereas others may only partially fail if the response is under-scaled. Over-scaled responses in terms of resource intensity means not just a lack of efficiency in terms of marginal utility (Baldwin 2000), but directly reduce a state's ability to mobilize sufficient resources to prevent or mitigate other types of foreign or indeed domestic threats or hazards to human life and health. The US War on Terror (WOT), including the US invasion of Iraq and Afghanistan, has been estimated by the Congressional Research Service to have cost US$1.6 trillion with a narrow focus on US military operations (Belasco 2014), whereas the academic 'Cost of War Project' arrived at an economic cost to the US of US$4.4 trillion (Crawford 2014). Even without monetizing lives or life-expectancy gained or lost, one can easily characterize this scale of spending as disproportionate in relation to the risk of terrorism and compared to alternative foreign or domestic uses of these resources. Secondly, a policy may be mis-designed in terms of scope when attempts to tackle a given threat the effects are (would have been) either counter-productive or create (would have created) significant displacement threats and risks. It has been argued, for instance, that US practices of renditions, torture, unlawful detention and drone-strikes used in the WOT have damaged the US ability to find allies and boosted radicalization and recruitment to violent jihadist groups. This conceptualization of over-reaction means also that a fair *ex post* assessment of the proportionality of policy needs to incorporate counterfactual reasoning about alternative consequences that result from either action or inaction with given resources (Baldwin 2000).

The third performative dimension that is implicit in Walker and Maliki's (2011) typology but not separated out is *timeliness*. A diagnostic judgement about the high probability of a state attack six months in advance would be very useful for maximizing policy options but also very difficult, whereas the same judgement is typically easier a couple of hours before an attack, when indications/signals are stronger but effective options will have dramatically narrowed. Similarly, whether a given policy reaction is proportional often depends on the evolution of a threat over time, its magnitude as well as its nature: an overwhelming military presence may be appropriate during a particular phase of military operation but counterproductive at earlier or later stages of conflict prevention and resolution. Similarly, countermeasures against pandemics are a race against time where the type of action depends on the spread, mutation and lethality of a virus. Hence, we propose to focus on accurate threat assessment, policy proportionality and timeliness as key challenges to avoid either under- or over-reaction to transboundary threats. In reality, cases will not map neatly onto each of the cells in Table 1, but may show the presence of both kinds of mistakes at different points in time.

Building on these considerations we can now describe both sides of the coin as *failures to mobilize the available cognitive and material resources of policy-making in a proportionate and time-sensitive way to the severity, probability and nature of a transboundary threat.* In the case of under-reaction, the failure lies in not acting early or decisively enough given available knowledge and means, whereas over-reaction are cases where action was taken in response to either an exaggerated or illusionary threat or could have been realistically addressed with significantly less costly or risky means. This definition does not necessarily limit our focus to one particular actor involved in the policy-process: analysts, policy-planners, decision-makers or, indeed, operatives involved in implementation. Scholars in intelligence studies spent considerable efforts to distinguish failures of the intelligence community from failures of policy-makers (Jervis 2010; Pillar 2011). These distinctions also matter to the definition of appropriate criteria to assess whether a given action was a mere technical mistake, negligence against professional norms, gross incompetence, or outright malfeasance, for instance, when senior decision-makers consciously suppress, obscure or hide 'inconvenient' threat assessments.

The other important aspect of this definition lies in the words 'available' and 'realistic' in recognition of the distinction between *ex ante* avoidable failures and those actions or lack of action that may have caused an over- or under-reaction in terms of *ex post* cost−benefit assessments, but which were ultimately unavoidable given the knowledge, skills, instruments and conditions at the time − a distinction often acknowledged but rarely heeded in scholarly works on mistakes and missed opportunities (Tuchman 1985; Zartman 2005). Most public inquiries launched after cases of 'under-reaction' revolve around two questions:

attributing individual or institutional accountability ('blame'); and learning lessons about how such harm may be avoided in the future (see Bovens and 't Hart 2016). The former task is not just hampered by the 'politics of blame' (Weaver 1986), but also arises from hindsight bias as human beings tend to overestimate what was knowable and likely given their knowledge of what actually happened. A good example is allegedly plentiful and high quality early warnings about genocide in Rwanda quoted in writings which, on closer examination, turn out to lack specificity and credibility, or did not satisfy basic criteria to qualify as a warning (Otto forthcoming). Moreover, academic works as well as public inquiries such as in the area of conflict prevention do not sufficiently acknowledge uncertainty about what works in preventing transboundary threats, including trade-offs, moral dilemmas and unintentional consequences (Meyer *et al.* 2010). Indeed, some transboundary threats may be too difficult to solve for even the most powerful states, regional bodies and global institutions of governance. It is instructive that many of the lessons learnt from the financial crisis of 2008 are yet to be fully implemented, including banks being 'too big to fail' or reducing global and regional imbalances in trade and capital flows.

When identifying relevant cases for the proposed pilot study we need not only to conduct *ex post* cost–benefit calculations in the full knowledge of the consequences and an assessment of the alternative causes of action, but also consider the relationship between knowledge, means, time and threat properties. Using the typology elaborated above, three cases each of potential over- and under-reaction to transnational threats were selected according to the following criteria: (1) equal coverage of both security as well non-conventional transboundary threats; (2) states as well as international organizations and agencies as actors (European Union [EU], Eurocontrol, WHO); (3) significant degree of news media salience as a potential foreign policy fiasco. The first two criteria are motivated by our aspiration to maximize variation on case properties and thus increase the theoretical yield if common factors or mechanisms can be found. The third criterion reflects a best case design as one would expect foreign policy fiascos, especially those on the under-reaction side, to have tangible consequences that draw news media attention and trigger controversies over who (if anyone) deserves blame and how to improve (on the attribution of blame in media narratives, see Oppermann and Spencer [2016]). These case features enabled also better access to relevant information about the performance of different actors and stages available from public inquiries, official reports and subsequent analysis in the academic literature. Hidden or forgotten foreign policy fiascos may well exist, but given the novelty of this approach the contribution starts from the low-hanging more visible fruits.

After the initial scanning for suitable cases according to the criteria above, a pilot case analysis was conducted drawing on the preliminary or final results of public inquiries (9/11 Commission 2004; Chilcot Inquiry 2010; Financial Crisis Inquiry Commission [FCIC] 2011; House of Lords 2015; Lord Butler 2004; WHO Review Commitee 2011: 7,), statements by the actors themselves (e.g. Eurocontrol 2010) and secondary literature. The evidential basis varies, but filling all the information gaps through original research would have required a highly resource-intensive process-tracing approach and, in some cases, the kind of access to documents and witnesses that only public inquiries enjoy (e.g. Chilcot Inquiry 2010). Space constraints do not allow listing all sources consulted or provide more empirical detail from the longer case summaries that were compiled to cover the different stages in the warning–response process: collection; forecasting; prioritization; mobilization; and implementation. The conclusions as to the type of failure should be regarded as preliminary, especially with regard to the more recent cases. The cases are not necessarily identical in their degree of failure, nor the extent to which key actors can be held accountable for mistakes made in the process given available knowledge and resources. For instance, US intelligence assessments of the WMD threat were on the whole correct given the available information, but politicians cherry-picked and distorted intelligence to justify their preferred cause of action (Fitzgerald and Lebow 2006; Jervis 2010).

WHEN TO EXPECT UNDER- AND OVER-REACTION

What do we know about the factors that cause over- and under-reaction in international public policy widely conceived? There is no shortage of good scholarly works on good judgement in foreign policy (e.g., George 1993; Renshon and Larson 2003). Similarly, intelligence studies and political psychology highlight biases in information processing and analytical judgements and provide advice on how to compensate for them (Betts 2007; Jervis 2010). Similarly relevant but hardly used in foreign policy analysis is the public administration literature, which looks at crisis and disaster prevention, preparedness and management (Bazerman and Watkins 2008; Comfort et al. 2010). The literature does not currently agree on which factors matter most for appropriate responses to non-conventional transboundary threats, but is also marred by the empirical and theoretical bias towards studying cases of under-reaction. Within the pilot case studies we systemically searched for those factors (see Table 2) that according to the evidence examined were (1) causally important enough to expect the scale and scope of the over-reaction to have been affected, although not necessarily sufficient for avoiding failure per se, and (2) with at least two of the three factors being present in all of the cases covering the over- and under-reaction divide.

The distinctiveness of this approach becomes apparent when we reflect on some factors with unidirectional effects. For instance, a high level of politicization or mediatization of a given risk arising either from the news media (Boin et al. 2005, 2008) or political actors' strategies is likely to be positively associated with over-reaction as it tends to exaggerate risk perceptions and paves the way for extraordinary and therefore more likely disproportionate measures. Conversely, a threat that is off-the-radar of the news media, public and political debates, such as mass atrocities in foreign countries of no strategic significance, will

Table 2 Overview of pilots case findings

Factor Case	H1: Misapplication of lessons learnt	H2: Obstacles from institutional silos	H3: Biases from salient preferences
9/11	+	+	+
Iraq 2003	+	−	!
Financial Crisis 2008	+	+	!
Swine Flu 2009	!	+	+
Ash Cloud 2010	+	!	−
Ukraine 2013/14	+	!	+

Note: − = insignificant; + = significantly affects scope and scale of failure; ! = necessary factor for overall failure.

attract less attention and resources from authorities and therefore makes missing warning signals and hesitant policy responses more likely (Power 2003). The other factor which is often considered as detrimental to good threat assessment and proportionate response is uncertainty (Boin *et al.* 2005: 3–54). But insofar as uncertainty can be considered a core challenge to threat assessment and proportionate response in foreign affairs, it is questionable how useful this observation is. For instance, the advice to analysts and policy-makers to 'reduce uncertainty' by taking more time to gather more information and conduct deeper and wider analysis will simultaneously reduce the capacity of actors to act early and effectively, thus making under-reaction more likely. High uncertainty makes it also more difficult to identify genuinely avoidable mistakes.

H1: Vivid lessons learnt from recent episodes involving similar threats lead to the over-application of these lessons to threats and scenarios which are in fact significantly different.

A rich literature in international relations argues that lessons learnt from historical cases and episodes structure how human beings, including senior decision-makers and policy communities, perceive reality. They tend to focus on surface similarities (Khong 1992: 14; May 1973) between current and past cases to fill in gaps in their knowledge to make sense and anticipate. Inferences drawn from past cases can inevitably turn out to be wrong, but are more likely to be wrong when experts and decision-makers over-estimate the similarity between past and current cases. In all cases examined above, experts and decision-makers held on to assumptions rooted in lessons learnt from previous cases that turned out to be wrong: national monetary policy was not able to deal with the repercussions of the financial crisis and markets were surprised that authorities allowed a major investment bank to fail; the swine flu virus (H1N1) was far less deadly than avian flu, but more contagious; Islamist terrorism had ceased to be solely regionally focused and had developed the level of organization, capabilities and intent to mount a major attack on the US mainland; significant segments of Iraqi society did not respond positively to regime change as Kosovo Albanians did in 1999.

In all these cases, experts as well as decision-makers based their assumptions on previous experiences of either successful or failed crisis management. US central bankers believed that they could handle a bursting asset bubble, given their experience of successfully handling the fall-out from the Dotcom bubble bursting in 2001, and paid little attention to the bubble building in mortgage-backed securities (FCIC 2011). The relatively successful hunt for the perpetrators of the 1993 attack on the World Trade Centre, the fact that the bombing itself had failed and the lack of subsequent attacks in the US gave the impression to many experts that jihadist terrorism was a nuisance but under control (9/11 Commission 2004). Their experience with the avian flu had convinced epidemiologists that a similarly lethal virus was very dangerous, but could be contained by acting early and decisively (WHO Review Commitee 2011). And policy-makers in the UK learned from the intervention in Kosovo that regime change can be accomplished militarily and that a successful aftermath would bring around initially hostile public opinion and opposed members of the United Nations (UN) Security Council. In the case of Russia's aggression against Ukraine, the EU Commission largely modelled its Neighbourhood Policy on the Eastern enlargement process of the EU. This resulted in over-applying a template designed for different circumstances and played an important role in underestimating the political vulnerabilities of Ukraine, as well as the risk of robust push-back from Russia (MacFarlane and Menon 2014: 96–7).

The experience of failure tends to lead to assumptions supportive of higher sensitivity to threats that look broadly similar, whereas success inspires confidence of being in control of these risks. The greater the sense of failure or, indeed, success in these episodes of crisis learning, the greater the probability that the lessons learnt will be over-applied to threats that may appear at first glance familiar, even when they are in fact different. This is partly because previous experiences constitute an availability heuristic that makes key actors remember more vividly those episodes that, for all kinds of reasons, caused stress and highly emotive reactions (Kahneman *et al.* 1982: 14). Furthermore, successful crisis managements tends to create complacency within institutions and leaders and to prolong the tenure of key decision-makers who have seen their previous judgements validated, whereas visible failure sparks critique and can empower the previously ignored 'doomsayers'. These may not be better at forecasting, just more disposed to pessimism. The net effect of personnel change and higher risk sensitivity could be a pendulum swing from under- to over-reaction.

H2: If threats are managed within rigid institutional silos, it is more likely that novel threats will be either missed or inappropriately dealt with by established diagnostic and policy routines.

Any system of risk governance experiences tensions between allocating the responsibility for preventive policy to one particular part of the administration and the challenge of evaluating risks that arise from either action or inaction of other units. Risk myopia can develop as a result of the inability of the existing institutional configuration to cope with the cross-cutting nature of the risks associated with either action or inaction. The problem is not the allocation of responsibility to one organizational unit *per se*, but the inability of that particular unit to develop ways of sharing information and consulting with relevant units within and outside the organization to accurately identify and assess novel risks, but also understand the wider impact of their potential responses. The problem of institutional silos for risk management and prevention is still relatively new to the study of foreign policy, although it is well-recognized in studies of disasters (Bazerman and Watkins 2008: 102–3; Weick and Sutcliffe 2007).

We have seen that bodies specialized in one particular area of risk, such as the WHO or national health ministries in the case of swine flu, failed to properly appreciate the economic and political costs of disproportionate preventive action and were thus biased in their approach to calibrating their responses. A similar phenomenon could be seen in the decision by civil aviation authorities led by Eurocontrol to completely close Northern European airspace in response to the eruption of the Icelandic volcano Eyjafjallajökull on 14 April 2010; initially invoking the zero-risk regulatory approach designed for a different situation and manifested in the long-standing guidance of the International Civil Aviation Organization (ICAO) to avoid ash clouds, regardless of any concentration thresholds, average daily flights dropped by more than 80 per cent in three days (Alemanno 2011: 3–4), disrupting the travel plans of 10 million passengers and costing the industry in excess of US$1.7 billion (Eurocontrol 2010). As the human and economic cost of this blanket ban became increasingly apparent, the authorities changed how ash clouds and their concentration was measured and allowed air travel to gradually resume, depending on three zones of ash cloud concentration five days after the eruption.

Similarly, defence ministries have been traditionally focused on the survival of the state and its population against the risk of state attacks, including nuclear war. They are used to assess the risk posed by actual or potential enemies, but they have neither the habit nor the competence of conducting a more wide-ranging risk assessment of their own actions and consider systematically unintended consequences. By concentrating deliberation about and planning for the invasion of Iraq in the Pentagon, decision-makers missed out on relevant expertise in the State Department relating to risks of sectarian violence in Iraq and an interest in avoiding damage to US reputation. Similarly, in the case of Ukraine, the EU Commission's Directorate General (DG) for Trade had the lead role in conducting the negotiations with Ukraine over the Deep and Comprehensive Free Trade Agreement (DCFTA) as part of the overall Association Agreement (AA), treating the DCFTA as just another FTA with attention focused on technical economic and legal issues, rather than a wider appreciation of the geopolitical and security risks (Smith 2014: 594). This under-appreciation could have been avoided by stronger internal co-ordination with the European External Action Service (EEAS), as well as more involvement of the Council of Ministers and representatives from EU member states with substantial expertise of Russia.

While over-reaction is more probable when institutional responsibilities for preventive policy are all allocated to the same unit, the risk of under-reaction often arises from the lack of institutional links between risk monitoring and management. A key problem in the lack of appropriate regulation of systemic financial risk was the underlap between different national and international financial regulators in monitoring the stability of increasingly interconnected financial systems. Within financial institutions themselves, the units responsible for monitoring institutional risk exposure were often unaware of the highly specialized work done in those small units of banks that devised the highly profitable but also very risky products (Tett 2011). The 9/11 attacks were facilitated by an underlap in institutional responsibilities between the Federal Bureau of Intelligence (FBI) and the Central Intelligence Agency (CIA) for monitoring and countering threats to the US homeland arising from international terrorism (9/11 Commission 2004). Recognizing and dealing with novel risks or novel responses to risks will always be a challenge to existing institutional configurations, but silo mentalities within and across institutions make blind-spots in risk monitoring, management and response more probable.

> H3: If the consequences of acting or not acting against a particular threat are highly salient for senior decision-makers, they are likely to misinterpret threats and mis-design policy responses.

We know from experiments that human beings are prone to be affected in their judgments of a phenomenon by their feelings relating to the 'goodness' or 'badness' of it (Finucane *et al.* 2000). These feelings influence judgments in a way that risks and benefits will be inversely correlated – so that a phenomenon, which is seen as very risky cannot be associated with benefits, while a phenomenon seen as beneficial leads actors to downplay the associated risks. These so-called affect heuristics, including the specific case of optimistic bias (Armor and Taylor 2002), play an important role in explaining extreme outcomes like wishful thinking or denial. In the cases of over- and under-reaction examined, we can find evidence that actors' strong political or financial preferences affected their balancing judgments. Such motivational biases can not only arise from the impact of the threat itself, but also from internal or external incentive structures such as career advancement, anticipated blame or legal liability.

One case is the inflated rating given by Credit Rating Agencies (CRA) for complex structured products involving sub-prime mortgages in the run up to 2008 (see Kruck 2016). The 'issuer-pays model', coupled with insufficient competition among agencies and a high fraction of income from such products, created a systemic conflict of interest in favour of analysts being overconfident in their technical ability to devise highly rated products for satisfied clients and thus attract further business from these clients (Mathis *et al.* 2009). It also made CRAs less open to internal sceptics just as some chief executive officers (CEOs) of banks were not open to warnings that the products they currently made considerable profits from could soon become a major source of loss (Tett 2011). In the case of swine flu, different factors were pushing in the same direction of early and vigorous action, such as the prevailing ethos to save lives by planning for the worst, coupled with subtle and undisclosed conflicts of interests affecting experts on influential WHO and national advisory committees (Cohen and Charter 2010). In the run-up to the 9/11 attacks, warnings about al-Qaeda were not welcome, since they appeared as a circumspect distraction to the foreign policy agenda of the new administration (Clarke 2004). Motivational biases are also visible in the planning of the Iraq invasion, which saw not only worst-case thinking about the risks posed by inaction, but also wishful thinking about the aftermath of regime change (Fitzgerald and Lebow 2006). In the case of Ukraine, one significant reason for why the EU underestimated the strain on the Yanukovych government arising from the Association Agreement and, subsequently, the Russian reaction to its fall, was firstly the desire to reach a successful conclusion to the long-standing negotiations over the Association Agreement (Smith 2014: 594), as well as the strong ideational support for the goals of the Euromaidan (House of Lords 2015).

We expect motivational biases to be particularly pronounced in settings where changing threat assessments and acting or not acting on a given risk has significant redistributive consequences, as in the case of the CRAs in the run up to the financial crisis. In the area of conventional foreign policy, positive or negative biases in the processing of warning signals may arise from balance-of-threat calculations in which policy-makers interpret potential preventive action from the perspective of whether it will strengthen or weaken potential rivals and enemies. International regulators are concerned about the consequences of being blamed for failures to act by their principals as well as external pressure groups. While a complete lack of external scrutiny can induce regulators to become complacent and more easily captured by stakeholders, extremely strong scrutiny that is averse to even the smallest risks can lead risk regulators to prioritize action to avoid blame, even if this action created new kinds of risks in other areas.

CONCLUSION

The contribution aimed at advancing our understanding of over- and under-reaction towards transboundary threats which pose specific challenges in terms of diagnosis and appropriate response. In contrast to the strategic surprise literature in intelligence studies and foreign policy analysis, it has been argued that over- and under-reaction are not completely distinct phenomena that require idiosyncratic explanations, but can be understood as inter-related failures in threat assessment, proportional response and timeliness. This approach places a greater emphasis on a substantive and in-depth assessment of performative acts of various actors in foreign policy-making, rather than a more narrow focus on either the legislative process as in some of the public policy literature (Marsh and Donnell 2010) or on senior decision-makers as in many studies of foreign policy performance (Walker and Malici 2011). The typology developed is sensitive to the risk of hindsight bias in *ex post* assessments of diagnostic judgements, as well as the need for counterfactual reasoning when assessing alternative choices and displacements risks. A second advantage to most of the literature in intelligence studies and foreign policy judgements lies in its wide applicability across institutional contexts (regulators, business, intelligence) and types of risks (violence, health, finance), and therefore its ability to highlight the generic problems modern government faces when trying to implement an all-risk approach to transboundary threats.

The second contribution of the article lies in identifying common causes of over- and under-reaction within six pilot studies. We have focused on the three factors common to all cases examined: (1) misapplied lessons learnt from recent vivid crises; (2) the rigidity of institutional silos, and finally (3) the strength of actor preferences in relation to the expected outcome of preventive action. It is their cumulative effects rather than the presence of a single factor, which can be expected to tilt the key judgments in a particular direction and to substantially increase the risk of over- or under-reaction. We do not claim that any of these factors are completely novel to the study of international relations and public policy, but our approach breaks new ground by linking these factors specifically to the challenge of avoiding both over- and under-reaction in foreign policy and shows their applicability to a wider range of threats.

Even though over- or under-reaction cannot be eradicated, those instances that could be classed as avoidable mistakes or outright disasters can be made less likely by monitoring for and, if possible, mitigating against the three factors. As a first step, practitioners should become more reflexive about the lessons learnt from recent and vivid cases of success or failure and, subsequently, more sceptical and demanding *vis-à-vis* arguments that pose similarities and widely applicable lessons to current problems. Secondly, practitioners should recognize the strong influence of motivational biases affecting potential producers and consumers of warnings and examine whether such biases are caused by misaligned internal incentives or external scrutiny structures that could be altered. Thirdly, it is important to regularly review the allocation of responsibilities for risk monitoring among states and international organizations, as well as the co-ordinating and communication mechanisms between them to allow for the better integration of relevant knowledge and the management of boundary and displacement risks.

ACKNOWLEDGEMENTS

The author expresses his gratitude for the helpful comments received from the editors, three anonymous reviewers, a discussant, as well as the participants at an ECPR workshop on Non-Proportionate Policy Response organized by Moshe Maor and Jale Tosun. An ERC Starting Grant for the FORESIGHT project (No 202022) helped fund some of the underlying research, and the author wishes to thank John Brante, Chiara de Franco and Florian Otto for helping to inform the author's thinking behind this article, as well as Nikki Ikani for advice on the Ukraine case.

REFERENCES

9/11 Commission (2004) *The 9/11 Commission Report*, Washington: United States of America Government Printing Office, available at http://govinfo.library.unt.edu/911/report/911Report.pdf (accessed October 2015).

Alemanno, A. (ed.) (2011) *Governing Disasters: The Challenges of Emergency Risk Regulation*, Cheltenham: Edward Elgar.

Aradau, C. and Van Munster, R. (2007) 'Governing terrorism through risk: taking precautions, (un)knowing the future', *European Journal of International Relations* 13(1): 89–115.

Armor, D.A. and Taylor, S.E. (2002) 'When predictions fail: the dilemma of unrealistic optimism', in T. Gilovich, D. Griffin and D. Kahneman (eds), *Heurestics and Biases: The Psychology of Intuitive Judgment*, Cambridge: Cambridge University Press, pp. 334–47.

Baldwin, D.A. (2000) 'Success and failure in foreign policy'. *Annual Review of Political Science* 3: 167–82.

Bazerman, M.H. and Watkins, M.D. (2008) *Predictable Surprises: The Disasters You Should Have Seen Coming, and How to Prevent Them*, Boston, MA: Harvard Business School.

Beasley, R. (2016) 'Dissonance and decision-making mistakes in the age of risk', *Journal of European Public Policy*, doi:10.1080/13501763.2015.1127276.

Belasco, A. (2014) 'The cost of Iraq, Afghanistan, and other global War on Terror operations since 9/11', Congressional Research Service, available at http://www.fas.org/sgp/crs/natsec/RL33110.pdf?utm_source=wordtwit&utm_medium=social&utm_campaign=wordtwit (accessed October 2015).

Betts, R.K. (1978) 'Analysis, war and decision: why intelligence failures are inevitable', *World Politics* 31(1): 61–89.

Betts, R.K. (1982) *Surprise Attack*, Washington, DC: Brookings Institution.

Betts, R.K. (2007) *Enemies of Intelligence: Knowledge and Power in American National Security*, New York: Columbia University Press.

Boin, A., 't Hart, P., Stern, E., and Sundelius, B. (2005) *The Politics of Crisis Management: Public Leadership under Pressure*, Cambridge: Cambridge University Press.

Boin, A., McConnell, A., and 't Hart, P. (2008) *Governing after Crisis: The Politics of Investigation, Accountability and Learning*, Cambridge: Cambridge University Press.

Bovens, M. and 't Hart, P. (1996) *Understanding Policy Fiascoes*, New Brunswick, NJ: Transaction.

Bovens, M. and 't Hart, P. (2016) 'Revisiting the study of policy failures', *Journal of European Public Policy*, doi:10.1080/13501763.2015.1127273.

Bovens, M., 't Hart, P. and Peters, B.G. (2001) *Success and Failure in Public Governance: A Comparative Analysis*, Cheltenham: Edward Elgar.

Chilcot-Inquiry (2010) 'Iraq inquiry', available at http://www.iraqinquiry.org.uk (accessed October 2015).

Clarke, R.A. (2004) *Against all Enemies: Inside America's War on Terror*, New York: Simon & Schuster.

Cohen, D. and Charter, P. (2010) 'WHO and the pandemic flu "conspiracies"'. *British Medical Journal* 340, doi: http://dx.doi.org/10.1136/bmj.c2912.

Comfort, L.K., Boin, A. and Demchak, C.C. (2010) *Designing Resilience: Preparing for Extreme Events*, Pittsburgh, PA: University of Pittsburgh Press.

Crawford, N.C. (2014) 'US costs of wars through 2014', available at http://costsofwar. org/sites/default/files/articles/20/attachments/Costs%20of%20War%20Summary% 20Crawford%20June%202014.pdf (accessed October 2015).

De Franco, C. and Meyer, C.O. (2011) *Forecasting, Warning, and Responding to Transnational Risks*, Basingstoke: Palgrave.

Desch, M.C. (2007) 'America's liberal illiberalism: the ideological origins of overreaction in US foreign policy', *International Security* 32(3): 7–43.

Dunn Cavelty, M. and Mauer, V. (2009) 'Postmodern intelligence: strategic warning in an age of reflexive intelligence', *Security Dialogue* 40(2): 123–44.

Eurocontrol (2010) 'Ash-cloud of April and May 2010: impact on air traffic', available at https://www.eurocontrol.int/sites/default/files/content/documents/official-docum ents/facts-and-figures/statfor/ash-impact-air-traffic-2010.pdf (accessed October 2015).

Financial Crisis Inquiry Commission (FCIC) (2011) *Financial Crisis Inquiry Report: Final Report of the National Commission on the Causes of the Financial and Economic Crisis in the United States*, Washington, DC: Financial Crisis Inquiry Commission.

Finucane, M.L., Alhakami, A., Slovic, P. and Johnson, S. (2000) 'The affect heuristic in judgments of risks and benefits', *Journal of Behavioural Decision Making* 13: 1–17.

Fishbein, W.H. (2011) 'Prospective sense-making: a realistic approach to "foresight for prevention" in an age of complex threats', in C. De Franco and C.O. Meyer (eds), *Forecasting, Warning, and Responding to Transnational Risks: Is Prevention Possible?* Basinstoke: Palgrave, pp. 227–40.

Fitzgerald, M. and Lebow, R.N. (2006) 'Iraq: the mother of all intelligence failures', *Intelligence and National Security* 21(5): 884–909.

George, A.L. (1993) *Bridging the Gap: Theory and Practice in Foreign Policy*, Washington, DC: United States Institute of Peace Press.

House of Lords (2015) *The EU and Russia: Before and beyond the Crisis in Ukraine*, HL Paper 115, London: House of Lords, European Union Committee, available at http://www.publications.parliament.uk/pa/ld201415/ldselect/ldeucom/115/115. pdf (accessed July 2015).

Jervis, R. (1976) *Perception and Misperception in International Politics*, Princeton, NJ: Princeton University Press.

Jervis, R. (2010) *Why Intelligence Fails: Lessons from the Iranian Revolution and the Iraq War*, Ithaca, NY: Cornell University Press.

Kahneman, D., Slovic, P. and Tversky, A. (1982) *Judgment under Uncertainty: Heuristics and Biases*, Cambridge: Cambridge University Press.

Kam, E. (2010) *Surprise Attack: The Victim's Perspective*, Cambridge, MA: Harvard University Press.

Khong, Y.F. (1992) *Analogies at War: Korea, Munich, Dien Bien Phu, and the Vietnam Decisions of 1965*, Princeton, NJ: Princeton University Press.

Kruck, A. (2016) 'Resilient blunderers: credit rating fiascos and rating agencies' institutionalized status as private authorities', *Journal of European Public Policy*, doi: 10. 1080/13501763.2015.1127274.

Lord Butler (2004) *Review of Intelligence on Weapons of Mass Destruction: Report of a Committee of Privy Counsellors*, London: House of Commons.

MacFarlane, N. and Menon, A. (2014) 'The EU and Ukraine', *Survival* 56(3): 95–101,.

Maor, M. (2012) 'Policy Overreaction', *Journal of Public Policy* 32(3): 231–59.

Maor, M. (2014) 'Policy persistence, risk estimation and policy underreaction', *Policy Sciences* 47: 425–43.

Marsh, D. and Donnell, A. (2010) 'Towards a framework for policy success', *Public Administration* 88(2): 564–83.

Mathis, J., McAndrews, J. and Rochet, J.C. (2009) 'Rating the raters: are reputation concerns powerful enough to discipline rating agencies?', *Journal of Monetary Economics* 56(5): 657–74.

May, E.R. (1973) *'Lessons of the Past. The Use and Misuse of History in American Foreign Policy*, New York: Oxford University Press.

McDonnell, A. (2010) 'Policy success, policy failure and grey areas in-between', *Journal of Public Policy* 30(3): 345–62.

Meyer, C.O., Otto, F., Brante, J. and De Franco, C. (2010) 'Re-casting the warning-response-problem: persuasion and preventive policy', *International Studies Review* 12(4): 556–78.

Oppermann, K. and Spencer, A. (2016) 'Telling stories of failure: narrative constructions of foreign policy fiascos', *Journal of European Public Policy*, doi: 10.1080/ 13501763.2015.1127272.

Otto, F. (forthcoming) 'Hindsight bias and warning: misinterpreting warnings of the Rwandan genocide', in C.O. Meyer, J. Brante, C. De Franco and F. Otto (eds), *Heeding Warnings about War? Persuasion and Advocacy in Foreign Policy*, Cambridge: Cambridge University Press.

Pillar, P.R. (2011) *Intelligence and US foreign policy: Iraq, 9/11, and misguided reform*, New York: Columbia University Press.

Posner, R.A. (2004) *Catastrophe: Risk and Response*, Oxford: Oxford University Press.

Power, S. (2003) *A Problem from Hell: America and the Age of Genocide*, New York: Harper.

Renshon, S.A. and Larson, D.W. (2003) *Good Judgment in Foreign Policy: Theory and Aapplication*, Lanham, MD: Rowman & Littlefield.

Smith, N.R. (2014) 'The underpinning realpolitik of the EU's policies towards Ukraine: an analysis of interests and norms in the EU–Ukraine Association Agreement', *European Foreign Affairs Review* 19(4): 581–96.

Tett, G. (2011) 'Silos and silences: the role of fragmentation in the recent financial crisis', in C. De Franco and C.O. Meyer (eds.), *Forecasting, Warning and Responding to Transnational Risks: Is Prevention Possible?*, Basingstoke: Palgrave, pp. 208–16.

Tuchman, B.W. (1985) *The March of Folly: From Troy to Vietnam*, New York: Ballantine Books.

Walker, S.G. and Malici, A. (2011) *US Presidents and Foreign Policy Mistakes*, Stanford, CA: Stanford Security Series.

Weaver, R.K. (1986) 'The politics of blame avoidance', *Journal of Public Policy* 6(4): 371–98.

Weick, K.E. and Sutcliffe, K.M. (2007) *Managing the Unexpected: Resilient Performance in an Age of Uncertainty*, San Francisco, CA: Jossey-Bass.

WHO Review Commitee (2011) *Report of the Review Committee on the Functioning of the International Health Regulations (2005) and on Pandemic Influenza A (H1N1) 2009*, Geneva: World Health Organisation.

Wohlstetter, R. (1962) *Pearl Harbour: Warning and Decision*, Stanford, CA: Stanford University Press.

Zartman, W.I. (2005) *Cowardly Lions: Missed Opportunities to Prevent Deadly Conflict and State Collapse*, Boulder, CO: Lynne Rienner.

Resilient blunderers: credit rating fiascos and rating agencies' institutionalized status as private authorities

Andreas Kruck

ABSTRACT   The authority of credit rating agencies (CRAs) has been surprisingly resilient even in the face of recurrent, widely recognized and severe rating failures. This contribution analyses why rating fiascos have had little impact on CRAs' status as transnational private authorities. This resilience is not only owing to CRAs' own (genuinely private) sources of authority. Rather, previous public authorization of CRAs as quasi-regulators and the path-dependent politics of post-fiasco re-regulation have institutionally entrenched and legitimated their status as private authorities. Relying on a historical institutionalist approach and focusing on the regulatory setting of the European Union (EU), the article retraces how flawed public policy choices in the past, i.e., granting CRAs a recognized regulatory role, and non-intended institutional dynamics have spawned later regulatory dilemmas in dealing with CRAs' rating fiascos. Thus, CRAs' recent mistakes have paradoxically fostered a progressive institutionalization rather than a downgrade of their role as private governors.

INTRODUCTION

More recent accounts of credit rating agencies (CRAs) and their role in financial market governance have largely been stories of failure. Allegations of 'rating fiascos' abound not only in the United States (US) but increasingly also in the European Union (EU). CRAs have been scathed for rating fiascos on numerous occasions, including sovereign ratings decisions in the Asian Crisis (1997–8), several corporate bankruptcies in the 2000s and the recent US sub-prime, global financial and European sovereign debt crises. These 'rating fiascos' signify severe and economically costly perceived rating mistakes or failures; i.e., they comprise instances of credit rating which are considered by a large majority of political and market actors as negligently or recklessly misleading assessments of credit risks that have in turn been strongly detrimental to national, regional or even global financial stability (see Meyer 2016).

Given the recurrent, widely recognized and costly nature of their rating fiascos, one would expect CRAs' authority[1] to make judgements of credit-worthiness to suffer. Especially since the recent financial crisis, EU regulators have set out to reduce CRAs' power in a set of three CRA Regulations (2009, 2011, 2013). But, despite their fiascos and regulatory reform efforts, CRAs continue to co-determine access to capital markets and costs of borrowing for public and private debtors. Investors still follow CRAs' standard of creditworthiness, and even powerful states in Europe and elsewhere zealously seek to preserve their top ratings. CRAs' status as transnational private authorities has been surprisingly resilient, even in the face of widely recognized rating fiascos. This is puzzling also for major theoretical perspectives on private authority: a functionalist rational choice approach according to which the authority of private-sector actors is contingent on their performance (in providing valued governance contributions) and their ensuing reputation would lead us to expect that CRAs' authority should be damaged by rating fiascos. Similarly, a statist realist view would suggest that in the face of costly failures of private governors, states will reassert their public authority and effectively rein in CRAs' influence (see Bruner and Abdelal 2005).

I draw on historical institutionalist reasoning to resolve this puzzle. I argue that CRAs' resilience is not only owing to their own genuinely private sources of authority, most notably their expertise and role as gatekeepers. Rather, previous public authorization of CRAs as quasi-regulators and the path-dependent politics of post-fiasco re-regulation are crucial to understand CRAs' persistent authority. Focusing on the regulatory setting of the EU, I retrace how CRAs' status as private authorities has become institutionally entrenched and legitimated through past and current financial market regulations. In the decades before the global financial crisis, regulators not only in the US but around the world, including the EU, granted CRAs a recognized regulatory role, as CRAs' ratings were increasingly used for regulatory purposes, e.g., in the Basel II standards on banking supervision (Bruner and Abdelal 2005; Darbellay 2013: ch. 4; Hiß and Nagel 2012: 49; Kerwer 2002; Nölke and Perry 2007). While this regulatory use and recognition was not the sole cause of CRAs' much-cited power in global financial markets (Kerwer 2005; Nölke 2004; Sinclair 2005), it significantly contributed to institutionalize a powerful position of CRAs in the financial system and narrowed down future paths in the (re-)regulation of CRAs. Non-intended material and immaterial dynamics of path-dependency have rendered public regulators' later attempts at reducing the centrality of CRAs complicated and largely futile, creating a regulatory dilemma: in the wake of the recent crises, public regulators have seen hardly any alternative but to respond to CRAs' fiascos by shoring up regulation and oversight (Hiß and Nagel 2012). However, this in turn institutionally inscribes CRAs as flawed but legitimate and perfectible private governors, rather than mere purveyors of opinions or mundane service providers. Paradoxically, CRAs' mistakes have fostered a progressive institutionalization rather than a downgrade of their role as private governors.

The contribution promotes a more nuanced understanding of the consequences of private governance fiascos. It illustrates how path-dependent public (re-)regulation may distort the 'rationally efficient' competition-based relationship between (bad) performance/reputation and (the loss of) private expertise-based authority. Moreover, the article underlines that unintended institutional dynamics can be a major impediment to effective learning from costly private policy fiascos and their future prevention through adequate (re-)regulation. It thus also illuminates why and when statist realist beliefs in states' capacity to reassert control over and to dis-empower resilient private authorities may be misguided. In the remainder, I first outline widely recognized rating fiascos and point out perceived structural flaws of CRAs. I then analyse the interplay of public and private sources of CRAs' authority and retrace how the path-dependent EU approach to the (re-)regulation of CRAs tends to solidify rather than effectively reduce CRAs' status as private governors in the wake of rating fiascos. I conclude with some broader implications for the study of policy fiascos.

RATING FIASCOS AND THE PATHOLOGIES OF THE RATING INDUSTRY

Severe rating mistakes in the Asian Crisis (1997–8) and the Enron (2001), WorldCom (2002) and Parmalat (2003) corporate bankruptcies created a first wave of broad-based criticism (Langohr and Langohr 2008: 439; Ryan 2012: 4, 10). In the Asian Financial Crisis, CRAs downgraded sovereign ratings far too late, but then to an excessive extent (Ferri *et al.* 1999). In the context of the bankruptcy of the US energy company Enron, CRAs assigned excellent credit quality assessments to the company even the day before it went bankrupt. Similar rating fiascos occurred in the WorldCom and Parmalat bankruptcies (Darbellay 2013: 67).

In the wake of the US sub-prime mortgage crisis (2007), which evolved into the most severe global financial and economic crisis after the Second World War, CRAs were singled out as one of the main targets of criticism by politicians, market professionals, researchers and journalists. CRAs greatly underestimated the credit risk of 'toxic' complex structured finance products (Porter 2010: 69), most notably mortgage-backed collateralized debt obligations (CDOs). Investors around the world relied on the excellent (AAA) ratings for these packaged securities and bought them without being aware of the credit risks implied in them. CRAs were blamed for downgrading mortgage-backed securities far too late and for failing to identify risks and value of those complex products properly (Brunnermeier *et al.* 2009: 54; Hiß and Nagel 2012: 170–3; Quaglia 2013: 61). They promoted an enormous growth of sub-prime lending and contributed to both the intensity and the geographical reach of the global financial crisis (Financial Stability Forum 2008: 32–3). Moreover, CRAs put the insurer AIG, rescued by a bailout package in 2009, in the AA category and rated Lehman Brothers an A just a month before it collapsed in 2008. Accordingly, EU parliamentarians argued that CRAs 'have failed in the crises of the 1990s and also in the Enron case. ... They have provided wrong analyses of the financial products which were based on US mortgages and gave the Lehman Brothers bank good grades when it was already faltering.'[2] The European Commission claimed in 2009 that CRAs 'have to a high degree contributed to the current problems on the financial markets. They have clearly underestimated the risk that issuers of certain complex financial instruments could not repay their debts.'[3]

Sovereign ratings in the European debt crisis have put CRAs even more into the centre of political contestation in Europe. European politicians accused CRAs that they failed to predict the crisis and then precipitated it by downgrading sovereign ratings of eurozone countries too far and too fast (Ryan 2012: 5; see Ferri *et al.* 1999). CRAs were scolded for reinforcing pro-cyclical behaviour and herding effects, causing credit crunches in times of crisis and triggering acute liquidity problems for ailing European states. European politicians criticized CRAs for their timing of downgrades, for example in advance of Greek rescue packages to increase pressure on negotiators (Ryan 2012: 11–12). CRAs were viewed as active driving forces during Europe's crisis as the markdown of Portugal, Italy, Greece and Spain resulted in significantly higher interest rates on government bonds which in turn aggravated the European debt crisis (Gärtner *et al.* 2011). Internal Market Commissioner Barnier criticized in 2011 that CRAs 'have made fatal mistakes in the past. The timing of some sovereign ratings has also surprised me – for example when they were released in the midst of negotiations for a bailout package for a country. We must not allow ratings to reinforce the volatility of the markets.'[4] Jean-Claude Juncker, then leader of the Euro Group, denounced sovereign downgrades of numerous eurozone members in 2011 as 'unfair' and 'completely excessive': 'I believe it would be better if we took the ratings less seriously.'[5] Standard & Poor's erroneous downgrade of France in 2011 further politicized the role and control of CRAs (Ryan 2012: 5).

This series of rating fiascos has led to heightened attention to structural pathologies such as persistent flaws in rating methodologies and models, the oligopolistic market structure undermining market discipline (which, as argued below, is at least partly owing to states' previous regulatory empowerment and furthered by current re-regulation), the pro-cyclical effect of ratings and especially the conflict of interests CRAs faced (Financial Stability Forum 2008: 33). Their 'issuer-pays' business model implies that CRAs earn fees for providing ratings for financial instruments from the originators of the securities. (Brunnermeier *et al.* 2009: 54; Porter 2010: 69). Thus, EU Commissioner Almunia stated in 2011 that 'among the many problems caused by rating agencies are conflicts of interest, opaque methodologies and possible abuse of market power.'[6] This view combined with growing resentment about the perceived lack of understanding US-based CRAs showed for European accounting standards, corporate financing customs and sovereign borrowers' financial situation (Bruner and Abdelal 2005: 192).

PUBLIC (RE-)REGULATION AND THE INSTITUTIONALIZATION OF CRAS' STATUS

The dynamic interplay of public and private sources of CRAs' authority

The global and European financial crises fostered a shared perception of CRAs' proneness to fiascos. A near consensus that overreliance on credit ratings constituted an instance of market and policy failure, as well as public pressure arising from costly bailouts, created political resolve among European policy-makers and regulators to take a firm stance against one of the culprits for the crisis and to reduce the central role of CRAs in financial market governance. Despite that seemingly large window of opportunity for institutional change, the re-regulation that *has* materialized has hardly curbed CRAs' power. To understand that, we have to take a closer look at both public and private sources of CRAs' authority.

On the one hand, these private firms are not just commercial information providers, but governance actors capable of wielding authority (Sinclair 2005). By defining and monitoring criteria of credit risk for investors and borrowers around the world, CRAs have established a (nearly global) private standard of credit-worthiness (Kerwer 2002). Without public interference, reliance on and compliance with this private standard is based on CRAs' expert authority and their ensuing legitimacy (Nölke 2004: 163–4). Because of CRAs' presumed expert status, investors have relied extensively on their standard of credit-worthiness for screening non-transparent capital markets. Borrowers are aware of CRAs' published criteria for credit-risk assessment and tend to adjust their behaviour to them, since – by assigning and constantly reviewing credit ratings – CRAs do not only define a standard of credit-worthiness, but also verify compliance with the standard and promote its adoption. The letter-grade rating is vital for borrowers' financing conditions and their access to capital (Kerwer 2006: 91). Thus, both investors and borrowers are dependent on CRAs – for analytical resources and credibility respectively – which leads them to recognize CRAs as private authorities that set standards and co-ordinate actors' behaviour (Nölke 2004). This is the first genuinely private component to CRAs' authority: their epistemic authority, enhanced by the 'moral authority of the non-state, non-self-interested referee' (Bruner and Abdelal 2005: 191; see Porter 2010: 59) and the resulting structural power as gatekeepers of global financial markets.

A second major source of CRAs' authority has been public regulatory empowerment, i.e., the incorporation of ratings into financial regulation. This practice has allowed regulators to impose flexible, risk-sensitive investment restrictions, disclosure requirements or capital reserve requirements (Bruner and Abdelal 2005: 192–3; Kerwer 2006: 95; Nölke and Perry 2007: 124; Sinclair 2005: 42–6). Rather than conducting risk assessments needed for risk-sensitive regulation *themselves*, public regulators transferred this task to CRAs when using credit ratings in regulation (on delegating responsibility for the management of risks, see Beasley 2016).

While this regulatory use originated and remained most extensive in the US, a global trend towards the use of private ratings for regulatory purposes gained traction in the 1990s and 2000s. Within the EU, it started in 1993 with the Capital Adequacy Directive. From 1993 to 2006, all European members of the Basel Committee on Banking Supervision (BCBS) except for Germany used credit ratings in their prudential supervision of banks. A further shift towards ratings-dependent regulation occurred through the 2006 EU Capital Requirements Directive (Darbellay 2013: 49; Langohr and Langohr 2008: 431, 435–7; Weber and Darbellay 2008: 2). It transformed into EU law the main provisions of the Basel II Accord (2004), which promulgated non-binding international standards for banking supervision (Council of Ministers and European Parliament 2006). The Basel II Accord provided for the use of credit ratings from approved CRAs in the calculation of banks' capital reserve requirements (Sinclair 2005: 47–9). Owing to the lobbying of large international banks (Lall 2012) and the insistence of Continental European countries, most notably Germany, banks could deviate from this external 'standardized approach' to credit risk assessment and, upon application, use internal rating procedures (Nölke and Perry 2007: 130). Nonetheless, Basel II and the 2006 Capital Requirement Directive entailed a significant recognition of a regulatory role for CRAs in European financial regulation.

When credit ratings were used in financial regulation, CRAs' private standard of credit-worthiness was made binding by a public third party (Kerwer 2002: 16; Nölke 2004; Nölke and Perry 2007). Thus, 'ratings [were] given the force of law' and 'receive[d] a public imprimatur' (Bruner and Abdelal 2005: 191). Regulatory authority was delegated to CRAs. At the same time, regulatory recognition also entrenched CRAs' role as (authoritative) gatekeepers. It rendered ratings more valuable, gave CRAs a privilege *vis-à-vis* other providers of financial information and provided a lucrative boost to CRAs' business. Regulatory use further damaged competition: it created regulatory barriers to market entry and reinforced an effective oligopoly of recognized, certified and regulation-eligible market incumbents. It also attenuated reputational pressures to ensure high informational quality and credibility of credit ratings since the business of the regulatorily privileged CRAs shifted to selling 'regulatory licenses' that issuers *had* to buy (Bruner and Abdelal 2005: 193; Darbellay 2013: 45; Langohr and Langohr 2008: 439). Finally, regulatory use strengthened the private expert authority and the perceived reliability and legitimacy of CRAs. Regulatory reliance on CRAs signalled to investors that it was safe to rely on CRAs' risk assessment: ratings which were deemed reliable enough to be used for regulatory requirements should also be adequate for making investment decisions (see European Commission 2013; Financial Stability Forum 2008). Public regulatory use thus implied a delegation of regulatory authority and a reinforcement of CRAs' genuinely private sources of authority. Coupled with low levels of regulation and oversight, it was an important driver of CRAs' excessive power in the past two or three decades (Bruner and Abdelal 2005: 193).

The historical institutionalist argument about path-dependent regulatory dynamics

Drawing on historical institutionalist concepts and reasoning (see Mahoney 2000; Pierson 2000), I argue that regulatory use and recognition of CRAs, i.e., past public policy choices which have institutionalized a powerful position of CRAs in the financial system, structure and narrow down future paths in dealing with CRAs' rating fiascos. The regulatory institutionalization of CRAs' status reflects features of an increasing returns process meaning that 'the probability of further steps along the same path increases with each move down that path' (Pierson 2000: 252).

The combination of CRAs' autonomous (re-)sources of private authority and the public empowerment of CRAs via regulatory recognition has propelled material and ideational dynamics of path dependency. Continued and large-scale reliance of both public and private actors on CRAs' analytical resources has generated significant *material feedback loops*. Regulators' and market actors' capacity gaps with regards to credit risk assessment and their structural dependencies on CRAs have progressively grown as state regulators and investors alike have neglected the maintenance or build-up of adequate risk assessment capacities which could substitute for CRAs' analytical resources. The costs of exiting the path of continued reliance on CRAs have thus increased over time.

Regulatory use has also generated *ideational feedback loops* bolstering CRAs' authoritative status. It has fostered a normalization and legitimation of broad-based reliance on CRAs, contributing to turn reliance on credit ratings into a normalized behavioural regularity. Public regulatory recognition further enhanced the private epistemic authority of CRAs to a point where it is hard to cut it back by formal regulatory action. This implies that authority shifts are sticky, i.e., hard to effectively reverse even if the formal rules of the game can be and indeed are rewritten.

These material and immaterial reasons for path-dependency have *firstly* rendered post-fiasco *dis*-empowerment through states' revoking the initial transfer of regulatory authority to CRAs complicated, costly and only moderately consequential (in terms of reducing CRAs' *de facto* authority in the eyes of other market actors). *Secondly*, EU regulators have therefore rather responded to rating fiascos with intrusive re-regulation of CRAs' behaviour in an effort to impose meaningful control. But, *thirdly*, such intrusive re-regulation on the one hand has negative material side-effects on competition in the rating market (strengthening incumbent CRAs' structural power) and, on the other hand, entails the ideational reproduction and validation rather than the down-grading of CRAs' status as crucial governance actors. As a result, re-regulation contributes to perpetuate and further institutionalize the path-dependent dynamics of CRAs' private authority in the face of rating fiascos.

In the following, I empirically unfold this three-step causal argument in the form of a coherent 'analytical narrative' which methodologists deem particularly fit for historical institutionalist research interested in illustrating dynamic causality (Büthe 2002). For the sake of analytical clarity, I do however provide subsections which disentangle material and ideational reasons for path-dependency.

Complicated and (largely) futile attempts at reducing regulatory reliance on CRAs

Hesitant and cautious institutional reform
The above-mentioned material and ideational dynamics of dependency have severely constrained EU regulators' attempts at dis-empowering CRAs in the wake of their politicized rating fiascos. The European Commission issued a consultation report in 2008 stressing the need for 'policy options to address the problem of excessive reliance on credit ratings' (European Commission 2008: 1). But neither the 2009 CRA I Regulation nor the 2011 CRA II Regulation (Council of Ministers and European Parliament 2009, 2011) covered regulatory over-reliance on CRAs and its connection to investors' overreliance. Besides banks' internal ratings, the new Basel III accord (2010) still relies on credit ratings to calculate risk-weighted minimum capital standards and minimum liquidity ratios (Basel Committee on Banking Supervision 2010: 52–3; Goldbach and Kerwer 2012: 256–7). The EU Capital Requirements Directive IV of 2011, which implemented the main Basel III provisions within the EU, included measures to reduce overreliance on external credit ratings by stipulating that banks' investment decisions be based not only on external ratings but also on their own internal credit opinion (European Commission 2013: 3). However, the EU was not ready to withdraw the regulatory use of credit ratings from banking regulation without ensuring that suitable alternatives are available (Darbellay 2013: 63; Lall 2012: 630).

Amidst growing political pressure to limit CRAs' power, the 2013 CRA III Regulation addressed the problem of regulatory overreliance (see Council of Ministers and European Parliament 2013: 4–5). The CRA III Regulation demanded that the European Supervisory Authorities should remove credit ratings 'where they have the potential to create mechanistic effects' (European Commission 2013: 4–5; see Darbellay 2013: 62–3). Moreover, Preamble 9 states that, instead of relying 'solely and mechanistically' on external credit ratings, '[c]redit institutions and investment firms should be encouraged to put in place internal procedures in order to make their own credit risk assessment and should encourage investors to perform a due diligence exercise.'

But the 2013 CRA Regulation was very explicit that EU regulators do not want to rush a complete withdrawal of credit ratings from financial regulation. It cautiously held that the EU:

is working towards reviewing, at a first stage, whether any references to credit ratings in Union law trigger or have the potential to trigger sole or mechanistic reliance on such credit ratings and, at a second stage, all references to credit ratings for regulatory purposes *with a view to deleting them by 2020, provided that appropriate alternatives to credit risk assessment are identified and implemented.* (Preamble 6; my emphasis)

Why did the EU take this quite hesitant approach?

Material obstacles to the dis-empowerment of CRAs
Despite all their frustration with rating fiascos, European politicians and regulators continue to proclaim that a world without CRAs is 'no longer conceivable' and that diverse market actors are still 'dependent' on CRAs (both quotes from Reuters [2007]). Internal Market Commissioner Barnier, one of the most vocal critics of CRAs, admitted in 2011 that CRAs 'are necessary for risk assessment. But these assessments must be precise, transparent and reliable.'[7] EU regulators just could not miss how mightily US regulators struggled with the implementation of the ambitious 2010 Dodd–Frank Act provisions on stopping the use of CRAs' ratings in US regulation.

Proper and ready alternatives at reasonable costs have proved hard to come by (Hill 2011: 147–8). Owing to previous experiences with largely uniform, non-risk-weighted regulatory requirements such as the Basel I capital reserve provisions which had effectively encouraged riskier investments of banks to increase their returns on regulatory capital (Pagliari 2012: 48–9; Weber and Darbellay 2008: 3), regulators have viewed it as imperative to stick with risk-sensitive (though pro-cyclical) regulations that are contingent on regulatees' exposure to credit risk and that adjust to changing market circumstances.

Regarding alternatives to risk assessment by CRAs, US and EU regulators have agreed that references to *credit spreads* as a market-based substitute for credit ratings would only boost pro-cyclical effects (Langohr and Langohr 2008: 440). They would rather enhance the role of *internal ratings-based procedures* of financial institutions (e.g., in Basel II and III). However, they anticipated significant difficulties and costs especially for smaller, less-sophisticated banks in the implementation of an internal ratings-based approach (Lall 2012: 630). Regulators and even banks themselves expressed doubts about whether smaller financial institutions could do a better job of analysing securities than CRAs (Federal Reserve Board 2011: 4). Moreover, policy-makers feared moral hazard of banks using exclusively internal ratings (Weber and Darbellay 2008: 11). Rare proposals of *public regulators' taking over risk assessment* themselves drew strong opposition with concerns about missing public expertise and resources, lack of independence and even less competition leading to worse rating quality being voiced throughout the financial policy community, including supervisors such as the FED (Federal Reserve Board 2011: 4).

From a material path-dependency perspective, extensive reliance on CRAs has led states and private market actors to neglect the maintenance and build-up of capacities that could substitute for the outsourced risk assessment tasks. The costs of exiting the path of reliance on CRAs and displacing these incumbent private authorities have progressively grown. And '[t]he experience in the US has shown that it is difficult to remove references to ratings without having viable alternatives in place' (European Commission 2013: 11). The creation of a publicly sponsored and supported European CRA is not considered such a viable alternative. The European Commission argues that:

> setting up a CRA with public money would be costly (approximately 300–500 million euros over a period of 5 years), could raise concerns regarding the CRA's credibility especially if a publicly funded CRA would rate the Member States which finance the CRA, and put private CRAs at a comparative disadvantage. (European Commission 2013: 9)

Even if one might consider these issues with finding alternatives to CRAs as primarily transitional problems, further fundamental complications remain. Revoking the public regulatory empowerment of CRAs, i.e., stopping the use of credit ratings in financial regulation, would now have only a limited effect on CRAs' *de facto* authority – both in terms of structural power and recognition – in the eyes of market participants. This is owing to a double dynamic in CRAs' authority. First, even after severe mistakes CRAs possess their own genuinely private sources of business profit and power. States' leverage from cutting references to credit ratings in financial regulation is therefore limited, as regulatory reliance has been a boost to, but is not a precondition for CRAs' influence and business viability. Second, the effects of public empowerment are 'sticky'. Having previously authorized a public function of private CRAs, public regulators have difficulties reaching the contrary effect by simply revoking the formal authority transfer. This is because CRAs have not only kept their own (re-)sources of authority, but actually *profited* from their regulatory privilege to consolidate their state-independent power in financial markets. To fully grasp this dynamic, we also have to look beyond material factors.

Ideational obstacles to the dis-empowerment of CRAs

Boosted by regulatory recognition, investors' reliance on CRAs', meaning mostly the Big Three's, risk assessment has turned into a normalized behavioural regularity not even shattered by rating fiascos. '[O]ver the past decades behavioral reliance has added to regulatory reliance' (Darbellay 2013: 86). CRAs' position as authoritative judges of credit-worthiness whose actual or preconceived assessments are consequential and must be taken into account seems largely intact in the eyes of market participants. After a strong dip in 2008, market shares and profit margins of the leading CRAs have risen again (Hill 2011: 143–4). Bankers and brokers in both the US and Europe claim that market norms dictating the use of dominant CRAs are sticky regardless of rating failures: 'You basically have to go to Moody's and S&P ... The market doesn't accept it if you don't go to both of them' (broker Dessa Bokides, quoted in Hill 2011: 140). Besides previous regulatory empowerment and current re-regulation of CRAs (discussed below), these sticky market norms or rather market actors' ideational preconception – amounting to a collective self-fulfilling prophecy – that they have to continue to rely on the most prominent CRAs because other market participants have long done and will likely keep doing so have contributed to the persistence of an oligopoly of failing, but still powerful incumbent CRAs.

In sum, the closely linked interplay of normalized behavioural regularities and the more material, structural power position CRAs occupy as oligopolistic gate-keepers – both of which have profited from regulatory empowerment, but are not wiped away by formal regulatory dis-empowerment, i.e., deleting references to credit ratings in financial regulation – mean that the market practice of relying on credit ratings from a few powerful CRAs will not disappear in the medium term, even if formal regulatory references to credit ratings are removed. Thus, regulatory dis-empowerment, i.e., states' renouncing the regulatory use of CRAs, is not only complicated and costly, it will also have only limited impact on CRAs' overall authority.

Shoring up regulation and oversight

Faced with the difficulty and ineffectiveness of revoking previously delegated regulatory authority, EU regulators responded to CRAs' rating fiascos with quite intrusive re-regulation. In a series of three CRA Regulations (2009, 2011 and 2013), the EU devised relatively tight rules (Darbellay 2013: 72–3; Hiß and Nagel 2012: 243–5; see Council of Ministers and European |Parliament 2009, 2011, 2013). Using two main sources of inspiration, namely the evolving US legal framework on CRAs and the provisions of the (voluntary) International Organization of Securities Commissions (IOSCO) Code of Conduct, the EU Regulations provided that all CRAs whose ratings are to be used in the EU needed to apply for registration through a centralized European-level system (Darbellay 2013: 73; Quaglia 2013: 62; White 2010: 223). The newly created European Securities and Markets Authority (ESMA) was entrusted with exclusive registration and supervisory powers over CRAs registered in the EU, including European subsidiaries of US headquartered firms. It was given powers to administer the registration process, request information, launch investigations and perform on-site inspections (Quaglia 2013: 62). It was also mandated to specify the CRA Regulations by issuing binding 'technical standards' and to manage the European Rating Platform, a tool to improve the comparability and visibility of ratings of financial instruments (European Commission 2013: 8).

Regulatory requirements imposed on CRAs included measures to prevent conflicts of interests through in-house rotation and a ban on an analyst's rating an entity in which she/he has an ownership interest; disclosure requirements concerning CRAs' risks models, rating methods and basic assumptions; a ban on rating consultancy services for companies that are to be rated; and the issuance of transparency reports that list large customers and outline the measures taken by the CRA to ensure the quality of its ratings, e.g., through ongoing monitoring procedures (European Commission 2013: 2). The EU Regulations explicitly stipulated that rating methodologies must be, *inter alia*, 'rigorous' and 'systematic' leaving it to the ESMA to specify, monitor and implement this requirement (European Commission 2013: 2). With regard to sovereign ratings, the CRA III Regulation defined specific procedural require-ments (*ibid.*: 5; see Council of Ministers and European Parliament 2013). Among other things, CRAs must set up a calendar indicating when they will rate EU member states with ratings being limited to three per year for unsoli-cited sovereign ratings. Moreover, the Regulation provided that investors and EU member states must be informed of the underlying facts and assumptions on each sovereign rating.

Finally, the CRA III Regulation introduced a civil liability regime for CRAs (Art. 35a) for cases in which a CRA infringes intentionally or with gross negli-gence the CRA Regulations, thereby causing damage to an investor (European Commission 2013: 10). To claim damages, an investor must establish that it has 'reasonably' and 'with due care' relied on a CRA for an investment decision. While the elements of 'damage', 'intentionally', 'gross negligence', 'reasonably' or 'due care' may be hard to prove, the liability rule is still a significant departure from previous conceptions of credit ratings as 'mere opinions' (Darbellay 2013: 79–84). How these new liability rules will be implemented and enforced within the EU remains to be seen. But a brief look at post-crisis efforts in the US to expose CRAs to legal liability is instructive in several regards. In February 2015, S&P agreed on a 1.5 billion dollar settlement with the US Department of Justice and some 20 states after having come to a much smaller agreement with the SEC in January 2015 (Robinson and McLaughlin 2015). This ended a two-year court battle over inflated ratings for sub-prime mortgage bonds. On the one hand, the fine indicated that (states' threat of) litigation could lead to meaningful financial consequences for rating fiascos. On the other hand, with the deal US public authorities have let CRAs get away without admitting legal wrongdoing while also making financial concessions compared to their initial 5 billion dollar claim (*ibid.*). What is more, US public authorities backed down from exposing CRAs to stricter legal liability and accountability after the CRAs reacted on such plans by refraining from rating certain types of debt, thereby causing major market disruptions. This illustrates how extensive reliance on CRAs and resulting path-dependencies have put CRAs into a position of structural power allowing them to mitigate, if not prevent, painful public encroachment.

Despite these notable (re-)regulation efforts, reasonable doubts about their effectiveness in terms of ensuring the reliability and integrity of the rating process are in order (Darbellay 2013: 89; Hill 2011: 145–6). Owing to oper-ational and legal issues, regulators have not cut the link between CRAs and issuers by encouraging the replacement of the 'issuer-pays' model with an 'investor-pays' model or the establishment of a 'common pool' financed by issuers from which CRAs would be selected. This clearly hampers the impact of regulatory reform.

(Side-)effects of re-regulation: entrenching rather than down-grading CRAs' status as private authorities

A fundamental dilemma has shaped post-fiasco re-regulation in a way that has driven further the path-dependent institutionalization of CRAs' status as private authorities. In the wake of the global and European crisis, the costs from rating fiascos and political pressure piled up, while attempts at reducing the centrality of CRAs via public *dis*-empowerment have proved complicated and largely futile owing to the material and ideational obstacles outlined above. In that situation, it was very plausible, if not compelling, for policy-makers to respond to rating fiascos with tighter regulation and oversight, in particular since the extant oligopolistic structure of the rating market would make it 'highly unlikely that market pressure alone is sufficient to discipline the CRAs to change their conduct' (Pagliari 2012: 55).

However, this approach of shored up regulation and oversight has had severe unintended consequences (Hiß and Nagel 2012: 248–61). In a paradoxical process of mistakes-driven progressive institutionalization of CRAs' status, the new rules have tended to inadvertently perpetuate and reinforce a further institutionalization rather than a downgrade of CRAs' status as private authorities. In terms of unintended material consequences, re-regulation has failed to change those very structures that put a few CRAs into the centre of the information and access regime of current financial markets. Moreover, the new rules re-articulate and reproduce CRAs as recognized and trustworthy private authorities and thus create unintended ideational consequences which will likely propel the future path-dependent evolution of CRAs' authority.

Perpetuating structural power: unintended material consequences
Post-fiasco re-regulation has tended to undermine the declared policy goals of downgrading CRAs' structural centrality in the financial system, increasing competition in the rating market and reducing overreliance on CRAs. According to the conception of the Dodd–Frank Act and the EU CRA Regulations, public oversight is necessary to discipline CRAs. But re-regulating CRAs is a tricky business: tight(er) regulation which takes seriously the systemically important function of CRAs in the current financial architecture may inadvertently undermine regulators' medium-/long-term goals of diminishing CRAs' crucial role as private governors and discouraging investors' overreliance on credit ratings. Contrary to regulators' declared intentions to lower barriers to market entry, enhanced regulatory oversight actually *empowers* CRAs, especially market leaders (Darbellay 2013: 87), keeping the Big Three (Moody's, S&P's and Fitch) at the core of the financial architecture rather than reducing their centrality and enhancing competition.

Re-regulation of CRAs creates more rather than fewer barriers to entry as regulatory compliance is particularly onerous for new entrants (Darbellay 2013: 87; Hill 2011). As Lawrence White (2010: 224) put it, recent regulatory efforts:

unavoidably restrict flexibility, raise costs, and discourage entry and innovation in the development and assessment of information for judging the
creditworthiness of bonds. Ironically, such efforts are likely to increase the
importance of the three large incumbent rating agencies.

Thus, re-regulation after CRAs' rating fiascos inadvertently contributes to the
persistence of an oligopoly of a few flawed but structurally powerful CRAs
which remain largely unaffected by market competition.

Reproducing recognition and trust: unintended ideational consequences
In addition, from an ideational view, formal public regulation and oversight
gives 'too much of an official endorsement to ratings' (Brunnermeier *et al.*
2009: 54) and reassures the financial markets of the credibility of CRAs.
Rather than creating incentives to reduce overreliance on (a limited number
of) CRAs, it thus contributes to ideationally entrench the status of CRAs as
authoritative governors rather than providers of mere opinions. This is
because public re-regulation constructs CRAs as fallible but indispensable gatekeepers that need to be regulated judiciously to fulfil a systemic oversight function in financial markets: CRAs are regulatorily constituted as flawed, but
generally legitimate and so significant for the financial system that they
require closer public control to 'function properly' and be trusted again by
market actors.

However, this kind of tying CRAs even more tightly into the regulatory
system is likely to exacerbate rather than resolve the key problem of over-reliance
by making CRAs appear trustworthy (again) (Darbellay 2013: 86–7). Although
ESMA seems serious about its supervisory role, the EU Regulations help
'enhance the legitimacy of what is a form of outsourced due diligence'
(Paudyn 2013: 806–7) and underscore CRAs' position at the core of the financial market governance system. Aspiring to learn from the mistakes of CRAs in
the global financial and European sovereign debt crises, the rules tend to reproduce rather than decrease CRAs' authoritative status.

CONCLUSION

This contribution has characterized CRAs as resilient blunderers. Rating fiascos,
e.g., in the US sub-prime, global financial and European sovereign debt crises,
have largely failed to undermine CRAs' status as private authorities. The latter
has become institutionally entrenched and legitimated through past and current
financial market regulations – to a degree that it is no longer shattered by rating
fiascos. Previous public authorization of CRAs (i.e., flawed public policy choices
in the past) as well as non-intended path-dependent dynamics have constrained
and shaped later re-regulation in the wake of rating fiascos. In particular, evolving resource dependencies and increasing costs of switching from reliance to
non-reliance on CRAs are key to making sense of CRAs' persistent authority.
Together with the ideational normalization of (public and private actors')
reliance on CRAs resulting in sticky behavioural regularities, they go a long

way capturing the difficulties of effective regulatory dis-empowerment, the intricacies of imposing regulatory oversight and CRAs' getting away with blatant blunders without losing their authoritative position as private governors.

On a more general level, the case of the path-dependent re-regulation of CRAs is reflective of broader post-crisis reforms in financial regulation which have been shaped by strong path dependency (see Helleiner 2014; Porter 2014). The global regulatory response to the most severe financial crisis after the Great Depression has overall been incremental and underwhelming in terms of improving regulatory capacity and financial stability. This contribution has illuminated why even stark and widely recognized failures of previously empowered private actors may fail to result in effective regulatory dis-empowerment and a loss of the blunderers' authority, challenging both simple rational-functionalist and statist realist approaches to the impact of failure on private authorities.

My analysis thus underlines the limits to (states' and private stakeholders') learning from costly failures committed by private agents (see Howlett 2012). More specifically, it points out the problems in preventing governance fiascos of powerful private governors from re-occurring through formal public re-regulation. While, even after the privatization of governance tasks, state regulators still feel – and, arguably, are publicly held – responsible for 'cleaning up' after private actors' failures, their capacities to effectively correct and prevent the mistakes of private governors tend to decline as the public and self-empowerment of private governance actors progresses.

NOTES

1 Political actors, including private agents, have authority when the addressees of their actions recognize that these actors can make competent judgments and binding decisions. They exercise authority in that they successfully claim the right to perform governance functions like the formulation of rules and rule monitoring, implementation or enforcement (Zürn *et al.* 2012: 70, 86).

2 Jürgen Klute (EP Member, 2010), in: http://www.europarl.europa.eu/news/de/newsroom/content/20100607FCS75591/9/html/Die-Rating-Agenturen-spielen-eine-Rolle-die-ihnen-eigentlich-nicht-zusteht (accessed March 2014). All following translations of non-English quotes are mine.

3 http://europa.eu/rapid/press-release_IP-09-629_de.htm?locale=en (accessed March 2014).

4 http://ec.europa.eu/deutschland/press/pr_releases/10287_de.htm (accessed March 2014).

5 http://www.t-online.de/nachrichten/ausland/eu/id_52074968/angela-merkel-und-nicolas-sarkozy-nehmen-ankuendigung-von-ratingagentur-gelassen.html (accessed March 2014).
6 http://www.europarl.europa.eu/news/de/news-room/content/20111121IPR31952/html/Eurobonds-Vorbehalte-der-EU-Abgeordneten-gegenüber-Kommissionsvorschlägen (accessed March 2014).
7 http://www.europarl.europa.eu/news/de/news-room/content/20111121IPR31952/html/Eurobonds-Vorbehalte-der-EU-Abgeordneten-gegenüber-Kommissionsvorschlägen (accessed March 2014).

REFERENCES

Basel Committee on Banking Supervision (2010) *Basel III: A Global Regulatory Framework for More Resilient Banks and Banking Systems*, Basel: Bank for International Settlements, available at http://www.bis.org/publ/bcbs189_dec2010.pdf (accessed March 2014).
Beasley, R. (2016) 'Dissonance and Decision-Making Mistakes in the Age of Risk', *Journal of European Public Policy*, doi:10.1080/13501763.2015.1127276.
Bruner, C.J. and Abdelal, R. (2005) 'To judge Leviathan: sovereign credit ratings, national law, and the world economy', *Journal of Public Policy* 25(2): 191–217.
Brunnermeier, M., Crocket, A., Goodhart, C., Persaud, A.D. and Shin, H. (2009) 'The fundamental principles of financial regulation', *Geneva Reports on the World Economy* 11, Geneva: International Center for Monetary and Banking Studies.
Büthe, T. (2002) 'Taking temporality seriously: modeling history and the use of narratives as evidence', *American Political Science Review* 96(3): 481–493.
Council of Ministers and European Parliament (2006) 'Directive 2006/49/EC of 30th June 2006 on the capital adequacy of investment firms and credit institutions', Brussels: Council of Ministers and European Parliament, available at http://eur-lex.europa.eu/legal-content/EN/TXT/?uri=CELEX:32006L0049 (accessed January 2014).
Council of Ministers and European Parliament (2009) 'Regulation (EC) No. 1060/2009 of 16 September 2009 on credit rating agencies', Brussels: Council of Ministers and European Parliament, available at http://www.esma.europa.eu/system/files/L_302_1.pdf (accessed February 2014).
Council of Ministers and European Parliament (2011) 'Regulation (EC) No. 513/2011 of 11 May 2011 amending Regulation No. 1060/2009 on credit rating agencies', Brussels: Council of Ministers and European Parliament, available at http://www.esma.europa.eu/system/files/CRA2_Reg_513_2011_EN.PDF (accessed February 2014).
Council of Ministers and European Parliament (2013) 'Regulation (EC) No. 462/2013 of 21 May 2013 amending Regulation No. 1060/2009 on credit rating agencies', Brussels: Council of Ministers and European Parliament, available at http://eur-lex.europa.eu/legal-content/EN/ALL/?uri=CELEX:32013R0462 (accessed February 2014).
Darbellay, A. (2013) *Regulating Credit Rating Agencies*, Cheltenham: Edward Elgar.
European Commission (2008) 'Tackling the problem of excessive reliance on ratings', *Consultation Report of the DG Market Services*, Brussels: European Commission, available at http://ec.europa.eu/internal_market/consultations/docs/securities_agencies/consultation-overreliance_en.pdf (accessed February 2014).
European Commission (2013) 'Memo: new rules on credit rating agencies (CRAs) enter into force', 18 June 2013, Brussels: European Commission, available at http://europa.eu/rapid/press-release_MEMO-13–571_de.htm (accessed March 2014).

Federal Reserve Board (2011) *Report to the Congress on credit ratings*, July 2011, Washington: Board of Governors of the Federal Reserve System.

Ferri, G., Liu, L., and Stiglitz, J.E. (1999) 'The procyclical role of rating agencies: evidence from the East Asian Crisis, *Economics Notes* 28(3): 335–55.

Financial Stability Forum (2008) *Report of the Financial Stability Forum on enhancing market and institutional resilience*, April 2008, Washington: Financial Stability Forum, available at http://www.ifrs.org/News/Announcements-and-Speeches/Documents/FSF_Report_to_G7_11_April.pdf (accessed March 2014).

Gärtner, M., Griesbach, B. and Jung, F. (2011) 'PIGS or lambs? The European debt crisis and the role of rating agencies', *International Advances in Economic Research* 17(3): 288–99.

Goldbach, R. and Kerwer, D. (2012) 'New capital rules? Reforming Basel banking standards after the financial crisis', in R. Mayntz (ed.), *Crisis and Control: Institutional Change in Financial Market Regulation*, Frankfurt: Campus, pp. 245–60.

Helleiner, E. (2014) *The Status Quo Crisis: Global Financial Governance After the 2008 Meltdown*, Oxford: Oxford University Press.

Hill, C.A. (2011) 'Limits of Dodd–Frank's rating agency reform', *Chapman Law Review* 15(1): 133–48.

Hiß, S. and Nagel, S. (2012) *Ratingagenturen zwischen Krise und Regulierung*, Baden-Baden: Nomos.

Howlett, M. (2012) 'The lessons of failure: learning and blame avoidance in public policy-making', *International Political Science Review* 33(5): 539–55.

Kerwer, D. (2002) 'Standardising as governance: the case of credit rating agencies', in A. Héritier (ed.), *Common Goods: Reinventing European and International Governance*, Lanham, MD: Rowman and Littlefield, pp. 293–316.

Kerwer, D. (2005) 'Holding global regulators accountable: the case of credit rating agencies', *Governance* 18(3): 453–75.

Kerwer, D. (2006) 'Governing financial markets by international standards', in M. Koenig-Archibugi and M. Zürn (eds), *New Modes of Governance: Exploring Publicness, Delegation and Inclusiveness*, Basingstoke: Palgrave, pp. 77–100.

Lall, R. (2012) 'From failure to failure: the politics of international banking regulation', *Review of International Political Economy* 19(4): 609–38.

Langohr, H.M. and Langohr, P.T. (2008) *The Rating Agencies and their Credit Ratings: What they are, how they Work and Why they are Relevant*, Chichester: Wiley.

Mahoney, J. (2000) 'Path dependence in historical sociology', *Theory and Society* 29(4): 507–48.

Meyer, C. (2016) 'Over- and under-reaction to transboundary threats: two sides of a misprinted coin?', *Journal of European Public Policy*, doi:10.1080/13501763.2015.1127275.

Nölke, A. (2004) 'Transnational private authority and corporate governance', in S.A. Schirm (ed.), *New Rules for Global Markets: Public and Private Governance in the World Economy*, Basingstoke: Palgrave, pp. 155–75.

Nölke, A. and Perry, J. (2007) 'Coordination service firms and the erosion of Rhenish capitalism', in H. Overbeek, B. van Apeldoorn and A. Nölke (eds), *The Transnational Politics of Corporate Governance Regulation*, London: Routledge, pp. 121–36.

Pagliari, S. (2012) 'Who governs finance? The shifting public–private divide in the regulation of derivatives, rating agencies and hedge funds', *European Law Journal* 18(1): 44–61.

Partnoy, F. (1999) 'The siskel and ebert of financial markets? Two thumbs down for the credit rating agencies', *Washington University Law Review* 77(3): 619–712.

Paudyn, B. (2013) 'Credit rating agencies and the sovereign debt crisis: performing the politics of creditworthiness through risk and uncertainty', *Review of International Political Economy* 20(4): 788–818.

Pierson, P. (2000) 'Increasing returns, path dependence, and the study of politics', *The American Political Science Review* 94(2): 251–67.

Porter, T. (2010) 'Risk models and transnational governance in the global financial crisis: the cases of Basel II and credit rating agencies', in E. Helleiner, S. Pagliari and H. Zimmermann (eds), *Global Finance in Crisis: The Politics of International Regulatory Change*, London: Routledge, pp. 56–73.

Porter, T. (ed.) (2014) *Transnational Financial Regulation after the Crisis*, London: Routledge.

Quaglia, L. (2013) 'Financial services governance in the European Union after the global financial crisis: incremental changes or path-breaking reform?', in M. Moschella and E. Tsingou (eds), *Great Expectations, Slow Transformations: Incremental Change in Post-Crisis Regulation*, Colchester: ECPR, pp. 57–75.

Reuters (2007) 'Germany's ruling conservatives want rating agency regulation', *Financial Express Online*, 23 August, available at http://www.financialexpress.com/news/Germanys-ruling-conservatives-want-rating-agency-regulation/212176/ (accessed January 2009).

Robinson, M. and McLaughlin, D. (2015) 'S&P ends legal woes paying $1.5 billion fine to US, states', Bloomberg, 3 February, available at http://www.bloomberg.com/news/articles/2015–02–03/s-p-ends-legal-woes-with-1-5-billion-penalty-with-u-s-states (accessed June 2015).

Ryan, J. (2012) 'The negative impact of credit rating agencies and proposals for better regulation', *Working Paper FG 1, 2012/Nr. 01*, Berlin: German Institute for International and Security Affairs.

Sinclair, T.J. (2005) *The New Masters of Capital: American Bond Rating Agencies and the Politics of Creditworthiness*, Ithaca, NY: Cornell University Press.

Weber, R.H. and Darbellay, A. (2008) 'The regulatory use of credit ratings in bank capital requirement regulations', *Journal of Banking Regulation* 10(1): 1–16.

White, L.J. (2010) 'Markets: the credit rating agencies', *Journal of Economic Perspectives* 24(2): 211–26.

Zürn, M., Binder, M. and Ecker-Ehrhardt, M. (2012) 'International authority and its politicization', *International Theory* 4(1): 69–106.

Dissonance and decision-making mistakes in the age of risk

Ryan Beasley

ABSTRACT   Scholars of public and foreign policy have emphasized the role of decision processes in the creation of policy failures and fiascos and have demonstrated the importance that psychological factors play in policy mistakes. Using Ulrich Beck's notion of *world risk society* and drawing on advances in our understanding of a key psychological factor central to decision-making pathologies – cognitive dissonance – this contribution explores the ways in which features of the risk era could alter important decision dynamics and increase decision-making mistakes. In combination with the catastrophic potential of *world risk society*, this would suggest an increase in the frequency of policy-making fiascos. Bridging the gap between the 'macro' conditions of globalization and the 'micro' processes of decision-making also challenges our conception of both the nature and sources of policy-making mistakes and suggests that our scholarly understanding of 'decision-making mistakes' may need rethinking.

IINTRODUCTION

A general consensus has emerged that many policy failures and fiascos can be linked to problems within decision-making processes (see McConnell 2016). While various organizational and institutional sources have been identified as contributing to policy-making errors, psychological factors (e.g., heuristics and biases; the framing of prospects; small group dynamics) play a key role. While such 'micro-processes' can influence decisions, they always occur within a larger context that shapes their impact on policy outcomes. Sensitive to this, researchers have argued for an interplay between individual psychological factors and the broader organizational context within which they occur. Janis's *Groupthink* is an early example of work that incorporated both 'structural faults' (e.g., insulation of the group) and a 'provocative context' (e.g., external threats and situational complexity) as antecedents to psychological pitfalls and poor decision-making processes (Janis 1982).

The broadest sociological context and contours of the international system, however, have rarely been examined with regard to their direct impact upon the psychological dynamics of decision-making. Local conditions have had pride of place. In practice they are linked, but analytically they are all too often examined separately. Yet, arguments abound regarding the prevalence

129

of dramatic changes at the broadest levels of international society, ranging from 'globalization' to the rise of civilizational fissures defining the future of conflict (*cf.* Huntington 1996), to the development of global civil society (*cf.* Kumar 2008). With some notable exceptions (e.g., Jervis 1998), little work has systematically explored the effect of such 'macro' international conditions on 'micro' decision-making processes.

This contribution offers one approach to connecting broad international changes in the 'age of globalization' to decision-making dynamics among policy-makers. For this purpose I draw upon prominent sociologist Ulrich Beck's *world risk society* (WRS) thesis (Beck 1992; 1999; 2009), arguing that his view of the changing global context should also create specific cognitive dynamics that promote decision-making mistakes and contribute to policy fiascos. A key aspect of this argument is that risk decisions – decisions involving significant uncertainty and the need to prevent self-generated, unpredictable, uncontrollable outcomes with global catastrophic potential – specifically activate a range of sources of cognitive dissonance, the reduction of which is at the heart of a wide variety of decision-making mistakes. I begin by offering a brief overview of Beck's WRS thesis, followed by a brief introduction to the theory of cognitive dissonance. I then connect key features of WRS to dynamics of cognitive dissonance and associated decision-making mistakes that are increasingly likely to occur in the age of risk, referring in particular to the post-September 11 'War on Terror' policy responses and the 2003 Iraq War to illustrate the argument. I end the contribution with some observations about the future study of policy-making mistakes and fiascos.

RISK AND WORLD RISK SOCIETY: OVERVIEW

Scholarship on risk has burgeoned over the last few decades, despite the concept of risk not having a commonly agreed definition (Garland 2003). While a variety of major sociological approaches to risk exist (Zinn 2006), I will focus on the WRS thesis of Ulrich Beck (Beck 1999). Beck's work has generated an avalanche of scholarship following from his *Risk Society* (1992), but it has also drawn heavy criticism (Elliott 2002; Mythen 2004; Scott 2000). Beck's WRS thesis, however, offers some important features that lend it to the type of theorizing relevant here, such as its explicit focus on decisions as a source of the reputed transformations at work in the current era and its explicit if provocative and much critiqued inclusion of terrorism, which I use for my illustrations. I recognize, however, that WRS is a much-contested assertion, to which I will briefly return in my conclusions.

According to Beck, modern industrial society has been successful in addressing individuals' needs by greatly reducing scarcity and providing the necessary governance and resources to foster technological progress and provide material improvements. But society now faces a transformation where these widespread successes are altering key social institutions and practices (e.g., class, sex roles, the nuclear family) and even beginning to undermine themselves. 'The term *risk society* . . . epitomizes an era of modern society that no longer merely casts off traditional ways of life but rather wrestles with the side effects of successful modernization' (Beck 2009: 8; emphasis original). Beck sees the success of modernity as having created a transformation to a second modernity, a period he calls 'reflexive modernity' that has itself resulted in the uncontrollable risks we now face. The irony is that the remarkable human progress encapsulated within the scientific and technological breakthroughs of the modern era (which Beck essentially celebrates) has also resulted in widespread risks such as financial meltdown, the effects of climate change, and international terrorism.

A key distinction Beck makes is between 'hazards' and 'risks'. Hazards represent catastrophes that happen to humanity which have essentially been ever-present – such as tsunamis, earthquakes and volcanic eruptions. Risks represent, on the other hand, potential catastrophes that humanity has itself created. These, in turn, are rooted in decision-making that has included a sense of acceptability of some risk in exchange for benefits. '[R]isks presume industrial, that is, techno-economic decisions and considerations of utility. . . . They differ from pre-industrial natural disasters by their origin in decision-making' (Beck 1992: 98). These conditions also give rise to great uncertainty, as society shifts toward the 'reflexive rationality' of preventing crises arising from the essentially uncontrollable techno-scientific realities rather than the 'linear rationality' of pursuing positive goals. Reflexive modernization thus represents a condition wherein there is awareness of, and effort to reduce, the self-generated risks of modern industrial society through processes of regulation and employing the precautionary principle.

In sum, the WRS thesis describes a context wherein the types of problems that policy-makers are grappling with are replete with uncertainty, self-generated, catastrophic in potential, causally elusive, difficult to predict and largely uncontrollable. These risks are not localized but can become global in scope, their probabilities incalculable and their consequences uninsurable (Beck 2008). States face the difficulty of not knowing the nature, source and magnitude of the next international crisis to which they must attend, alongside heightened accountability by publics that demand to feel secure from the anxiety of unknown risks without possibility of compensation. Moreover, the source of such crises will increasingly be non-state and even 'non-actor' in nature (e.g., nuclear meltdown, global financial collapse, disease outbreak, global terrorist networks), generated by the very actors tasked with dealing with the consequences. I will argue that these very conditions affect policy-makers by heightening cognitive dissonance, which negatively impacts the quality of their decision-making.

COGNITIVE DISSONANCE THEORY: OVERVIEW

Despite the frequent casual use of the term, 'dissonance' is a sophisticated and detailed psychological theory that is one of the most influencial within the field of social psychology (Harmon-Jones and Mills 1999; Randles *et al.* 2015) and continues to generate much research. Festinger (1957) proposed that cognitions, when brought together, could either be consonant or dissonant with one another. Dissonant pieces of knowledge give rise to an unpleasant, aversive feeling within the individual, motivating dissonance reduction (and dissonance avoidance in the first instance). 'Dissonance' is the aversive feeling within individuals that arises owing to inconsistencies (Gawronski 2012), and such inconsistencies can originate from various cognitions, including cognitions about the world, the self, and behaviours, and dissonance can vary in intensity with a correspondingly intense motivation to reduce it.

Dissonance can be reduced in various ways, such as through rational but comparatively rare behavioural changes ('I smoke. I know smoking causes cancer. I'll quit smoking'), to more moderate cognitive distortions ('I smoke, but not as much as somebody who might get cancer'), to full blown denial ('They say smoking causes cancer, but it really doesn't'). Reducing dissonance can be very functional and adaptive for an individual, motivating us to reduce our cognitive workload, protect our sense of self-worth, or even resolve internal conflicts so that behaviour can occur (Harmon-Jones *et al.* 2015). Dissonance reduction, however, most often results in some level of distortion, self-deception, and infidelity between our beliefs about the world and the world itself. In the majority of cases the reduction of dissonance is achieved by altering information used to form beliefs, preferences, and make decisions, which can result in reasoning errors and mistakes in individuals' perceptions and judgments.

While Festinger's original conception of dissonance has been robust, there have been several advances in our understanding of the sources of dissonance that have relevance to decision making in the age of risk. Nearly 60 years of research have found that dissonance is associated with commitment to difficult choices, can be enhanced by uncertainty, implicates the 'self', is intensified by ethical failure and involves the desire to reduce the impact of aversive consequences. These features make dissonance theory remarkably apt for applying to policy decision-making in the risk era.

WORLD RISK SOCIETY, DISSONANCE AND DECISION-MAKING

World risk society entails several factors that should activate cognitive dissonance in decision-makers, increasing the likelihood of several types of decision-making errors. Combined with the catastrophic potential of WRS, this could result in a recipe for policy fiascos. Table 1 presents a summary of the key 'world risk society factors' proposed to be relevant to policy decision-making (column 1). Associated with each of these is the proposed 'source of dissonance' that should become activated, according to cognitive dissonance theory (column 2), and the 'dissonance reduction by policy-makers' likely utilized by decision-makers to alleviate the uncomfortable feeling of dissonance (column 3). Finally, the 'negative impacts on decision-making process' likely to follow from dissonance and its reduction are offered (column 4). Each of these connections will be clarified in the following sections.

Table 1   World risk society, dissonance, and decision-making

World Risk Society factors	Source of dissonance	Dissonance reduction by policymakers	Negative impacts on decision-making process
Prevention of unpredictable & uncontrollable risks	Uncertainty & violated expectations	Deny failure Increase confidence in policies Enhance self-images	Poor information search and biased processing Poor group dynamics (overestimate group; pressure towards uniformity; etc.)
Self-generated risks	Committed self implicated		
Global catastrophic potential	Aversive consequences & moral dissonance	Avoid & distort dissonant information Deny responsibility Deny harm	Poor survey of objectives Confirmation bias/ overconfidence Reduce reliance on outside experts

I will primarily draw examples from the 'War on Terror' and the US-led invasion of Iraq. These are not meant to test my argument, but rather as plausible illustrations for purposes of clarity. The 'War on Terror' is well suited for this purpose. Beck explicitly focuses on 'terrorism' (Beck 2002, 2003), and a large body of scholarship has emerged exploring risk society and aspects of terrorism and counter-terrorism (cf. Aradau and van Munster 2007; Heng 2002, 2006; Krahmann 2011). The policy responses to 9/11 are arguably a good example of risk society dynamics. 'Just as war against terror is a global war, risk society is amongst other things a paradigm of globalization, and as such is particularly suited to the interpretation of the response to September 11 2001, and its effects' (Spence 2005: 284). More-over, the decision to incorporate Iraq into the 'War on Terror' has itself been scrutinized for the presence of decision-making mistakes (Badie 2010; Mintz and Wayne 2014) and is widely seen as a policy failure (cf. Western 2013). It thus serves as a convenient illustration of the ways in which cognitive dissonance might operate within the realm of policy-making and contribute to policy-making mistakes and fiascos.

World risk society factors and sources of dissonance

Prevention of unpredictable, uncontrollable risks/uncertainty and violated expectations
The first major dimension of WRS likely to give rise to dissonance is uncertainty. Beck argues that the 'regime of non-knowing' is created when policymakers cannot discern the agents of threat, their potential, or their intentions (Beck 2009). 'World risk society is confronted with the awkward problem of

having to make decisions about life and death and war and peace on the basis of a more or less frank lack of knowledge' (Beck 2008: 6). Risks are not only difficult to predict or control (Beck 1999; Beck 2009), but they are also uninsurable and beyond compensation. Governments thus turn to the precautionary principle and seek to prevent risks from materializing in the first instance. This puts policy-making in a more 'reflexive' state of risk management under uncertainty, which involves committed efforts to prevent the worst from happening, and defining 'success' as 'non-failure' (see also Meyer 2016).

There is little definitive information that confirms the effectiveness of chosen policies when trying to 'prevent a bad outcome' instead of trying to 'create a good outcome', so policy-makers live in a sort of continuous informational limbo which in turn drives the need to convince themselves that actions or policies have indeed resulted in the expected prevention. This should create information-based dissonance, as no real consonant information can demonstrate policy success. Decision-makers must increasingly plan for the unexpected, the unknown. Risk management's preventive orientation only specifies that dangers exist and may materialize, but the time and place of those dangers is unclear. For policy-makers, there is significant inconsistency between their claims of having successfully caused non-events and the attributions of policy failure when an event occurs despite their efforts to prevent it. The nearly impossible prevention of negative outcomes should more frequently and reliably generate violated expectations.

Conditions of uncertainty and violated expectations are particularly prone to producing dissonance. Cognitive dissonance theory has been directly linked to uncertainty (Heine *et al.* 2006), in that they both 'describe inconsistent cognitions or unexpected events as leading to an aversive arousal state, which leads to predictable behavioural change in the service of reducing the arousal' (Randles *et al.* 2015). Violated expectations themselves were seen by Festinger (1957) as central to dissonance. He recounts a fringe cult that incorrectly predicted the end of the world and struggled to reconcile their intense commitment to the cause with the reality of their continued existence. The group's leader reduced dissonance in the unexpected morning by reporting to the others that their steadfast commitment was what prevented the destruction of the Earth (Festinger *et al.* 1956). In this way, the group claimed success for a 'non-event' and thereby reduce dissonance. More recently, Proulx *et al.* (2012: 285) have proposed an 'integrative perspective [that] construes "inconsistencies" as any detected expectancy violation', thus placing expectations as the central dynamic producing aversive arousal and efforts to reduce it.

Dissonance reduction by policy-makers

Dissonance by its very nature motivates the reduction of intra-psychic uncertainty. We should expect to see an increased tendency for decision-makers to deny that events represent a failure of policy, focusing instead on positive outcomes and indicators of success. Beck sees the political motivations of élites as they grapple with the challenge of providing security in the context of WRS, suggesting that they can essentially 'feign control' and claim that they have successfully managed risks. 'Given their task of averting dangers, politicians, in particular, may easily find themselves compelled to proclaim that the observance of security standards is assured even though such guarantees are impossible. They do so nonetheless because the *political* costs of omission are much higher than those of an overreaction' (Beck 2009: 53–4). While realized crises may present such opportunities to frame policy (Boin *et al.* 2009), they are also an opportunity to reduce dissonance by reframing them as positive outcomes. Even many years after the fact, former National Security Advisor Condoleezza Rice hints, for example, that the Arab uprisings would have been impossible without the administration having removed Hussein from power in Iraq (Keen 2011).

In order to reduce dissonance associated with the lack of information supporting preventive policies, policy-makers will likely seek information in a biased fashion to support their expectations (Scherer *et al.* 2013). This may have been evident in former Vice-President Dick Cheney's assertion, just prior to the United States-(US-)led invasion of Iraq, that the US would be greeted as liberators because Iraqis *currently opposed* to Hussein indicated that it would happen. Pointing to discussions with Kanan Makiya, whom he notes is part of the resistance to the Hussein regime, Cheney indicates that '[t]he read we get on the people of Iraq is there is no question but what they want to get rid of Saddam Hussein and they will welcome as liberators the United States when we come to do that' (Cheney 2003).

We can also see overconfidence in advance of a policy as an effort to mobilize support. Maor (2012: 243) explicitly examines policy 'overreaction' from a psychological point of view, and argues that 'policy-makers may look for proactive framings of crisis management, especially the use of non-language in the form of highly visual and dramatic information that is easily remembered'. Secretary of State Colin Powell's crucial speech at the United Nations in advance of the Iraq War is illustrative, involving his holding up a mock vial of anthrax and displaying charts of mobile production facilities (Vogel 2008). When policies fail to prevent an unexpected outcome, dissonance may prompt the seeking of enhanced feelings of self-worth and self-affirmations. Indeed, we may even see more overconfidence (Blanton *et al.* 2001) and an enhanced belief in the ability to predict and control events as a dissonance reduction compensation for policy failures. As is often the case with dissonance reduction, disconfirming information results in bolstering beliefs instead of challenging them. Early on, the Bush administration was keen to argue that the invasion was successful, reducing the threat of nuclear weapons falling into the hands of terrorists (CNN 2003). When counter-attacks began to occur in Iraq and elsewhere, the focus shifted to changing the measures of success, a task that befuddled key policy-makers like Secretary of Defense Donald Rumsfeld (*USA Today* 2003).

Self-generated risks/committed self-implicated

The second major dimension of WRS with implications for cognitive dissonance involves the origin of risks. In Beck's view, risks are generated by deliberate techno-scientific decisions, and this directly implicates those responsible when such decisions result in unintended crises. He notes that 'with the origin of industrial risks in decision-making the problem of social accountability and responsibility irrevocably arises. ... As we sociologists say, the social roots of risks block the "externalizability" of the problem of accountability' (Beck 1992: 98). In some instances specific decision-makers are directly implicated in choices that have been made, and at other times governments carry forward policies of their predecessors – such as maintaining reliance on nuclear energy or supporting a set of financial regulatory practices. The first instance represents a direct commitment to an action or decision, while the second instance can be viewed from the 'induced compliance' dissonance paradigm wherein individuals willingly but reluctantly engage in counter-attitudinal behaviour. In either case policy-makers become connected to the policy in question.

Under such circumstances, the 'self' is implicated as being responsible for outcomes by having committed – even if reluctantly – to a course of action. Scholars have demonstrated this to be central for the arousal of dissonance (Cooper 2007). Although Beck has been critiqued for his stark distinction between 'natural hazards' and 'manufactured risks' (Furedi 2002; Mythen 2004), from a dissonance perspective it is the degree to which events follow from prior decision that matters most. Indeed, self-consistency theory (Aronson 1999), as an approach to cognitive dissonance, says the self must be involved to arouse dissonance. Steele's (1988) 'self-affirmation' theory goes further in saying that we want to see ourselves as good, competent people, and the 'drive' associated with inconsistencies is better understood as the pursuit of self-esteem and self-worth. If our actions are responsible for a negative outcome, then dissonance is likely to arise – even if the reduction of that dissonance involves denying our involvement.

Global catastrophic potential/aversive consequences and moral dissonance

The third major dimension of WRS that arguably evokes cognitive dissonance involves its catastrophic potential. Governments are tasked with preventing risks from materializing that are potentially catastrophic in nature, indiscriminate in consequence, and global in scope.[1] These include regional or global catastrophes such as Chernobyl, Fukushima or the global financial collapse, alongside the more calculated but equally 'non-state' threats of global terrorism. Beck views these as so significant that they move beyond the realm of compensation, such that they are uninsurable and, indeed, incalculable (Beck 2008). Even when such crises do not materialize, they are anticipated and constructed as potential threats to be prevented. The desire to avoid catastrophic consequences is a key feature of WRS.

Cognitive dissonance is centrally concerned with the avoidance of negative consequences, and several approaches to dissonance emphasize that it is not merely about cognitive inconsistencies, but rather the desire to make unwanted consequence less aversive (Cooper and Fazio 1984; Johnson *et al.* 1995; Scher and Cooper 1989). The significant negative consequences also mean that moral implications of policy fiascos are profound, and combined with the self-generated nature of these risks, the moral culpability of policy-makers is evident. As Adams notes, '[r]isk-management decisions are moral decisions made in the face of uncertainty' (Adams 2003:87). The uninsurable nature of these risks further highlights the moral implications, as governments can no longer exchange failed security from risks for compensation. In such circumstances individuals are more likely to experience 'ethical dissonance', connecting their own shortcomings and decision-making errors with the outcome.

Steel's self-affirmation theory rests not only on self-esteem but also on the idea that 'seeing oneself as good and moral is the objective' (Cooper 2007: 98). Barkan and colleagues (2012) explicitly identify 'ethical dissonance' as a special type of dissonance, defined as an inconsistency between one's drive to preserve a moral self-image and an individual's immoral acts. They argue that in addition to the violation of social norms (Cooper and Fazio 1984), when individuals behave in ways contrary to their own belief and values (Aronson 1992) and additionally are responsible for behaving in ways that threaten their self-integrity (Steele 1988), dissonance is even more likely (Barkan *et al.* 2012; Shu *et al.* 2012).

Dissonance reduction by policy-makers
Both the 'self-generated risks' and 'global catastrophic potential' of WRS appear particularly likely to generate dissonance. Associated with each of these are dissonance reduction strategies designed to alleviate the attendant psychological discomfort. These have also been noted by scholars as aspects of the policy-making and management process. When formulating policies in dissonance-arousing contexts, decision-makers are generally more likely to avoid inconsistent information or to distort information to make it consistent with their views or preferred policies. When a serious risk becomes a reality (e.g., Fukushima), or becomes a prominent feature of political discourse (e.g., global warming), dissonance reduction techniques such as denying culpability will be most prominent (Gosling *et al.* 2006). Dissonance reduction offers another perspective on 'blame avoidance behaviour' by policy-makers (Hinterleitner and Sager 2015; Hood 2010; Weaver 1986). While the 'blame game' results from a wide variety of organizational, political and even individual difference factors (Boin *et al.*, 2010), dissonance and its reduction can help to account for some of the underlying psychological dynamics that lead individuals to deny personal responsibility for failures and mistakes. Although such denials and rationalizations can be politically motivated, there is some recent evidence that the desire to reduce dissonance can actually result in false memories (Rodriguez and Strange 2015), giving

another plausible psychological explanation for why policy-makers might claim to have supported (or opposed) policies that they in fact did not.

Additionally, there will be efforts to deny or diminish the magnitude of negative consequences, and decision-makers may engage in systematic rationalizations in order to justify their policies or reduce negative reactions to their decisions. Dissonance can motivate policy-makers to alter their view of harmful consequences, making them seem less negative, as 'the motivation for dissonance reduction arises from the perception of aversive consequences and that changes of attitudes that generally follow from dissonance arousal are at the service of rendering those consequences nonaversive' (Cooper 1999: 150). The Bush administration, for example, grossly underestimated costs of invading Iraq in advance of the actual invasion (*Guardian 2013*), despite credible higher estimates available at the time. After the invasion, when the swift victory and 'mission accomplished' sensibilities began to fade in the face of stiff resistance in Iraq, the administration continued to minimize the sense of negative consequences, such as by offering low estimates of Iraqi casualties (*Washington Post* 2005).

Negative impacts on decision-making processes

In general the nature of decision-making mistakes prompted by dissonance and its reduction should not be dissimilar to those already familiar to scholars of policy-making. Dissonance reduction will most often result in some level of distortion of information, selective information avoidance, and various other techniques for re-aligning inconsistencies among beliefs, preferences and behaviours. But given the nature of policy-making described by WRS, we can see some aspects of these types of mistakes in a new light.

The 'linear rationality' of modernity focuses on achieving objectives by applying means toward ends, and thus one noted mistake is failing to survey objectives (Janis 1972; Schafer and Crichlow 2010). But the 'reflexive rationality' of WRS suggests that specifying objectives and determining appropriate alternative courses of action are much broader in nature, being built around prevention of 'bad outcomes'. In a sense, this places 'normal' policy-making more squarely in the realm of grand strategy, with overly broad objectives and underspecified means. The challenge of addressing such ill-structured problems (Sylvan and Voss 1998) is compounded by the dissonance associated with a risk management, reflexive approach and will likely result in excessive cognitive simplifications designed to simplify ill-structured problems and to align information with a limited range of policy objectives.

Decision-makers may seek experts to help overcome the complexities of a given risk, which could be viewed as a positive strategy as both *knowledge* and *experience* are factors that have been associated with more effective decision-making (Schafer and Crichlow 2010). For Beck, however, risk society greatly reduces confidence in expertise, as the complexity and unpredictability of techno-scientific risks eludes expert control. The British Petroleum (BP) oil spill in the Gulf of Mexico in 2010 is illustrative, as the crisis spun out of control and the technological complexity of trying to plug the oil deep underwater gave way to hapless efforts with comical names such as 'top kill' and 'junk shot' and involved complex challenges around the use of expertise (*cf.* Mills and Koliba 2015). For complex and unbounded risks 'there is typically little data or evidence on which to base management decisions and practices, and there is little confidence that management strategies will actually reduce the risk in a tangible way' (Handmer and James 2007: 129).

While cognitive dissonance has generally been considered intra-personal, decision-makers rarely grapple with policy-making alone, and Beck explicitly recognizes this fact (Beck 1992: 98). Festinger himself considered the social group to be a source for the experience (and alleviation) of dissonance (Festinger, 1957).[2] Recently scholars have connected cognitive dissonance to group dynamics (McKimmie 2015; McKimmie *et al.* 2009), and studies have observed dissonance reduction through diffusion of responsibility within groups (Cooper and Stone 2000) and have found that consensus following disagreement among group members is a source of dissonance reduction (Matz and Wood 2005).[3] But the nature of decision-making in WRS may actually increase dissonance. 't Hart (1990: 105) indicates that intensive competition with an out-group is likely to influence 'high group cohesiveness and anticipatory compliance in the face of strong leadership ... [and] symptoms of groupthink, such as a belief in the inherent morality of the group and stereotypes of out-groups'.[4] Facing crises that originate in the backlash of techno-scientific progress, however, the ability to 'scapegoat' the source of risk onto the 'other' will be difficult and implicate the self. Efforts to reduce dissonance may intensify and result in cognitive distortions that reduce personal responsibility, perhaps even by creating an 'other' to which negative outcomes can be attributed – such as mistaking Saddam Hussein to be colluding with al Qaida and to be the source of risks associated with weapons of mass destruction and international terrorism (Badie 2010).

CONCLUSIONS

I have argued from a 'process conception' of mistakes, connecting the conditions *of* WRS to the dynamics of decision-making through the vehicle of cognitive dissonance. Alongside the behavioural and institutional changes that Beck argues accompany WRS, we should also consider the impact on policy decision-making dynamics, as the types of decision scenarios increasingly likely to be facing governments may fundamentally influence the 'micro processes' of decision-making. Even if the WRS thesis is not itself fully empirically accurate (Jarvis 2007), the more recent expansion of risk bureaucracies, risk regulation regimes and political risk analysis itself suggests that many governments are indeed taking a reactive and preventive approach to many areas of policy-making (Hood *et al.* 2001; Jarvis and Griffiths 2007). Connecting this to decision-making processes highlights the possible influence of the broadest sociological context on decision-making mistakes and emphasizes different dynamics and decision pathologies that can occur when policy-makers are dealing with WRS-type events and crises.

Other psychological approaches to the study of risk and policy decision-making exist, of course, such as framing (cf. Kahneman and Tversky 1979), individual personality differences (cf. Kowert and Hermann 1997) and cultural beliefs in relation to risk perceptions (cf. Wildavsky and Dake 1990). What has been less emphasized is a direct connection to the more macro international context. While there has been some speculation that international features can influence psychological processes, such as *cognitive capitalism* (Moulier-Boutang 2012), or the more general systemic effects on the information processing of foreign policy-makers (Jervis 1998), little work has tried to directly connect broad sociological features to the psychological foundations of decision-making mistakes. While cognitive dissonance is not itself a theory of risk or risk-taking, it is instead a more generally applicable theory of how people respond to inconsistencies and is particularly well suited to examining 'mistakes and failures' and how we deal with them (Tavris and Aronson 2008). Moreover, psychologists are beginning to reinterpret many of their findings in the light of dissonance theory, recognizing that 'the basic notion of cognitive consistency can integrate a wide range of social psychological phenomena that have rarely been analysed from a consistency perspective' (Gawronski 2012: 653; see also Gawronski and Strack 2012). Combined with the concepts of WRS, then, dissonance offers a compelling connection to policy mistakes and fiascos.

By its very nature – connecting the 'macro level' to the 'micro-cognitive level' – the empirical demonstration of these effects is extremely difficult. Indeed, idiosyncratic features of any choice situation will continue to be a primary influence on the prevalence of dissonance and its reduction. Dissonance does not indicate what specific types of mistakes decision-makers are likely to make, since it does not in itself specify the nature of dissonance reduction that will be utilized in any particular situation. Individuals are relatively free to deny events, distort information to put it in line with beliefs and behaviours, bolster their beliefs, enhance their sense of self-worth or self-esteem, and even (though more rarely) change their behaviour in response to the arousal of dissonance. The gritty work of examining decision-making remains essential for scholars interested in such process explanations of policies, mistakes and fiascos.

NOTES

1 For a critique of Beck's assertions regarding the 'global' nature of risks society, see Caplan (2000).
2 Festinger himself was deeply interested in group dynamics, having published on it prior to his formal presentation of cognitive dissonance (Festinger and Thibau 1951).
3 Even Janis (1972) may have recognized aspects of dissonance within his concept of groupthink, and perhaps saw groupthink as a space *absent of dissonance*. He notes that the term 'groupthink' is Orwellian in origin and of the same order as terms like 'doublethink', which Orwell's book *1984* (1949/2006) presents as the ability to hold two completely contradictory beliefs in mind simultaneously and to believe them both equally without doubt or hesitation – a remarkable description of the complete absence of dissonance.
4 Interestingly, the majority of the case studies of groupthink, groupthink-avoidance, and those that have helped to move us 'beyond groupthink' are grounded in decisions that involved 'others' – that is, rooted in the linear rationality of linking means with ends against a calculating alter. Focusing on foreign policy, Schafer and Crichlow's (2010) 39 case studies only involve two that could plausibly be argued to involve a 'non-other' actor: case #38 where the Bush administration decided to impose a steel tariff, and case #17 wherein the Reagan administration took the decision to develop the 'Strategic Defense Initiative' (SDI).

REFERENCES

Adams, J. (2003) 'Risk and morality: three framing devices', in R.V. Ericson and A. Doyle (eds), *Risk and Morality*, Toronto: University of Toronto Press, pp. 87–103.

Aradau, C. and van Munster, R. (2007) 'Governing terrorism through risk: taking precautions, (un)knowing the future', *European Journal of International Relations* 13(1): 89–115.

Aronson, E. (1992) 'The return of the repressed: dissonance theory makes a comeback', *Psychological Inquiry* 3(4): 303–11.

Aronson, E. (1999) 'Dissonance, hypocrisy, and the self-concept', in E. Harmon-Jones and J. Mills (eds), *Cognitive Dissonance: Progress on a Pivotal Theory in Social Psychology*, Washington, DC: American Psychological Association, pp. 103–26.

Badie, D. (2010) 'Groupthink, Iraq, and the War on Terror: explaining US policy shift toward Iraq', *Foreign Policy Analysis* 6(4): 277–96.

Barkan, R., Ayal, S., Gino, F. and Ariely, D. (2012) 'The pot calling the kettle black: distancing response to ethical dissonance', *Journal Of Experimental Psychology: General* 141(4): 757–73.

Beck, U. (1992) *Risk Society: Towards a New Modernity*, London: Sage.

Beck, U. (1999) *World Risk Society*, Malden: Polity.

Beck, U. (2002) 'The terrorist threat world risk society revisited', *Theory, Culture & Society* 19(4): 39–55.

Beck, U. (2003) 'The silence of words: on terror and war', *Security Dialogue* 34(3): 255–67.

Beck, U. (2008) 'World at risk: the new task of critical theory', *Development and Society* 37(1): 1–21.

Beck, U. (2009) *World at Risk*, Cambridge: Polity.

Blanton, H., Pelham, B. W., DeHart, T. and Carvallo, M. (2001) 'Overconfidence as dissonance reduction', *Journal of Experimental Social Psychology* 37(5): 373–85.

Boin, A., 't Hart, P. and McConnell, A. (2009) 'Crisis exploitation: political and policy impacts of framing contests', *Journal of European Public Policy* 16(1): 81–106.

Boin, A., 't Hart, P., McConnell, A. and Preston, T. (2010) 'Leadership style, crisis response, and blame management: the case of Hurricane Katrina', *Public Administration* 88(3): 707–23.

Caplan, P. (2000) *Risk Revisited*, London: Pluto.

Cheney, D. (2003) Meet the press interview, 16 March, available at www.mtholyoke. edu/acad/intrel/bush/cheneymeetthepress.htm (accessed March 2015).

CNN (2003) *'Bush makes historic speech aboard warship'*, 2 May, available at http:// edition.cnn.com/2003/US/05/01/bush.transcript/ (accessed March 2015).

Cooper, J. (1999) 'Unwanted consequences and the self: in search of the motivation for dissonance reduction' E. Harmon-Jones and J. Mills (eds), *Cognitive Dissonance: Progress on a Pivotal Theory in Social Psychology*, Washington, DC: American Psychological Association, pp. 149–73.

Cooper, J. (2007) *Cognitive Dissonance: 50 Years of a Classic Theory*, London: Sage.

Cooper, J. and Fazio, R.H. (1984) 'A new look at dissonance theory', in L. Berkowitz (ed.), *Advances In Experimental Social Psychology*, vol. 17, San Diego, CA: Academic Press, pp. 229–62.

Cooper, J. and Stone, J. (2000) 'Cognitive dissonance and the social group', in D.J. Terry and M.A. Hogg (eds), *Attitudes, Behavior, and Social Context: The Role of Norms and Group Membership*, Mahwah, NJ: Lawrence Erlbaum Associates, pp. 227–44.

Elliott, A. (2002) 'Beck's sociology of risk: a critical assessment', *Sociology* 36: 293–315.

Festinger, L. (1957) *A Theory of Cognitive Dissonance*, Stanford, CA: Stanford University Press.

Festinger, L., Riecken, H.W. and Schachter, S. (1956) *When Prophecy Fails: A Social and Psychological Study of a Modern Group that Predicted the End of the World*, New York: Harper.

Festinger, L. and Thibau, J. (1951) 'Interpersonal communication in small groups', *Journal of Abnormal and Social Psychology* 46: 92–9.

Furedi, F. (2002) *Culture of Fear: Risk Taking and the Morality of Low Expectation*, London: Continuum.

Garland, D. (2003) 'The rise of risk', in R.V. Ericson and A. Doyle (eds), *Risk and Morality*, Toronto: University of Toronto Press, pp. 48–86.

Gawronski, B. (2012) 'Back to the future of dissonance theory: cognitive consistency as a core motive', *Social Cognition* 30(6): 652–68.

Gawronski, B. and Strack, F. (eds) (2012) *Cognitive Consistency: A Fundamental Principle in Social Cognition*, New York: Guilford.

Gosling, P., Denizeau, M. and Oberlé, D. (2006) 'Denial of responsibility: a new mode of dissonance reduction', *Journal of Personality and Social Psychology* 90(5): 722–33.

Guardian (2013) 'How the US public was defrauded by the hidden costs of the Iraq war', 11 March, available at http://www.theguardian.com/commentisfree/2013/ mar/11/us-public-defrauded-hidden-cost-iraq-war.

Handmer, J.J. and James, P.P. (2007) 'Trust us and be scared: the changing nature of contemporary risk', *Global Society* 21(1): 119–30.

Harmon-Jones, E., Harmon-Jones, C. and Levy, N. (2015) 'An action-based model of cognitive-dissonance processes', *Current Directions in Psychological Science* 24(3): 184–9.

Harmon-Jones, E. and Mills, J. (1999) 'An introduction to cognitive dissonance theory and an overview of current perspectives on the theory', in E. Harmon-Jones and J. Mills (eds), *Cognitive Dissonance: Progress on a Pivotal Theory in Social Psychology*, Washington, DC: American Psychological Association, pp. 3–21.

Heine, S.J., Proulx, T. and Vohs, K.D. (2006) 'The meaning maintenance model: on the coherence of social motivations', *Personality and Social Psychology Review* 10(2): 88–110.

Heng, Y. (2002) 'Unravelling the "war" on terrorism: a risk-management exercise in war clothing?', *Security Dialogue* 33(2): 227–42.

Heng, Y. (2006) *War as Risk Management: Strategy and Conflict in an Age of Globalised Risks*, London: Routledge.

Hinterleitner, M. and Sager, F. (2015) 'Avoiding blame – a comprehensive framework and the Australian Home Insulation Program fiasco', *Policy Studies Journal* 43(1): 139–61.

Hood, C. (2010) *The Blame Game: Spin, Bureaucracy, and Self-Preservation in Government*, Princeton, NJ: Princeton University Press.

Hood, C., Rothstein, H. and Baldwin, R. (2001) *The Government of Risk: Understanding Risk Regulation Regimes*, Oxford: Oxford University Press.

Huntington, S.P. (1996) *The Clash of Civilizations and the Remaking of World Order*, New York: Simon & Schuster.

Janis, I.L. (1972) *Victims of Groupthink: A Psychological Study of Foreign Policy Decisions and Fiascos*, Oxford: Houghton Mifflin.

Janis, I.L. (1982) *Groupthink: Psychological Studies of Policy Decisions and Fiascos*, Boston: Houghton Mifflin.

Jarvis, D.L. (2007) 'Risk, globalisation, and the state: a critical appraisal of Ulrich Beck and the world risk society thesis', *Global Society* 21(1): 23–46.

Jarvis, D.L. and Griffiths, M. (2007) 'Learning to fly: the evolution of political risk analysis', *Global Society* 21(1): 5–21.

Jervis, R. (1998) *System Effects: Complexity in Political and Social Life*, Princeton, NJ: Princeton University Press.

Johnson, R.W., Kelly, R.J. and LeBlanc, B.A. (1995) 'Motivational basis of dissonance: aversive consequences of inconsistency', *Personality and Social Psychology Bulletin* 21(8): 850–5.

Kahneman, D. and Tversky, A. (1979) 'Prospect theory: an analysis of decision under risk', *Econometrica* 47(2): 263–91.

Keen, J. (2011) 'Rice reflects on Bush tenure, Gadhafi in New Memoir', *USA Today*, 31 October, available at http://usatoday30.usatoday.com/news/washington/story/2011-10-31/condoleezza-rice-memoir-bush/51006960/1.

Kowert, P.A. and Hermann, M.G. (1997) 'Who takes risks? Daring and caution in foreign policy making', *Journal of Conflict Resolution* 41(5): 611–37.

Krahmann, E. (2011) 'Beck and beyond: selling security in the world risk society', *Review of International Studies* 37(1): 349–72.

Kumar, K. (2008) 'Civil society, globalization, and global civil society', *Journal of Civil Society* 4(1): 15–30.

Maor, M. (2012) 'Policy Overreaction', *Journal of Public Policy* 32(3): 231–59.

Matz, D.C. and Wood, W. (2005) 'Cognitive dissonance in groups: the consequences of disagreement', *Journal of Personality and Social Psychology* 88(1): 22–37.

McConnell, A. (2016) 'A public policy approach to understanding the nature and causes of foreign policy failure', *Journal of European Public Policy*, doi:10.1080/13501763.2015.1127278

McKimmie, B.M. (2015) 'Cognitive dissonance in groups', *Social and Personality Psychology Compass* 9(4): 202–12.

McKimmie, B.M., Terry, D.J. and Hogg, M.A. (2009) 'Dissonance reduction in the context of group membership: the role of metaconsistency', *Group Dynamics: Theory, Research, and Practice* 13(2): 103–19.

Meyer, C. (2016) 'Over- and under-reaction to transboundary threats: two sides of a misprinted coin?', *Journal of European Public Policy*, doi:10.1080/13501763.2015. 1127275

Mills, R.W. and Koliba, C.J. (2015) 'The challenge of accountability in complex regulatory networks: the case of the Deepwater Horizon oil spill', *Regulation & Governance* 9(1): 77–91.

Mintz, A. and Wayne, C. (2014) 'Group decision making in conflict: from groupthink to polythink in the war in Iraq', in P.T. Coleman, M. Deutsch and E.C. Marcus (eds), *The Handbook of Conflict Resolution: Theory and Practice*, San Francisco, CA: Jossey-Bass, pp. 331–52.

Moulier-Boutang, Y. (2012) *Cognitive Capitalism*, London: Polity.

Mythen, G. (2004) *Ulrich Beck: A Critical Introduction to the Risk Society*, London: Pluto.

Orwell, G. (2006) *1984*, New York: Editions Underbahn.

Proulx, T., Inzlicht, M. and Harmon-Jones, E. (2012) 'Review: understanding all inconsistency compensation as a palliative response to violated expectations', *Trends In Cognitive Sciences* 16: 285–91.

Randles, D., Inzlicht, M., Proulx, T., Tullett, A.M. and Heine, S.J. (2015) 'Is dissonance reduction a special case of fluid compensation? Evidence that dissonant cognitions cause compensatory affirmation and abstraction', *Journal of Personality and Social Psychology* 108(5): 697–710.

Rodriguez, D.N. and Strange, D. (2015) 'False memories for dissonance inducing events', *Memory* 23(2): 203–12.

Schafer, M. and Crichlow, S. (2010) *Groupthink: High-quality Decision Making in International Relations*, New York: Colombia University Press.

Scher, S.J. and Cooper, J. (1989) 'Motivational basis of dissonance: the singular role of behavioral consequences', *Journal of Personality and Social Psychology* 56(6): 899–906.

Scherer, A., Windschitl, P. and Smith, A. (2013) 'Hope to be right: biased information seeking following arbitrary and informed predictions', *Journal of Experimental Social Psychology* 49(1): 106–12.

Scott, A. (2000) 'Risk society or angst society? Two views of risk, consciousness and community', in B. Adam, U. Beck and J. van Loon (eds), *The Risk Society and Beyond: Critical Issues for Social Theory*, London: Sage, pp. 33–46.

Shu, L.L., Gino, F. and Bazerman, M.H. (2012) 'Ethical discrepancy: changing our attitudes to resolve moral dissonance', in D. De Cremer, A.E. Tenbrunsel (eds), *Behavioral Business Ethics: Shaping an Emerging Field*, New York: Routledge, pp. 221–39.

Spence, K. (2005) 'World risk society and war against terror', *Political Studies* 53(2): 284–302.

Steele, C.M. (1988) 'The psychology of self-affirmation: sustaining the integrity of the self', in L. Berkowitz (ed.), *Advances in Experimental Social Psychology*, vol. 21. San Diego, CA: Academic Press, pp. 261–302.

Sylvan, D.A. and Voss, J.F. (1998) *Problem Representation in Foreign Policy Decision-making*, Cambridge: Cambridge University Press.

Tavris, C. and Aronson, E. (2008) *Mistakes were Made (but Not by Me): Why we Justify Foolish Beliefs, Bad Decisions and Hurtful Acts*, London: Pinter & Martin.

't Hart, P. (1990) *Groupthink in Government: A Study of Small Groups and Policy Failure*, Amsterdam: Swets and Zeitlinger.

USA Today (2003) 'Rumsfeld's war-on-terror memo', 16 October, available at http://usatoday30.usatoday.com/news/washington/executive/rumsfeld-memo.htm.

Vogel, K.M. (2008) '"Iraqi Winnebagos of death": imagined and realized futures of US bioweapons threat assessments', *Science & Public Policy* 35(8): 561–73.

Washington Post (2005) 'What's the story behind 30,000 Iraqi deaths?', 18 December, available at http://www.washingtonpost.com/wp-dyn/content/article/2005/12/17/AR2005121700017.html.

Weaver, R. (1986) 'The politics of blame avoidance', *Journal of Public Policy* 6(4): 371–98.

Western, J. (2013) 'From wars of choice to the mistakes of wars: presidential decision making and the limits of democratic accountability', *Perspectives on Politics* 11(2): 532–37.

Wildavsky, A. and Dake, K. (1990) 'Theories of risk perception: who fears what and why?', *Daedalus* 119(4): 41–60.

Zinn, J.O. (2006) 'Recent developments in sociology of risk and uncertainty', *Historical Social Research/Historische Sozialforschung* 31(2): 275–86.

Index

Note: Page numbers in *italic* type refer to tables
Page numbers followed by 'n' refer to notes